AWA7K26

AWA7K26

The OPEN Process Specification

This book was written with other contributions from members of the OPEN Consortium, particularly B. Unhelkar.

The OPEN Series

Consulting Editor: Brian Henderson-Sellers

Related Titles

The OPEN Toolbox of Techniques *Brian Henderson-Sellers and Houman Younessi*
Object-Oriented Development using OPEN: A complete Java application *Donald G Firesmith, Greg Hendley, Scott Krutsch and Marshall Stowe*

ACM PRESS BOOKS

This book is published as part of ACM Press Books – a collaboration between the Association for Computing (ACM) and Addison Wesley Longman Limited. ACM is the oldest and largest educational and scientific society in the information technology field. Through its high-quality publications and services, ACM is a major force in advancing the skills and knowledge of IT professionals throughout the world. For further information about ACM, contact:

ACM Member Services	**ACM European Service Center**
1515 Broadway, 17th Floor	108 Cowley Road
New York, NY 10036-5701	Oxford OX4 1JF
Phone: 1-212-626-0500	United Kingdom
Fax: 1-212-944-1318	Phone: +44-1865-382388
E-mail: acmhelp@acm.org	Fax: +44-1865-381388
	E-mail: acm_europe@acm.org
	URL: http://www.acm.org

Selected ACM titles

The Object Advantage: Business Process Reengineering with Object Technology (2nd edn) *Ivar Jacobson, Maria Ericsson, Agneta Jacobson, Gunnar Magnusson*

Object-Oriented Software Engineering: A Use Case Driven Approach *Ivar Jacobson, Magnus Christerson, Patrik Jonsson, Gunnar Overgaard*

Software for Use: A Practical Guide to the Models and Methods of Usage Centered Design *Larry L Constantine & Lucy A D Lockwood*

Bringing Design to Software: Expanding Software Development to Include Design *Terry Winograd, John Bennett, Laura de Young, Bradley Hartfield*

CORBA Distributed Objects: Using Orbix *Sean Baker*

Software Requirements and Specifications: A Lexicon of Software Practice, Principles and Prejudices *Michael Jackson*

Business Process Implementation: Building Workflow Systems *Michael Jackson & Graham Twaddle*

Interacting Processes: A Multiparty Approach to Coordinated Distributed Programming *Nissim Francez & Ira Forman*

Design Patterns for Object-Oriented Software Development *Wolfgang Pree*

The OPEN Process Specification

Ian Graham
Brian Henderson-Sellers
Houman Younessi

ACM Press
New York

Harlow, England • Reading, Massachusetts
Menlo Park, California • New York
Don Mills, Ontario • Amsterdam • Bonn
Sydney • Singapore • Tokyo • Madrid
San Juan • Milan • Mexico City • Seoul • Taipei

Addison Wesley Longman Limited
Edinburgh Gate
Harlow
Essex CM20 2JE
England

and Associated Companies throughout the World.

Cover designed by Senate
Typeset in Computer Modern by 56
Printed and bound in The United States of America

First printed 1997

ISBN 0-201-33133-0

British Library Cataloguing-in-Publication Data
A catalogue record for this book is available from the British Library

Library of Congress Cataloging-in-Publication Data
Graham, Ian.
      The OPEN process specification / Ian Graham, Brian Henderson-Sellers, Houman
Younessi.
            p.   cm.
      Includes bibliographical references and index.
      ISBN 0-201-33133-0 (alk. paper)
      1. Object-oriented methods (Computer science) 2. Computer software–Development–
Management. I. Henderson-Sellers, Brian. II. Younessi, Houman. III. Title.
QA76.9.035H47   1997
005.1'17'0212–dc21   97-2671
                                                                              CIP

Contents

Foreword

After nearly twenty years of commercial practice, it appears that object technology has not only grown up, but is on the verge of becoming the dominant approach in the software development industry. And after nearly ten years of textbooks, discussions, debates, and offerings from various vendors, it appears that the field of object-oriented 'methodologies' has grown up, too. The book you are holding in your hands, co- authored by Ian Graham, Brian Henderson-Sellers, and Houman Younessi but also based on the co-operative work of more than 30 people around the world, is convincing evidence of the new-found maturity in this field.

Having been involved in the 'methodology business' for some 25 years, I've always found it curious how these things develop. In other engineering disciplines, we expect the leading-edge ideas to emerge from universities and research institutions, so that practitioners faced with 'real-world' problems can be suitably enlightened. In a field like computing, one might expect leading-edge ideas to be the exclusive domain of such giants as IBM or Microsoft – or, depending on where your loyalties lie, perhaps Apple and Netscape. But while academia and industry monoliths have certainly played crucial roles in many aspects of both hardware and software development, they haven't provided much leadership in software development 'methods' – at least, not until now.

I'm oversimplifying matters, of course, but it's hard to deny that most of the widely used software development methods and techniques have been associated with individuals or small consulting firms. We don't hear much talk about following the 'IBM method' or the 'Microsoft way' of designing software. And, notwithstanding the enormous influence of such academicians as Dijkstra, Wirth, and Hoare, we don't hear much about following the 'MIT method' or the 'Carnegie-Mellon way' of designing software. Instead, software development organizations have focused their attention on the writings of a hodgepodge collection of individuals: Grady Booch and James Martin and Tom DeMarco and Peter Coad and James Rumbaugh and a dozen others. Having had the good fortune to be associated with some of these individuals, I can report from first-hand experience that while they were (and still are!) very intelligent, sincere, and well-intentioned, they often pursued their efforts with limited resources and a limited perspective on the broad spectrum of software problems. And thus, it is with no disrespect that many current researchers, including the authors of this book, refer to the works of these individuals as 'first-generation' methodologies.

This is a less relevant issue for the so-called 'structured' methodologies of the 1970s, for they only survived for one generation before the first generation of researchers retired, gave up, or moved on to the more interesting area of object technology. One could claim that a second generation of structured methods did emerge in the 1980s, but by then hardly anyone cared. Meanwhile, the field of object technology also experienced a first generation of methodology-developers; among other things, this resulted in a flurry of textbooks in the late 1980s, which met with varying degrees of success. Unfortunately, as Messrs. Graham, Henderson-Sellers, and Younessi point out, much of the emphasis in the first-generation methodologies was concerned with *notation* – i.e., how to draw the appropriate diagrams to represent some aspect of an object-oriented specification or object-oriented design.

Perhaps because object technology is more intellectually rewarding and challenging than structured methods, it has continued to evolve; during the early and mid-1990s, we began to see the emergence of 'second-generation' OO methodologies. In some cases, this represented the evolution and increased sophistication of the first-generation methodologists themselves; a good example of this can be found, for example, in the work of Peter Coad, who has moved far beyond the initial OO concepts that he co- authored with me in the late 1980s. But more often, the second-generation OO methods involved *integration* and *synthesis* of ideas from other first-generation researchers. The FUSION method developed by Hewlett-Packard is one such notable example; another example, which met with somewhat less recognition and success, was the 'Mainstream Objects' approach that I helped Software AG develop. A good example of the 'synthesis' that occurred in almost every example of second-generation OO methods was the notion of 'use cases' introduced by Ivar Jacobson's 'Objectory' method.

While these second-generation methods were certainly an improvement, it could be argued that most of them continued to place too much emphasis on diagramming notations, and that too many of them suffered from limited scope, as well as fuzzy details and other shortcomings. Perhaps this wouldn't have mattered so much if the overall field of object technology had been ignored; but throughout the 1990s, the growing influence of client-server technology, distributed computing, graphical user interfaces, and Internet/Web computing, has continued to put more and more emphasis on 'industrial-strength' object technology. Object technology, as suggested earlier, is growing up; and there is a concomitant need for OO methods to grow up.

All of which explains why I'm so delighted to see the work of the OPEN Consortium come to the fruition represented by this book. Led by both the academic expertise represented by Professor Henderson-Sellers and the industry-practitioner experience represented by Messrs. Graham and Younessi – not to mention the academic and industrial talents of the other 30-plus members of the consortium – the OPEN Process Specification truly represents a third-generation approach to industrial-strength object technology. While it contains a comprehensive notational scheme (known as OML, for 'Object Modeling Language'), it puts considerable emphasis on the *process* of object-oriented development. As you'll see in the middle chapters of this book, OPEN represents an integrated combination of 'activities,' 'tasks,' and 'techniques.' And while it makes no pretense of reducing the complex task of systems development to a mindless 'paint-by-the-numbers' exercise, it does significantly increase the chances that reasonably intelligent people will be able to follow some detailed, well-organized guidelines for achieving success with their projects.

Anyone who is familiar with the subject of OO methods will inevitably want to make a comparison between OPEN and the Unified Method Language (UML) developed by the 'three amigos' (Messrs. Booch, Rumbaugh, and Jacobson) at Rational Software Corp. Both approaches, along with a few others, have been submitted to the Object Management Group (OMG) as a proposed formal approach to OO development; and the long-term success of both OPEN and UML may well depend on the OMG's decision in this area. In the short-term, Rational has gained considerable attention by gaining the endorsement of major vendors such as Microsoft; but as noted in the Preface of this book, the OPEN Consortium has also garnered the support of a large number of computer vendors, CASE vendors, and other commercial organizations.

In the long run, it's possible that either UML or OPEN may dominate the field; but it's also quite possible that both will co-exist, each serving different needs. In any case, the only thing we can be sure about in the long term is that we'll all be dead. In the short-term, which seems to preoccupy many of us far more than it should, we need appropriate methods that can help us build the increasingly more complex systems that society wants us to build. And one of the things that's most interesting about OPEN versus UML, in the short term, is that while both have a very rich and comprehensive diagramming notation, only OPEN provides the thorough, comprehensive emphasis on process. If you're a software engineer or a project manager who has learned that diagramming notation is important, but inadequate without a firm supporting process, this means OPEN may well be the preferable choice.

Of course, that's up to you to decide. But you'll be in a much better position to make a choice after reading through this excellent book. Graham, Henderson-Sellers and Younessi have done a marvelous job in coordinating and distilling the work of over two dozen OO methodologists, and you have much to learn by digesting their explanation of this highly respectable third-generation OO method. I highly commend it to you.

Ed Yourdon
Polson, Montana
June 1997

Preface

Does anyone ever read the Preface? Well, in case you do, we should give you a brief rundown on what the book is about, who should read it and what the benefits of reading it may be.

OPEN is a third-generation object-oriented (OO) methodology containing a set of process patterns. What does that mean? The original methodological approaches, really just sets of techniques, were single authored; their support was minimal. Second-generation approaches started to actively borrow from other sources but still the merging of methodologies was second-hand. In third-generation OO approaches, the methodology developers are actively working *together* to produce widely supported and, at least in the case of OPEN, full lifecycle support. OPEN (which stands for Object-oriented Process, Environment and Notation) is developed by a group of (currently) 32 members known as the OPEN Consortium. While only three of this group have actually written the words in this book, all have contributed in terms of ideas, discussions and reviewing of this particular manuscript. Future books in the OPEN series will see different authors brought to the fore.

In this book, we describe the process underlying the OPEN methodology. We focus on the lifecycle (the 'contract-driven' lifecycle), the activities and tasks. The OPEN techniques will be the focus of a different book in the OPEN series. The way these are put together is flexible – each is a process pattern designed for a specific industry sector, for a specific project team size etc.

In this book, we do *not* discuss basic OO concepts, ideas and modeling techniques. We assume that the reader has read introductory texts (two of the three authors have written such books for your edification: Graham, 1994; Henderson-Sellers, 1997) and is ready to use a methodology on a real project (or to use OPEN in a teaching/learning mode).

The book is a little unusual in its structure: it has two components. First we describe OPEN in a normal format of, in this instance,[†] seven chapters. These describe the background to the OPEN project and why industry needs a third-generation OO methodology. Chapter 2 begins the focus of OPEN which is its strong, yet flexible, process specification and the patterns that are supported

---

† Ed.: OO jargon already – in the preface?

within its architecture. In this chapter, we discuss the need for process at a general level initially, moving slowly towards the specifics of the contract-driven lifecycle and then, through Chapter 3 on the need for seamlessness in OO methods, through to Chapter 4 with its detailed discussion on the activity objects which make up OPEN's contract-driven lifecycle. Chapter 5 details the tasks of OPEN while the remaining two chapters give a brief overview of the techniques and associated deliverables. Both of these will be reserved for detailed discussion in future books. There just was no room to fit them into this one!

Now the second portion of the book: a collection of appendices, the first of which at least is fairly major. Here is more of a dictionary, i.e. the reference manual to the OPEN tasks. The tasks are described in detail and ordered, as in a dictionary, alphabetically. Thus you can read Appendix A to get a detailed view of any specific task and then read the appropriate chapter (probably Chapter 4 or 5) to see how it fits in with the rest of the methodology, or vice versa. There is some repetition between the book itself and Appendix A. This is in order that each part can be studied relatively independently and is thus intentional.

There are another three appendices following this dictionary – all quite short. Appendix B summarizes the light version of the preferred OPEN notation known as COMN – itself the topic of a separate book. Appendix C gives an overview of a current (1997–1999) project to link OPEN with a commercial OO process known as MeNtOR. Finally, we offer Appendix D as an entity focusing on migration strategies. We have kept it separate here, although many of the ideas interweave the entire text, since it makes a nice and complete story in and of itself. We thought you might like to read it in its entirety.

As well as our colleagues in the OPEN Consortium (who are all listed in Section 1.4), we would also like to thank especially, for their constructive review comments, Don Firesmith, Tom Beale, Peter Horan, Marco Scheurer, W. M. Jaworski and the students of the Class of '97 studying IT921 at Swinburne University of Technology.

If you require local support for OPEN, contacts are given below. For more up-to-date information, consult the OPEN web site (details in Chapter 1.4) or the Addison-Wesley catalog entry for this book.

North America

>   Genesis Development Corporation: http://www.gendev.com
>   Knowledge Systems Corporation (KSC): http://www.ksccary.com/
>   Thomsen Dué: http://ourworld.compuserve.com:80/homepages/rtdue/
>   Tower Technology Corporation: http://www.twr.com

South America

>   Intuitive Technology: http://www.intuitive.com.br

Europe and Middle East

>   Bezant Limited : bezant@compuserve.com
>   Object House: steif@objectus.co.il

OIG Ltd: trish@oig.compulink.co.uk
Sen:te: http://sente.ch/
Wayland Informatics: http://www.wayland.co.uk

India

Fourfront: rajeshp@giaspn01.vsnl.net.in

Australasia

COTAR: http://www.csse.swin.edu.au/cotar/ and brian@csse.swin.edu.au

In addition, we wish to acknowledge the following copyright holders for permission to reproduce copyright material.

Addison Wesley Longman for Figures 2.4, 4.2, 4.5, 4.8, 4.9, 5.5, 5.6, 5.19, 7.2, A.1, A.4, A.6, A.7 and Tables 5.1, A.3, A.4, A.6; Cutter Corporation for Table A.7; Macmillan for Table A.8; Manning for Figures 2.6, 5.18; Prentice Hall for Figures 2.1, 2.2 and Table A.9; SIGS for Figures 3.1, 3.2, 4.10, 5.4, 5.7–5.9, 5.12–5.17, 7.1, 7.3, A.8–A.14, A.15, A.16, A.18–A.20, A.21 and Table A.1; Springer for Figures 4.3, 5.1 and Wiley for Table A.10.

We would also like to thank the following people for supplying diagrammatic material: J. M. Edwards for his contribution to Figure 1.4; D.G. Firesmith for Figures 5.10 and 5.11; P. Haynes for Figure 5.3; W. Hertha for Figure 2.7; and M. Scheurer for Table 3.1.

Ian Graham, Brian Henderson-Sellers
and Houman Younessi, July 1997

References

Graham I. (1994). *Object-Oriented Methods* 2nd edn. 473 pp. Harlow, UK: Addison-Wesley

Henderson-Sellers B. (1997). *A BOOK of Object-Oriented Knowledge* 2nd edn. 253 pp. Englewood Cliffs, NJ: Prentice-Hall

Trademark list

The following trademarks are used in the text:

Apple, MacApp and Powerbook are trademarks of Apple Computer Inc.

C++ and Unix are trademarks of AT&T

CORBA is the trademark of the Object Management Group

Eiffel is the trademark of the Non-Profit International Consortium for Eiffel

EiffelBench is a trademark of Interactive Software Engineering

Graphical Designer is the trademark of Advanced Software Technologies Inc.

IBM, Presentation Manager, SOM, DSOM and VisualAge are trademarks of International Business Machines, Inc.

Java and Open Look are the trademark of Sun Microsystems Inc.

MetaEdit is the trademark of MetaCase Consulting Oy.

Motif is a trademark of OSF

MS Windows, MS-DOS, Visual Basic, Foundation Classes, OLE and MS Project are all trademarks of Microsoft Corporation

NeWi is a trademark of System Software Associates Inc.

NeXT is the trademark of NeXT Computer

Objective-C and Software-IC are trademarks of Productivity Products International

ObjectMaker is the trademark of Mark V Systems

Objectory is the trademark of Objective Systems

Object Windows Library is a trademark of Borland International, Inc.

OMTool is the trademark of GE

OOATool is the trademark of Object International Inc.

Orbix is a trademark of Iona Technologies

Paradigm Plus is the trademark of Protosoft

Process Engineer is the trademark of LBMS

ROSE is the trademark of Rational Software Corporation

Simply Objects is the trademark of Adaptive Arts Pty Ltd

Smalltalk and VisualWorks are trademarks of ParcPlace Systems Inc.

SOMATiK is the trademark of Bezant Ltd

System Architect is the trademark of Popkin Software

UNIX is a registered trademark of X/Open Company Ltd, licensed through collaboration of Novell, HP&SCO

Xt Intrinsics is a trademark of X-Open

X-Windows is a trademark of the Massachusetts Institute of Technology

List of abbreviations

ADT	Abstract Data Type
AKO	A-Kind-Of
AMI	Application of Metrics to Industry
APO	A-Part-Of
AS	Australian Standards
ATM	Automated Teller Machine
BNF	Backus-Naur Form
BOM	Business Object Model
BON	Business Object Notation
BPR	Business Process Re-engineering
CAS	Complex Adaptive Systems
CASE	Computer Assisted Software Engineering
CBA	Computer-Based Assessment
CBA	Cost-Benefit Analysis
CD-ROM	Compact Disk-Read Only Memory
CIRT	Class, Instance, Rôle or Type
CMM	Capability Maturity Model
COMMA	Common Object Methodology Metamodel Architecture
COMN	Common Object Modeling Notation
CORBA	Common Object Request Broker Architecture
CPM	Critical Path Method
CPU	Central Processing Unit
CRC	Class, Responsibility, and Collaborators (cards)
CSF	Critical Success Factor
DB	DataBase
DBMS	DataBase Management System
DCS	Distributed Computing System
DFD	Data Flow Diagram
DOS	Disk Operating System
DSOM	Distributed System Object Model
ER	Entity Relationship (modeling)
ERA	Entity Relationship Attribute (modeling)
GQM	Goal Quality Metric

GUI	Graphical User Interface
HCI	Human–Computer Interaction
HCM	'Hairies and Conscripts' Model
IC	Integrated Circuit
IDL	Interface Definition Language
I/O	Input/Output
IOM	Implementation Object Model
IS	Information Systems
ISO	International Standards Organization
IT	Information Technology
ITT	Invitation To Tender
LARC	Library of Adopted Reusable Components
LED	Light Emitting Diode
LPRC	Library of Potentially Reusable Components
MIS	Management Information Systems
MOSES	Methodology for Object-oriented Software Engineering of Systems
MS	Microsoft
MVC	Model View Controller
OB	ObjectBase
OBA	Object Behavior Analysis
OLE	Object Linking and Embedding
O&M	Organizational and Management
OML	Object Modeling Language
OO	Object-oriented
OOAD	Object-oriented Analysis and Design
OOA/D/P	Object-oriented Analysis/Design/Programming
OOPL	Object-oriented Programming Language
OOPSLA	Object-oriented Programming, Systems, Languages and Applications
OOSE	Object-oriented Software Engineering
OPEN	Object-oriented Process, Environment and Notation
ORB	Object Request Broker
OSF	Open Software Foundation
OT	Object Technology
OWL	Object Windows Library
PC	Personal Computer
PERT	Programme Evaluation and Review Technique
PSEE	Process Sensitive Software Engineering Environment
PSP	Personal Software Process
PSPPS	Purpose; Scope; Partitions; Patterns; Semantics
RAD	Rapid Application Development
RAM	Random Access Memory
RDB	Relational DataBase
RDD	Responsibility-Driven Design
ROOM	Realtime Object-Oriented Method

SADT	Structured Analysis and Design Technique
SDLC	Software Development Life Cycle
SEI	Software Engineering Institute
SEP	Software Engineering Process
SEPA	Software Engineering Process Architecture
SLOC	Source Line Of Code
SMART	Specific; Measurable; Attainable; Relevant; Trackable
SOM	System Object Model
SOMA	Semantic Object Modeling Approach
SPICE	Software Process Improvement and Capability dEtermination
SRS	Software Requirements Specification
STD	State Transition Diagram
SVDPI	Subject–Verb–Direct.Object–[Preposition–Indirect.Object]
TBD	To Be Decided
TOM	Task Object Model
TQM	Total Quality Management
UI	User Interface
UML	Unified Modeling Language
US	United States
V&V	Verification and Validation
WWW	World Wide Web

Chapter 1

Introduction to OPEN

1.1 Why object orientation?

Software as a product and software development as a process are each complex. The most successful development metaphor for dealing with such complexity has been identified as the object-oriented (OO) approach to software construction. Object orientation is significant as a framework for the production of high-quality software in that it offers techniques that, *inter alia*, facilitate software construction by dealing more effectively with complexity, through provision of reuse opportunities and through improvement of design efficacy and maintainability.

Many people and organizations are convinced of the wisdom of shifting their systems development activities towards an OO approach. This may be because they become aware of the benefits of object technology (OT), have seen other companies succeeding in this way or even for that worst of reasons: because OT is new and fashionable. Even in the latter, misguided, case these companies may gain from the experience because, even should the project in hand fail, they may gain a better understanding of existing systems and development practices through the construction of an object model. People and organizations have several reasons for replacing or extending older systems. For example, a package vendor may see the move to OT as closely tied to the move to an open platform and, in turn, see this as a way of achieving greater market share since there are usually potential customers who do not (and perhaps will not) own the proprietary platform on which the old product currently runs. Vendors may also wish to compete more effectively by adding value to the existing product with graphical user interfaces, management information system (MIS) features or delivery on distributed platforms. User organizations may wish to take advantage of new standards, downsizing or friendlier interfaces along with the benefits of the move to OT itself. Both types of organization will be looking to slash maintenance costs, which can account for a huge proportion of the MIS budget, and to reduce time to market.

Object orientation has for a long time been considered in terms of an analysis/design/programming 'method', i.e. a set of (one hopes interrelated) concepts, techniques and notations. This view of object orientation is, however, limiting in that it largely disregards the contextual, organizational and

1

technological aspects that can potentially exist within a unified OO view of the development process. An OO approach needs to define a process. For that process to be of high quality it needs to possess a wide range of characteristics, as noted above.

One of the greatest technical advantages of an OO lifecycle process is that of (almost) seamlessness (Chapter 3). 'Objects'[†] are used as the basic concept and unit of consideration during requirements engineering, in systems analysis and design, in the OO programming language and in future maintenance. 'Objects' are the common language of users as well as technical developers. Of course, the notion of seamlessness causes concern for project managers more used to being able to clearly delineate the end of the analysis phase and the end of the design phase – perhaps in terms of a waterfall lifecycle. Modern use of the words analysis and design and of suggested replacement terms is discussed in detail in Chapter 3.

Unfortunately, many extant OO approaches are of needlessly limited scope in that they mainly focus on the notational and model-building aspects to the detriment of other aspects of the methodological dimension (see Section 2.1), let alone the contextual and the technological dimensions. From this perspective, the Object-oriented Process, Environment and Notation (OPEN) approach to object orientation, as described in this book, is an exception in that it goes much beyond just a set of notations and some modeling rules and comprehensively defines an OO *process*.

The challenge before us is to recognize – indeed to cast – object technology as a process and to endeavor to identify and measure the efficacy, and eventually the quality, of its individual components, as a means of developing a framework for predicting the quality of products resulting from the employment of such a process.

1.2   What is a methodology?

An (OO) method or methodology (we will mostly use the words interchangeably) must cover the whole lifecycle both technically and managerially. That means a methodology must provide, at least (Figure 1.1):

- a full lifecycle process
- a comprehensive set of concepts and models, all internally self-consistent
- a full set of techniques (rules, guidelines and heuristics)
- a fully delineated set of deliverables
- a modeling language which includes a metamodel and a workable and intuitive notation

---

† At this stage, we do not want to enter into any arguments regarding the use of the words object, type, class, rôle and instance and will just use 'object' in a truly generic sense.

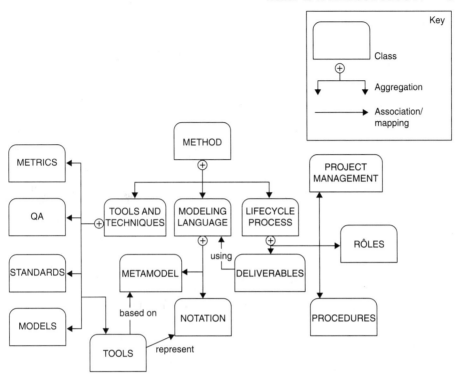

Figure 1.1   What is a method?

- a set of metrics

- quality assurance

- coding (and other) standards

- reuse advice

- guidelines for project management (including team structure and rôles, procedures and resource allocation and management).

If possible, a supporting set of tools should also be available.

In this book, we outline how this technique/process interaction ('lifecycle patterns') occurs in the context of the third-generation OPEN methodology for OO systems development. The model used, its metamodel and some appropriate notation is the focus of a companion book entitled *OPEN Modeling Language (OML) Reference Manual* (Firesmith et al., 1997). The OML describes the metamodel and the Common Object Modeling Notation (COMN) (Figure 1.2). A full description of the core of COMN, known as COMN Light, is given in Appendix 2.

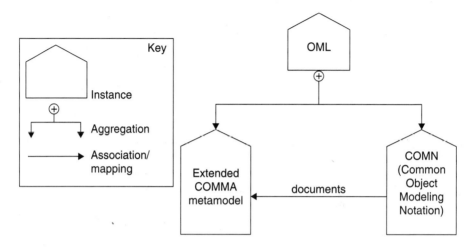

Figure 1.2. OPEN Modeling Language (OML) is composed of a metamodel (an extension to the COMMA core metamodel of Henderson-Sellers and Firesmith, 1997) and the COMN notation (Firesmith et al., 1997). The notation used is COMN itself.

1.3   What is OPEN?

OPEN is both an acronym and an invitation and opportunity to participate in a truly open, worldwide development of a rapidly emerging *full-lifecycle* OO methodological framework which can be loosely termed 'third generation.' It was initially created by a merger of three second-generation methods (MOSES, SOMA and the Firesmith method) commencing at the end of 1994 when it became clear, first, that there were too many first- and second-generation methods in the marketplace and that their scopes were too limited and, secondly, that the concepts underlying these three methods were almost completely compatible. (Other early influences and participants in the development of OPEN were Jim Odell and the responsibility-driven design (RDD) method.)

OPEN is essentially a framework for third-generation OO software development methods providing strong support for process modeling by using lifecycle patterns, strong support for requirements capture, and offering the ability to model intelligent agents. It has an embedded project management and reuse framework, supports business process modeling and offers guidelines on migration strategies. A prime concern of OPEN is software quality and the use of metrics. To that end, close links with quality frameworks including the Software Engineering Institute's Capability Maturity Model (CMM) are maintained and supported, and links to ISO 9000 and the SPICE software process improvement project are being developed. In addition to being released to the public domain, OPEN can also serve as the publicly available portion of commercial, largely proprietary methods. One such project, with the commercial MeNtOR method (Appendix C), has already begun.

In addition to synthesizing the best ideas and practices from MOSES, SOMA and Firesmith, OPEN also utilizes concepts from BON, Mainstream Objects, Martin/Odell, OBA, RDD, ROOM, Syntropy, UML and others. OPEN also offers a set of principles (see below) for modeling all aspects of software development, across the lifecycle. Individual methods may conform to the OPEN methodological framework by applying its principles and adopting all or part of the OPEN framework specification: lifecycle, tasks, techniques and modeling language (metamodel plus notation). OPEN will continue to evolve as new techniques are developed and enhanced by working methodologists, users and researchers.

OPEN extends the notion of a methodology not only by including a process model (a 'metaprocess') but also by providing guidelines for constructing versions of the method tailored to the needs of industry domains, individual organizations and problem types. Each of these versions is a lifecycle pattern in that it is derived from common usage, and is a solution to a problem in a context. The process model, the focus of this book, is an object model and, as such, is adaptable. One sample realization of this object model is the contract-driven lifecycle (Section 2.6) suitable for rapid application development within a MIS context, but other instantiations are not precluded. Indeed, how to tailor the OPEN process to other domains by selecting from a suite of lifecycle patterns will be the topic of future OPEN books (e.g. Duffy, 1997).

OPEN represents the summit of achievement in OO methods by tens of methodologists and the way forward into an uncertain future. It is open and remains in the public domain. It will not restrict innovation within conformant methods.

1.3.1 A tailorable lifecycle model

Underpinning any full lifecycle methodology must be a process (this argument is elaborated further in Chapter 2). However, it is generally believed that, no matter how hard we seek it, a single, generally applicable process will remain an unattainable and illusory Holy Grail of software engineering. Rather, different organizations, different development styles and different development domains will require their own specialized lifecycle process. The lifecycle process is essentially one part of the methodology, the key elements of which can probably best be grouped (Figure 1.3) into

- lifecycle process or (meta)model
- techniques
- representation

Thus, it may be argued, 'methodology' includes (lifecycle) process. However, at a large granularity, the (software engineering) process must include not only a methodology but also considerations of people/organizational culture and tools/

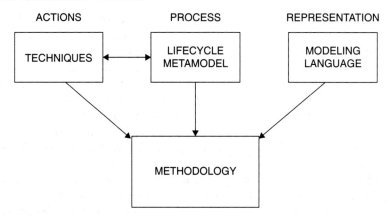

Figure 1.3. A methodology comprises, at least, a set of techniques plus a lifecycle model and a representational medium.

technology available. Techniques and processes interact strongly; while the representation (a combination of graphical notation and textual descriptors) provides the means of communication – developer to developer, developer to manager, developer to user, etc. Each of these software engineering processes (SEP) will be highly relevant under specific constraints and as such all are fairly widely useful. A SEP is a time-sequenced set of activities (often in parallel) which transform a user's requirements into software and provides a tested and well-defined approach to the development of OO software systems. Activities are connected in a flexible fashion by stating preconditions that must be satisfied before an activity can commence – as opposed to specifying the previous activity which must be completed as would be the case in a waterfall lifecycle metamodel. A single SEP, thus derived, is highly appropriate to a particular problem type and industry domain.

Generification of these SEPs permits us to seek for an underlying architecture, the software engineering process architecture (SEPA) (Figure 1.4). A SEPA for OO development, which as we shall see is embodied within OPEN, thus provides an integrating framework. No one project will ever use this; rather they will instantiate a particular part of the framework for their own circumstances. This 'tailoring of the lifecycle process' is in fact a major task within the overall OPEN architecture (Chapter 5). The SEPA is described by a set of objects representing lifecycle activities. Any type of interaction is possible within these objects in true OO fashion if the messages sent between these reifications of OPEN activities meet the client object's contract. The activities thus trigger or enable each other by message passing. The messages are guarded by pre- and post-conditions representing tests. The 'methods' of an activity are its tasks. Tasks can also be considered the smallest unit of work within OPEN (Figure 1.5). Tasks are carried out by actors (people) using techniques.

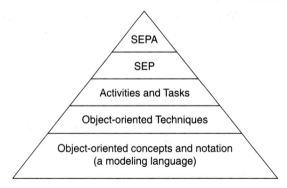

Figure 1.4. The pyramid of OO methodological sophistication. At the peak is the software engineering process architecture (SEPA) and at the base well-understood concepts.

In the seamless, iterative lifecycle of an OO development in which incremental delivery is the norm – and highly advantageous in keeping the user 'in the loop' providing immediate feedback, always a currently viable version for use and evaluation and producing higher-quality software – the elements which comprise the lifecycle describe the high-level activities which must be undertaken in order to produce the software product(s). The activities, described in detail in Chapter 4, are linked together in an organization's tailoring of the contract-driven lifecycle (as noted above) – which produces their specific SEP. The way in which activities are linked together depends on the organization and the problem. Case-study example SEPs are to be discussed in a future OPEN book: *Tailoring the OPEN Lifecycle – Case Studies.*

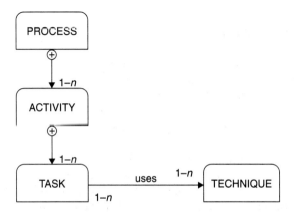

Figure 1.5. OPEN's activities have tasks which themselves are accomplished by the use of techniques.

The heart of OPEN tasks and techniques

Tasks

Techniques					
M	D	F	F	F
D	D	F	F	D
D	D	O	O	D
F	O	O	O	F
F	M	O	D	F
R	R	M	R	O
D	R	F	M	O
D	F	M	D	D
R	R	D	R	R
O	D	O	O	R
F	M	O	F	D

For each
task/technique
combination
we will recommend
five levels of
probability from
Always to Never

M = mandatory
R = recommended
O = optional
D = discouraged
F = forbidden

Figure 1.6.   A core element of OPEN is a two-dimensional relationship between techniques and the tasks. Each task may require one or several techniques in order to accomplish the stated goal of the task. For each combination of task and technique, an assessment can be made of the likelihood of the occurrence of that combination. Some combinations can be identified as mandatory (M), others as recommended (R), some as being optional (O), some are discouraged (D) but may be used with care and other combinations are strictly verboten (F = forbidden).

1.3.2   Tasks and techniques

We can think of these links (tasks to activities) in one of two ways: in a probabilistic manner or in a purer OO fashion by allocating tasks as methods of the activity objects. In the first case, we can assign, in very general terms or in more specific terms for any one highly specific project, probabilities or, to be more accurate, deontic certainty factors, for each of these task/activity links – see Chapter 5.

A two-dimensional matrix (Figure 1.6) then links the task (which provides the statement of goals, i.e. the 'what') to the techniques (which provide the way the goal can be achieved, i.e. the 'how'). Tasks are goals to be achieved – things to be done. You are at liberty to accomplish these tasks with whatever OO tools and techniques you are familiar with and which are compatible with the OPEN framework, also taking into account cost and other resource implications of these various choices. Again there is a fuzzy nature to the linkage of techniques and tasks. Some tasks are clearly best accomplished with a single, specific technique – a technique applicable to that task and nothing else (for example, implementation of services which support the coding task). Other techniques will be found useful in a range of tasks (for example, contract specification). And finally, for some tasks there may be a choice that the project manager has to make. The ways the activities–tasks–techniques linkages are established are at the heart of the lifecycle patterns of OPEN. Different combinations epitomize different patterns, useful in different contexts.

OPEN provides a large repository of techniques[†] taken from existing methods. These selected techniques range across project management, inspections and so on through to detailed theories and practices for requirements engineering and system modeling. An example here is the SOMA requirements engineering technology which is offered as a superior technique to the use-case technique. Others include the ROOM techniques for real-time architectural design, Reenskaug's rôle modeling, Buhr's time-threads and the pattern-oriented techniques of Catalysis.

In summary, the overall OPEN architecture sets the scene for the tasks that are needed within that lifecycle. The tasks, which may be grouped loosely into subject areas, are described here in some detail (Chapter 5 – with fuller details in the reference section of Appendix A); while only a brief summary is given of appropriate techniques (Chapter 6) that may be used to accomplish the goals of the task (full details will be the topic of forthcoming OPEN books by members of the OPEN Consortium – see Section 1.4). Deliverables associated with these tasks and techniques are outlined in Chapter 7.

1.3.3   OO principles

Finally, OPEN embodies a set of (OO) principles. It permits enhanced semantics for object-models based on the contributions of methods such as SOMA, BON, Syntropy, etc. Furthermore, OPEN is fully object-oriented in that encapsulation is a basic principle. To this end, bidirectional associations are strongly discouraged (Graham et al., 1997a). It is a logical consequence of this that class invariants are not an optional extra in the modeling semantics. Rule sets (which generalize class invariants) can be used to model intelligent agents as objects.

In OPEN, OO principles are basic and should be adhered to. These include:

- object modeling as a very general technique for knowledge representation
- encapsulation
- polymorphism

[†] In this book, focused on the OPEN process architecture, only a very brief summary is given. Later OPEN books will describe techniques in detail, e.g. a comprehensive overview in Herderson-Sellers and Younessi (1997).

together with

- clear, jargon-free and well-founded definitions of all terms
- extensive use of abstraction techniques, a foundation for semantically co-hesive and encapsulated 'objects'.

1.3.4   COMN – OPEN's recommended notation

While OPEN's focus has always been full lifecycle, during 1995 the call from OMG for a standardized metamodel and notation led some members of the OPEN Consortium to divert additional effort in these directions; thus was created the OML. OML is the name for the combination of metamodel and notation (Figure 1.2) – in parallel to a similar combination created by Rational method-ologists, known as Unified Modeling Language (UML). Both OML and UML are useful over a wide spectrum of situations (Whitehead, 1997). The OML metamodel is derived from the work of the meta-modeling COMMA project (Henderson-Sellers and Bulthuis, 1997) which itself has provided valuable input to the OMG meta-modeling effort. The notational element of OML also has its own name: COMN (Firesmith et al., 1997). While it was designed for use in OPEN, COMN is not so restricted and can be used in conjunction with other OO methods. Consequently, we have published the COMN notational standard separately from this book, merely summarizing the notation (COMN Light) in Appendix B.

OPEN strongly recommends the COMN notation which best supports its principles. However, we realize that many applications will only need a small subset (COMN Light) and that conformant methods will find some of it irrel-evant. Equally we understand that other notations will be preferred by some organizations. This is permissible within the OPEN framework. For example, the UML notation can be used to express OPEN models in many cases. However, some things that can be expressed well in COMN cannot be expressed or will not be properly expressible within the semantics of UML (e.g. responsibilities, rule-sets, exceptions, cluster encapsulation) and some UML practices (bidirectional associations) will violate OPEN principles.

1.4   Who are the people involved in OPEN?

The OPEN Consortium is a non-profit organization responsible for developing and maintaining the OPEN method and includes the original authors of the methods cited above together with over 25 other members drawn from the OO methodology, research and training communities worldwide. The current mem-bers of the OPEN collaborative team are: B. Henderson-Sellers, I. M. Graham and D. Firesmith together with D. Anastasiu, C. Atkinson, J. Bézivin, E. Col-bert, P. Desfray, R. Dué, D. Duffy, R. Duke, Y. Gill, K. Hung, G. Low, J. McKim,

D. Mehandjiska-Stavrova, S. Moser, K. Nguyen, A. O'Callaghan, M. Page-Jones, D. Patel, R. Pradhan, D. Rawsthorne, A. J. H. Simons, M. Singh, P. Swatman, B. Unhelkar, K. Whitehead, A. Wills, R. Winder, H. Younessi, E. Yourdon and H. Ziv. Initial work merged together the MOSES, SOMA and Firesmith methods; further collaborative mergers are anticipated.

Some of the first industry adopters (in alphabetical order) were:

(1) Users
Computer Vision India
Dow Jones
Customers of Fourfront
Israeli Electricity Company
KSC
There are several dozen companies, particularly in Australia, using the commercial product, MeNtOR, which is well aligned with OPEN (Appendix C)

(2) CASE tool vendors
Adaptive Arts Pty Ltd (Simply Objects)
Advanced Software Technologies Inc. (Graphical Designer)
Bezant (SOMATiK)
Mark V (Object Maker)
MetaCase Consulting (MetaEdit+)

(3) Process management
LBMS (Process Engineer)

(4) Consultancy support
COTAR (Australia)
Fourfront Information Technologies Private Limited (India)
Genesis Development Corporation (USA)
Intuitive Technology (Brazil)
KSC (USA)
Object House (Israel)
OIG Ltd (UK)
Sen:te (Switzerland)
Thomsen Dué and Associates (Canada)
Tower Technology Corporation (USA)
Wayland Informatics (UK)

(5) OPEN is also taught, to our knowledge, at
City University of Hong Kong (Hong Kong)
Concordia University (Canada)
De Montfort University (UK)
Hartford Graduate College (USA)
South Bank University (UK)
Swinburne University of Technology (Australia)
University of Technology, Sydney (Australia)
University of the West Indies (West Indies)

(6) Website

For more information, the OPEN home page is located at URL:

`http://www.csse.swin.edu.au/cotar/OPEN`

with mirrors at

USA: `http://www.markv.com/OPEN`

UK: `http://www.scism.sbu.ac.uk/cios/mirrors/OPEN`

Israel: `http://oop.cs.technion.ac.il/OPEN`

1.5 About this book

This book describes the process underlying the OPEN methodology. We do *not* discuss basic OO concepts, ideas and modeling techniques. Instead we address the user wishing to deploy an OO methodology in their organization (be it commercial software development, business and enterprise modeling and re-engineering or in a university or other teaching environment). Readers may thus be system architects, developers, managers or educators. Each will approach this text from a different viewpoint.

The structure of the book is as a sequence of seven chapters which follow through the OPEN process. We first focus on the overall need for a process in the context of software engineering. Moving from the general to the more specific, we introduce the 'contract-driven lifecycle' which is a major process pattern recommended within the OPEN methodological framework. This chapter is therefore of particular use to decision makers, managers, project managers and software engineers putting the ideas into practice. Chapter 3 evaluates the rôles of analysis and design in a seamless process, as supported in OO methods and advocated by object technologists.

In Chapter 4, the focus moves to the major elements of the OPEN methodology itself. In this and succeeding chapters, an overall description of activities (Chapter 4), tasks (Chapter 5), techniques (Chapter 6) and deliverables (Chapter 7) is followed by logical groupings of the elements and an overview discussion of each such topic area. Chapters 6 and 7 are purposefully lean since (i) the material needed to describe these areas in detail is too extensive to fit into one book and (ii) we wish to segregate the techniques into a separate volume since anyone skilled in OO in general, but not in OPEN in particular, will be all too aware of many of these techniques and thus not need to be burdened with them in this book.

While we discuss process patterns in general within this text on the OPEN process, there is still a need for detailed tailoring of the OPEN framework to specific domains. This will be the focus of a future series of case studies using OPEN in different domains and how the most appropriate pattern should be identified.

Most types of reader will benefit from reading the overview chapters (Chapters 4–7). However, they are still very much synoptic in nature. The full detail (much of which is quite dry reading) has been put in the reference sections (appendices) at the end of the book. Appendix A fully documents the tasks of OPEN (a similar full documentation of the OPEN techniques is in Henderson-Sellers and Younessi 1997); here is to be found a dictionary-type listing – one which is to be dipped into as necessary and *not* read sequentially. This reference portion of the book is described alphabetically, as you might expect. Any repetition between the book itself and Appendix A is intended so that each part (either the chapters of the book or the appendices) can be studied relatively independently.

Finally, there are another three appendices following this dictionary – all quite short. Appendix B summarizes the light version of the preferred OPEN notation known as COMN. This is fully described in a separate book (Firesmith et al., 1997). Appendix C gives an overview of a current (1997–1999) project to link OPEN with a commercial OO process known as MeNtOR. Last but by no means least, we offer Appendix D as an entity focusing on migration strategies. We have kept it separate here, although many of the ideas interweave the entire text, since it makes a nice and complete story in and of itself. We thought you might like to read this one as a novel (pun intended).

References

Duffy D. (1997). *Tailoring the OPEN lifecycle – case studies* (in preparation)

Firesmith D., Henderson-Sellers B. and Graham I. (1997). *OPEN Modeling Language (OML) Reference Manual.* pp. 271. New York: SIGS Books

Graham I. M., Bischof J. and Henderson-Sellers B. (1997a). Associations considered a bad thing. *Journal of Object-Oriented Programming,* **9**(9), 41–8

Henderson-Sellers B. and Bulthuis A. (1997). *Object-oriented Metamethods.* New York: Springer Verlag.

Henderson-Sellers B. and Firesmith D. G. (1997). COMMA: Proposed core model. *Journal of Object-Oriented Programming (ROAD),* **9**(8), 48–53

Henderson-Sellers B. and Younessi H. (1997). *OPEN's Toolbox of Techniques.* Harlow, UK: Addison-Wesley

Whitehead K. (1997). OO methodology issues: what are they and do they matter. *American Programmer,* **10**(3), 4–8

Chapter 2
Process as the keystone

2.1 The need for process

The 'software crisis' persists – user demand continues to outstrip our ability to supply quality software systems. Software systems are delivered late, with defects remaining (i.e. low quality) or not at all. Pressures for rapid delivery often lead to software developers concentrating on coding to the detriment of all other phases, particularly testing. Indeed, as pointed out recently by Dave Thomas, if software is being developed in 'webtime' (i.e. short time to market) for web applications with potentially small scope and short lifetime, lack of quality, durability, extensibility or maintainability may have less relevance. However, for core business information systems solutions, the growing exhortations that software development should become more of an engineering discipline must be heeded. Good engineering practices, which incorporate project management strategies, rely on the use of *processes* as a foundation for their 'manufacturing' environment. The need for a process to underpin software development is critical if information systems are to be built that have characteristics such as high reliability, extensibility, maintainability and correctness (to name only a few). Object technology has been heralded by many as providing significant advances in these areas but, as we shall discuss, it has not yet attained these goals in the areas of process, process improvement and project management. Innovation in software production must therefore continue and good practice must be documented and formalized. Adherence to such practices must be demanded of all practitioners.

Process is critical to the successful adoption of object technology for real-world applications. However, Tony Wasserman notes that 'the great variations among application types and organizational cultures make it impossible to be prescriptive about the process itself.'

To set this urgent need for process in the context of it being widely recognized as a *vital* component of an OO methodology, let us trace the history of OO 'methods.' In the late 1960s, object orientation was in its infancy; yet this decade was when many of the OO concepts were laid down. Object orientation had little real-world application and OO tools were generally confined to university and industry research laboratories. At this stage, it was understood that, with regards to object orientation, the word methodology could be interpreted as:

'Methodology' = set of programming-level standards, tips and hints.

Concepts are important but do not intrinsically contain information on how, when and where these should be used. In the 1970s and 1980s, techniques such as CRC cards, scenario analysis, the use of interaction diagrams and how to create object models became well developed. This laid the foundation for the development of OO design methods. At this stage, our understanding was extended to encompass these new considerations, such that the popular view of object orientation in this era was:

'Methodology' = set of design-level techniques, guidelines and supporting documentation.

In the early 1990s, this all came together in a veritable explosion of so-called OO methods (or methodologies) – see Table 2.1. The availability of these various methodologies, some of which were purer OO than others, some fuller lifecycle, some more influenced (or you may say biased) towards one particular programming language, supported the adoption of object technology (OT) in mainstream markets such as finance, insurance, banking, health and airlines.

Towards the end of 1994 it began to be realized that text books describing methods were inadequate for many organizational needs (Jacobson, 1994). It was argued that textbook-based methods were fine for learning the techniques

Table 2.1   Explosion of OO 'methods' (in alphabetical order of author).

Booch, 1991/1994
OOA/OOD of Coad and Yourdon, 1990; and then of Coad et al., 1995
Fusion from Coleman et al., 1994
Syntropy of Cook and Daniels, 1994
OSA from Embley et al., 1992
Firesmith method, 1993
SOMA: Graham, 1991/1995
MOSES: Henderson-Sellers and Edwards, 1994a
Objectory/OOSE: Jacobson et al., 1992
Martin/Odell, 1992/1995/1996
MeNtOr: Object-Oriented Pty Ltd, 1993
Synthesis: Page Jones, 1991
OOram: Reenskaug et al., 1996
OBA: Rubin and Goldberg, 1992
OMT: Rumbaugh et al., 1991
ROOM: Selic et al., 1994
Shlaer and Mellor, 1988/1991
BON: Walden and Nerson, 1995
RDD: Wirfs-Brock et al., 1990
and many others

---

and for pilot projects and small industries. However, even the best are somewhat
deficient with respect to real process support – in other words, many have no
or little method! Published methods were often limited to particular foci, for
example a data-modeling focus in OMT (Rumbaugh et al., 1991), a telecommunications influence on OOSE (Jacobson et al., 1992) etc. No single design
method (of those published up to 1995) is complete, mostly because they do not
deal fully with the difficult issues of project management, quality assurance and
project practicalities. Granted there is some embryonic evidence for some of the
issues in these books. For instance OOSE (Jacobson et al., 1992) includes some
discussion on testing, SOMA (Graham, 1995) on requirement analysis and user
interaction, MOSES (Henderson-Sellers and Edwards, 1994a) on metrics, quality
and project management. Neither do any of these pre-1995 methods integrate
well in hybrid environments in which interfacing with traditional code is vital.
Only one of the authors, to the best of our knowledge, in some of his *Object
Magazine* articles (e.g. Graham, 1993a, 1993b), discusses the ideas of interfaces
in terms of wrapper technology.

Overall, this led to disenchantment with Booch (Booch, 1994), OMT (Rumbaugh et al., 1991), OOSE (Jacobson et al., 1992) and the like by many organizations who, instead, chose to 'roll their own' by merging together bits of all
these familiar methods. There are, however, dangers in this (Henderson-Sellers
et al., 1994). This leads us to presume that what is now meant by methodology
is:

> *'Methodology' = client-specific methods that cover the lifecycle require-
> ments of the particular project.*

Over the period 1991–6, OMT, Booch, RDD, Coad and Yourdon, Shlaer/Mellor
and OOSE became the most widely known of the 'OO methods.' *However,*
as we began to suggest above, these well-known 'OO methods' are not really
methods at all but rather a somewhat coherent set of useful techniques and
notations. What is needed is full process support, but a process that is not
frozen as a particular model (e.g. waterfall), but is flexible and tailorable and
may be applied to many project domains. (To be fair, Booch (1994) was aware
of this issue, but his guidance remained somewhat vague. Firesmith (1993) also
had a short discussion on the need to tailor.) We need to consider the larger-
scale issues of organizational structures, corporate as well as departmental reuse
strategies, component-based development and costing models.

A good method or process, be it OO or not, has several rôles: it should
provide a set of standards, guidelines and heuristics for what is to be done, when
these actions are to be undertaken and in what order, what the elements are
that are involved in the process as well as what will be delivered. It should give
guidance and support through its techniques and guidelines (most important for
beginners); it should provide a framework for monitoring and control. At the
higher (software engineering process (SEP)) level this monitoring and control
may be achieved through advice on project management and quality procedures
and by the use of appropriate technologies. In an OO domain, these technologies

must be selected in such a way that they are sympathetic with an OO development approach. Consequently, as many have pointed out, an OO process is not simply a recipe book by which a series of steps is followed slavishly to produce the perfect 'meal.' Access to business knowledge is mandatory, as is creativity and skill in design. Rather than a 'cookbook,' a process or method may be better regarded as a good guidebook or road-map (Unhelkar and Mamdapur, 1995). Such a book provides the traveler with the basic layout of the streets, complete with hints, procedures and rules that apply, thus providing for a successful navigation. However, no one expects it to predict occasional disturbances such as burst water mains or pavements closed for renovation and the expert user will need to consult the map less than the novice, often bending the rules to create greater flexibility and permit more originality and creativity.

A well-defined process or method thus provides a standard, yet flexible, pattern-based framework for developing systems that blend engineering rigor with engineering creativity thus permitting success to be repeated and repetition of failures to be avoided. Adoption of such an approach will be instrumental in permitting the organization to improve their process capability as measured by capability maturity assessment models such as the Capability Maturity Model (CMM) of the Software Engineering Institute (SEI) or the ISO-SPICE software process improvement project. A match between a commercial process tool such as MeNtOR or Objectory (known as level 3 methods: Henderson-Sellers and Edwards, 1994b)[†] and a public domain method (level 2) such as OPEN or OOSE provides both full commercial-strength support and, at the same time, international validity and entry-level documentation through the corresponding public domain version (Appendix C).

2.2   What is a process?

A process is defined in the *Oxford English Dictionary* as: *A continuous and regular action or succession of actions, taking place or carried on in a definite manner and leading to the accomplishment of some result; a continuous operation or series of operations. (The chief current sense.)*

The software process produces software.

The three major areas of activity identified above support the notion that the *process* of software development ostensibly has three dimensions.

(1) Methodology: which can be viewed as the manifestation of attempts to introduce rigor into software development, at least by capturing and standardizing recognized good practice as well as seeking good underpinning theory. Examples might be an approach underpinned by a waterfall lifecycle model or else the typical framework sequence of

   (i) communicate with user
   (ii) develop a project plan

---

† Level 1 methods are simplified for teaching; level 2 are public domain full methods and level 3 are commercial products.

(iii) build an engineering model

(iv) construct the software using the model

(v) test and implement the software

(vi) obtain customer feedback (Pressman, 1996).

(2) People and organizational influences – directly related to the management of the human activities that lead to the development of software systems.

(3) Technology (tool support).

It is the balance of elements from these three dimensions that defines a specific software process and allows an approximation and subsequent comparison of the level of the capability, in process assessment terminology (e.g. CMM), of an instance of such a process. Indeed, it is a well-defined software process that is the central requirement for attaining a CMM or ISO-SPICE level 3 maturity.

We can therefore consider a process (any process, but a software process for our purposes) as being defined in terms of a mix of an instance of a methodology, a particular organizational context and a specific set of technologies. Given such a view of processes, and in the presence of adequately formal definitions and measures for each of the three elements involved, only then can one relate the quality of the resultant product to the quality of the process utilized.

As an example, consider the process of preparing a meal. The quality of the resultant meal is influenced by many factors including the quality of the recipe (the methodology), the level of skill of the person preparing the meal and the freshness and availability of the ingredients (the organizational context) and the availability of appropriate tools such as stoves, ovens, pots and pans (the technology). Similarly, in a software development context, the quality of a product is contingent upon the methodology used: Do we use OO analysis and design?; What validation technique is employed?; How well is the technique X specified? and so on. Consideration must also be given to the organizational context (the level of training and availability of staff, their morale, attitude, aptitude and experience, the availability of adequate funds and time, and so on), and the technology in use: What CASE tool do we use?; What automated testing system do we utilize?; and so on. The challenge before us is to identify and measure the efficacy of each of these elements of influence and to do so first in a prescriptive form and then by taking the scientific/engineering approach of evaluation of these elements in practice.

A high-quality software process, however, not only has to cover the three areas above, but also has to be understandable, enactable, repeatable, improvable and formally documented. To achieve these attributes, a software process has to be formal, granular, precise and measurement-based.

2.3   Clarification of terminologies

In the preceding sections we, and virtually every other author, have used terms such as 'process,' 'software process,' 'methodology,' 'technique' and 'method' without defining them and at times interchangably. This can be potentially confusing. For example: Are a software process and a methodology the same thing?; Are the terms 'methodology' and 'method' synonyms?; If not which encompasses which?; and so on. There is need for some clarification.

As we noted in Section 2.2, many software engineering authors, particularly those involved with the software process and software process assessment/improvement and quality domains, state that a software 'process' is composed of three major elements: (i) methodology; (ii) context and organizational influences (people); and (iii) technology – thus implying that a process includes or encompasses a methodology.

Many others, particularly object technology methodologists, have stated that a methodology is not just a set of notations and modeling rules and that an appropriate methodology must have a process dimension, thus implying that a methodology includes or encompasses a process.

To support their respective viewpoints, the former group put forward the argument that it is a common error that a 'software process' is often equated with the 'methodology' utilized. As this latter, more restricted, definition ignores the influence of technology and people, a variety of shortcomings or strengths demonstrated within a software development activity can no longer be explained adequately. For instance, it raises questions such as: Why is it that companies X and Y use the same 'process' yet produce vastly different results in terms of product quality? The answer is that most probably the software development *technologies* utilized (e.g. CASE, PSEE, compilers, static analyzers, etc.) differ in quality between the two firms or that the *organizational aspects* are not comparable. For example, it may be that employees at company X are better trained or more experienced than those at company Y or that they may have more stringent verification and validation (V&V) procedures than those in effect at company Y. The correct way of asking this question is: Why is it that companies X and Y use the same 'methodology' (e.g., both use SADT) yet one produces a vastly superior product to the other?

A second question might be: Why is it that our introduction of CASE as a means of process improvement did not have a significant effect? The answer may be associated with other aspects of the 'process' such as inadequacy of staff training in utilization of technology introduced, an important organizational aspect of a relatively mature process.

Another question: Why did our ability to build high-quality software diminish significantly when X left the team, although we have not changed the 'process?' has the answer that although the 'methodology' may not have changed, through the departure of X the 'process' obviously has. This is a common feature of immature software development firms within which expertise is resident in individuals rather than the organizational procedures. Hence the expertise is only available to the success of the process while that person is employed on the project; it is lost when that person leaves.

All – or at least the vast majority – of these issues would be resolved if we expanded the definition of the software process to encompass the technological and organizational aspects also. This is consistent with the bulk of informed

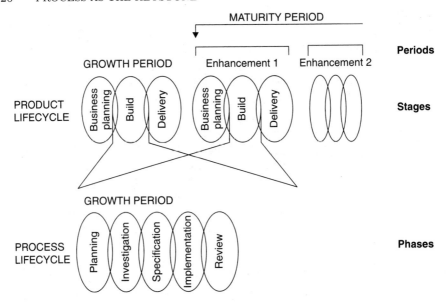

Figure 2.1. Product and process lifecycle in MOSES (after Henderson-Sellers and Edwards, 1994a).

current research (Bootstrap, Cleanroom etc.). Only through the inclusion of these other dimensions can we begin to 'compare apples with apples.'

In their own support, the latter group (OO methodologists) suggest that, as a methodology is 'an approach that covers lifecycle requirements of a particular project,' it is natural for it to be modeled and described as a network of interrelated tasks set out to achieve some specific end. As this is, not accidentally, also the definition of a 'process' as provided in the literature (e.g. Humphrey, 1989), it suggests that a methodology requires a process dimension. Pointing to many real-world instances where methods are described in terms of a series of 'transformations' or 'processes,' further controls such as project management and quality assurance are highlighted as also being necessary elements of a successful methodology. Furthermore, Wasserman (1996), in differentiating between notation and method, defines a method as a 'set of steps to be followed in deriving the analysis or design model.'

Which group is right? Well, they both are! The confusion arises from the granular nature of processes and what each party means when utilizing terms such as 'process,' 'method' and 'methodology.' What is meant is that when we speak of a software development project, we usually speak of at least two 'processes at differing levels of granularity' (for example, the product and process lifecycles of MOSES (Figure 2.1): Henderson-Sellers and Edwards (1994a)). Here we see two granularity levels: a high level which focuses on management issues and a lower level which has a more technical, modeling focus. The former encompasses the people factor, particularly in the business planning and delivery stages; it embraces technological ideas not only in the build stage but also in the business planning stage particularly with respect to feasibility studies and (possibly) the analysis of critical success factors (CSFs). The methodological element is essentially the build stage and this is equivalent to the embedded technical lifecycle. It is here, within the five phases of the process lifecycle (of MOSES) that we find the highly iterative descriptors for software development. Of course the people and technology issues of the higher-level management process cannot be totally ignored – they are just subjugated to the 'techie' sole focus of most software developers.

Most OO methodologies such as OMT or Booch focus on this finer-grained 'lifecycle process' and ignore[†] the more encompassing and more realistic SEP (a more sophisticated form of the product lifecycle with the embedded process lifecycle as in Figure 2.1). OPEN supports this newer, integrated, higher-level SEP while retaining the iterative lifecycle process (meta)model at the lower echelons.

Thus at the finer level of granularity, it is true that the elements and steps required to complete a task define a situation which may be described as a 'process.' In other words that method or approach by which the work is done may be described as a process; what is usually and popularly referred to as the 'methodology.' In this sense a 'methodology' has a 'process' dimension.

To illustrate, we shall further extend our meal preparation example. We have established that the quality of the meal will be partially influenced by the quality of the recipe. Most good recipes are, however, written out in terms of:

(1) The artifacts and structures involved. (What is there?) That is the ingredients needed and their attributes, for example quantity and state (melted, diced, heated, etc.).

(2) The procedure or transformations. (How do things change?) For example, put onions in frying pan and stir.

(3) Order and sequence. (When and in what sequence do things happen?) For example, first put the onions ... until golden brown.

Incidentally these three dimensions are the three dimensions of:

(1) structure

(2) transformation

(3) causality/sequentiality

present in the real world through which processes may be defined.

As such, a methodology may be thought of as a prescriptive model of a situation or artifact presented as a process. In this sense, then, the former encompasses the latter. In just the same way as a recipe models a meal, we

---

† We suggest that these methodological or method-level processes could perhaps be more appropriately thought of as a set of techniques, for example the Booch modeling technique.

might use either OML (Firesmith et al., 1997), or UML (Booch et al., 1996; Rational, 1997) to model a software system.

However, just as we cannot eat a recipe book, neither will merely a system model (a set of notations interrelated to capture some aspect of reality) suffice. Other elements, in addition to the modeling methodology, are needed to ensure the success of a project. As noted above, we also need the other two dimensions of context and organizational aspects, and that of technology.

In terms of our meal preparation example,

(1) we also need to utilize some pots and pans

(2) it matters if we have a gas or electric stove or a microwave oven

(3) we need to know whether an electric food processor is available, etc. (i.e. technology is important).

Also it is important whether

(1) the person is cooking for himself or herself, for a family dinner, for a dinner party, at a restaurant, or for a catering and food-packing company

(2) a person with an adequate level of expertise is leading the preparation of the meal

(3) there is adequate and sufficiently skilled help at hand.

Other important factors might be

(4) time availability

(5) morale and reward to be obtained for the completion of the task

(6) the appeal and ambience of the work area

to name but a few – all matters of a contextual and organizational nature.

The definition and realization of a combination of these technologies and circumstances, in addition to the recipe, will set out the 'meal preparation process.' One enactment of such a process will be a 'process instance' that, if re-created (repeated) identically at a later time or a different location, should produce the same result.

This is the 'process' at the higher level which clearly encompasses the 'method!'

At any rate, a consistent and clear set of terminologies must be utilized. In OPEN, the term 'methodology' refers to the method-level process (e.g. the equivalent of, say, the Booch approach), together with the term 'software process' at the higher level. The word 'technique' is at a very-low-level – examples here might be CRC cards, scenario analysis, textual analysis. Thus, the OPEN software engineering process specification can be thought of as a *strategy* which designates objectives, realized by the tasks. Many of the earlier OOAD approaches, in constrast, focus not on strategy but on *tactics*, realized in OPEN by the set of techniques.

2.4   The software process

As mentioned above, the overall prescriptive model (plan) of the software development activity within an organization may be termed the SEP. By this, we mean that the structures, artifacts, activities, rules, contexts and technologies utilized by an organization in their software development effort define a high-level abstract process composed of several interrelated blocks which interact to ensure the success of the development effort at hand. Reasonably mature (e.g. level 3 of CMM or ISO-SPICE) organizations define and follow such a high-level software process as their 'defined software process.' It should be noted that these definitions are in terms of not only the mandatory methodological steps (e.g. ISO-SPICE ENG $3^\dagger$, develop software design) but also those of context and organization (e.g. ISO-SPICE SUP 3, perform quality assurance; MAN 3, manage risk; ORG 4, provide skilled human resources) and that relating to technology (e.g. ISO-SPICE SUP 2, perform configuration management).

A given instantiation or enaction of such a process is usually called the 'process instance' or a 'software development project.' These instantiations are in fact the application of the SEP to the development domain.

There is, however, a need for a higher-level specification and abstraction. This requirement arises from the recognition that there are many different ways by which the building blocks composing a SEP may be interrelated. Furthermore, there is the recognition that there may be several different, functionally homologous building blocks from which to select in order to achieve some specific task. For these reasons, and ultimately to satisfy the flexibility requirement demanded of SEPs, we need a higher-level abstraction: one stated in terms of the building blocks available and the rules and conditions under which they may be interrelated to compose a software process which in turn may be instantiated. Such higher-level abstraction is the software engineering process architecture (SEPA) (Chapter 1, Figure 1.4).

Considerable interest is also emerging in less rigorously specified methodological 'steps' expressed in terms of *adaptive software development strategies* which are built using *complex adaptive systems* (CAS) theories originally developed at the Santa Fe Institute (see e.g. Highsmith, 1997). These theories have links into agents, self-organization and emergent outcomes and are compatible with RAD techniques. They elevate the plan–build–revise iterative or evolutionary lifecycle into one of speculate–collaborate–learn. The efficacy of these ideas in an OO process such as OPEN has still to be rigorously evaluated. However, a similar set of techniques, known as convergent engineering (Taylor, 1995) are fully and readily integrated into OPEN. Using convergent engineering techniques, a business design is implemented directly in software such that the business design and the software design become two viewpoints on the same, single system.

---

† In the ISO-SPICE terminology, each of the 28 processes covering the extent of the standard is identified by a three-letter and one-digit code (e.g. ENG 3). The three letters correspond to the process category (of which there are five: CUS, ENG, SUP, MAN, ORG) and the digit indicates an individual process within that category.

2.5 Process models

We need to emphasize that different process models will be needed under different circumstances. Different organizational cultures, project sizes, need for formality, safety criticality and so on, will require the adoption of a different project management strategy. Whatever the lifecycle model chosen (e.g. waterfall, fountain, spiral, pinball – see below), it will attempt to describe the fine-grained time sequencing (possibly in a fuzzy way) as the software development proceeds, as well as provide a sound basis for project management and the successful software delivery to the customer. In its simplest form, a lifecycle model is described by a linear sequence of phases in which specific activities are identified as occurring in each of these predefined phases – for example, the waterfall model. At the other extreme, phases may have absolutely no predetermined characteristics, that is their ordering is not only random, but changes from day to day, project to project – for example, the pinball model.

Consider a very simple process architecture, akin to the waterfall method of structured development. The activities of this process might be:

- delineate the problem to be solved
- consider possible solutions and, assuming a software solution is appropriate, then
- take the business decision to build the software.

While building the software, we might go through steps such as

- elicit user requirements
- undertake analysis of the problem ready for translation to a software design
- design the software
- code the software
- test the software (alpha and beta tests)
- put the software into use
- continue (possibly ad infinitum) to fix bugs and, probably in parallel,
- develop further enhancements to the software product.

The waterfall model is relatively rigid and linear. It does not support the need of object technology for iteration, incremental delivery, parallel development and flexibility and, appropriate for some projects, a more prototyping style. (The word prototyping can be emotive and we prefer in many projects to urge incremental delivery as the mindset rather than prototyping.)

Several alternatives to the waterfall lifecycle model have been proposed over the last few years. These include the spiral, the V, the X, the fountain and the pinball models (for a review of all these, except the very recently published pinball model, see *Migrating to Object Technology* (Graham, 1995)). MOSES,

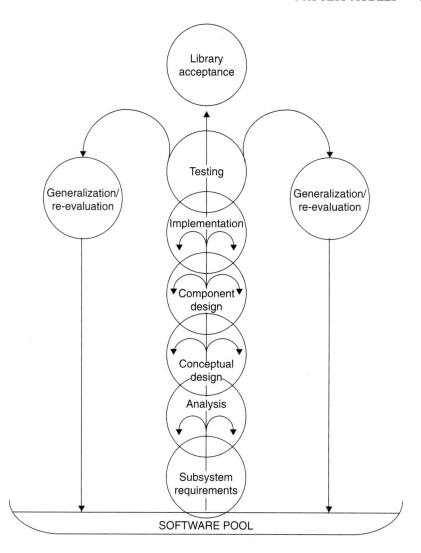

Figure 2.2.   The fountain model for the OO lifecycle of an individual class or cluster subsystem of classes. The basic model appropriate when a class needs to be specified from scratch (after Henderson-Sellers and Edwards, 1994a).

SOMA and OOram were significantly influenced by the fountain model (Figure 2.2). The fountain model only describes the technical or process lifecycle (MOSES terminology – see Figure 2.1) component of the methodology. This process lifecycle can itself be regarded as being embedded within the more business-focused product lifecycle (Figure 2.3). In this approach, the three stages of the product lifecycle (business planning, build, delivery) are highly business-focused;

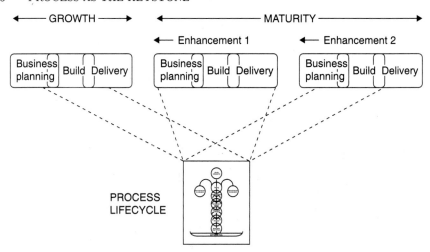

Figure 2.3   Fountain model embedded into business processes.

while the five MOSES phases (of planning, investigation, specification, implementation and review) are at the project management scale/technical level of an individual project. Enhancements or adjustments to existing software systems are catered for via the enhancement period which is a reapplication of the same three stages, probably with different weights.

While these three stages cover the lifecycle at a high level of granularity, it is clear that more detail is required. At a lower level, we can describe the lifecycle process as a set of activities, rather than the five lifecycle MOSES phases, and model these by objects. The activities have a fuzzy relationship to the stages (Figure 2.4) and encompass and extend the five phases of Figure 2.1. OPEN activities, particularly when modeled as objects, have entry and exit constraints (analogous to the pre- and post-conditions of the contracting model of Bertrand Meyer) and have clearly delineated deliverables and test conditions. However, unlike Meyer's pre- and post-conditions which act at the feature/operation level of a programming language, OPEN's contracts operate first at the activity level. There is a duality which we can apply here *either* by utilizing the notion of the *interface contract* of Wirfs-Brock et al. (1990) rather than Meyer's (1992) *service contract* (see comparison undertaken in Low et al., 1995) *or* by modeling the activities themselves as responsibilities of a higher-level project object (alternatively we might model the project object–activity object relationship using containment).

However, activities are a fairly high-level concept. The deliverables within the activities and the sign-offs from the activities are created by focusing on a number of tasks that might be needed to complete the activity and finalize the tested deliverables – of course the tasks might differ from project to project even for the same activity (guidelines on choosing what tasks are relevant are found elsewhere).

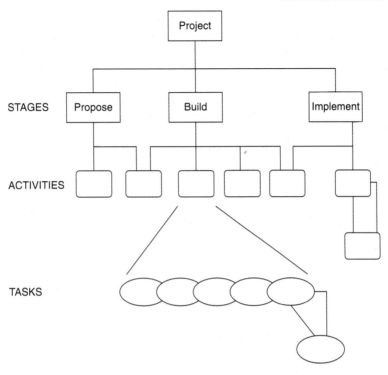

Figure 2.4 Stages, activities and tasks in SOMA (after Graham, 1995).

Tasks are 'actions' that have to be undertaken – things that have to be done. We will show later how tasks can be regarded as responsibilities/services of the activities – hence tasks can also have contracts with their own pre- and post-conditions. How each task is accomplished is described by one or more techniques. Formalization of this approach will be seen in the subsequent sections which describe in more detail the *contracting model* used to describe our recommended lifecycle development process in OPEN.

Implemented initially in MOSES and adopted in SOMA, these approaches (full lifecycle coverage and contracting) help move an OO methodology towards a full lifecycle coverage, based on the criterion discussed above. In other words, the model incorporates not only technical issues, as described in the lifecycle model and methodology (the *only* elements described in other methodologies such as OMT), but also business issues. This makes the overall architecture a comprehensive basis for not only technical project management but also for higher-level business decision making and end-user implementation and 'maintenance' (actually now able to be regarded as further extensibility to the product).

This approach is not unlike the one recently proposed by Daniels (1997). He clearly distinguishes between the project management/business perspective, which he calls the 'lifecycle,' and the software developer's viewpoint: the 'design process.' Daniels argues that much of the failure that has occurred in software development has been the result of force-fitting the 'lifecycle' and the 'design process' together as a single tool for both development and management. Thus progress (in project management terms) has typically been measured in developers' units (e.g. number of DFDs complete) rather than in users' units (e.g. the accounts-receivable functionality has been delivered). Thus, any given project has a lifecycle and a design process (which should each be chosen from a suite available at the organizational level); the development process then consists of activities, delivering 'products' (deliverables in OPEN) by means of task completion.

2.6   The contract-driven lifecycle

The contract-driven lifecycle, as used in our instantiation of OPEN, is shown in Figure 2.5. The model is, in essence, very simple (as in mathematics and science, the best answers are often the simplest – the principle of scientific parsimony and Occam's razor). In summary, a development program may be decomposed into a network of projects that produce deliverable, working software products. Projects are composed of activities (discussed in detail in Chapter 4). Each OPEN activity is shown as a box, either with rounded corners (an unbounded activity) or with rectangular corners (activity tightly bound in time). Since we are modeling these activities as objects, we can associate contracts with each activity object (discussed in Section 2.5) and with each task (modeled as a responsibility – see later) (hence the lifecycle name of 'contract-driven'). These contracts are expressed primarily by pre- and post-conditions; in other words, constraints that have to be met before an activity can be commenced and final conditions that have to be met (and signed off) before another activity can be initiated (i.e. one of its tasks triggered) – although of course parallelism is also supported in terms of non-dependent activity chains. Testing is an integral part of these exit conditions. Activities include well-specified testing tasks and should deliver test results against both use cases or task scripts (a higher form of use cases – see Graham, 1997) and a technical test plan of the normal kind; for example, tests that answer the following questions: Does an enhancement leave working things that worked previously? Does the system work well under stress and high-volume I/O? These activities thus provide a large-scale structuring in time. Different configurations, chosen to reflect the needs of different problems and different organizations, can be constructed from this flexible framework – thus fulfilling Pressman's call for an adaptive framework. Each combination of activities and interconnecting paths defines a SEP. Once chosen, the lifecycle process is fixed – although still, at least in an OO project, highly iterative, incremental, parallel, flexible and with a high degree of seamlessness (see Chapter 3).

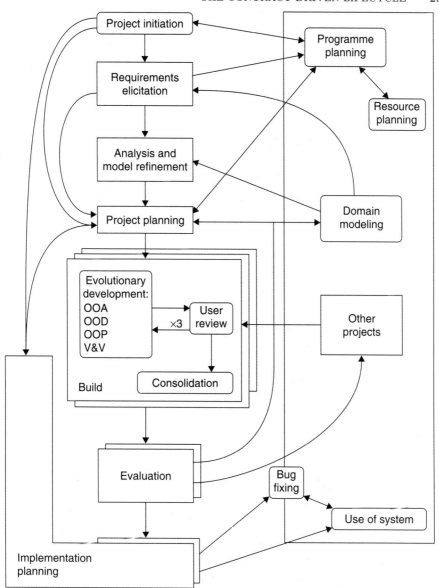

Figure 2.5 Contract-driven lifecycle model – one example instantiation.

The progression order is neither prescriptive nor deterministic. Rather, the contract-driven lifecycle permits

(1) ordering in an iterative and incremental fashion
(2) the tailoring by a given organization to its own internal standards and culture.

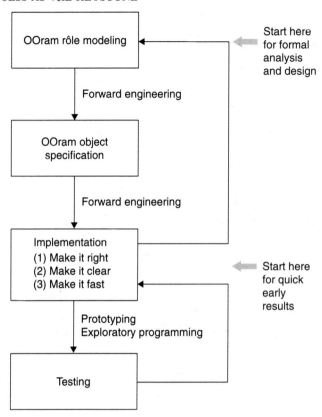

Figure 2.6.   OOram's 'simple implementation process' (after Reenskaug et al., 1996).

We indicate in Figure 2.5 some of the likely routes between activity objects, tailored for a MIS organization. But remember, the main governing constraint on the routes is whether you do or do not meet the preconditions of the tasks of the activity to which you wish to change.

Interestingly, the OOram lifecycle process (Figure 2.6) is essentially encapsulated within the evolutionary development activity. This rapidly cycles across class, instance, rôle or type (CIRT) identification, OOAD and OOP, followed by a test. What is added in this miniature prototyping lifecycle within the contract lifecycle (as exemplified in Figure 2.6) is the possibility of commencing in one of two alternative positions: either as a full lifecycle OOAD prior to implementation or as a 'structured hacking' or exploratory prototyping approach. Thus we could consider the OOram process as one particular lifecycle pattern within this framework.

OPEN's architecture also illustrates an instantiation of the proposed Architecture Reference Model which organizes information into four main categories:

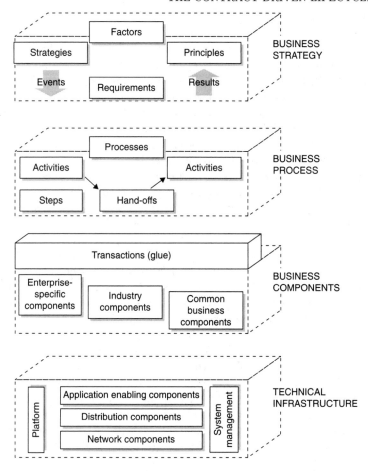

Figure 2.7   The Architecture Reference Model (after Hertha, 1995).

- business strategy
- business process
- business components
- infrastructure

(see Figure 2.7). The business strategy issues, the statements the business makes about its goals and objectives, form the backdrop to the business processes which implement the strategies in the form of workflows – seen here in the activities of program planning and domain modeling. The business components of the Architecture Reference Model are also represented in the domain modeling activity and in the analysis and model refinement activities (supported by the group of BPR-related techniques in OPEN, for instance) and, finally, the technical infrastructure is mirrored in the lifecycle model by the build activities.

2.6.1 Programmes and projects

Accumulated experience of years of software development indicates clearly to most commentators that only short projects and small teams succeed consistently. In OPEN, *projects* are typically small – from one to six months elapsed time – and utilize small teams (typically one to six people). Big project teams can be decomposed into small teams by layer, subsystem, or cluster such that the actual development is all done by small teams. A team size of 1 is too small; optimum size is 3–5 since within the team there must be adequate domain expertise, modeling expertise and implementation expertise. They are usually best managed by strict timeboxing and against prioritized objectives. The latter permit new features to be negotiated during the project provided that some low-priority ones can be dropped to compensate. This would be the only concept required if businesses only required software that took less than three person-years to develop. Unfortunately, the world is not so simple and large developments are sometimes needed: the software for the Boeing 777 or the space shuttle perhaps. To accommodate such developments, OPEN uses the concept of a *programme*. A programme is divided into multiple projects – in parallel or sequential or a mixture of the two. Programme decomposition is a classical software engineering task and we need not elaborate greatly on it in this text, although it should be noted that decomposition should be based on OO not functional principles – function points and use cases should not be used. What is new is the merger and recombination of the results of the separate timeboxes. Timeboxes may be concurrent or sequential combined with either centralized or distributed architecture. The consolidation activity within timeboxes ensures that the result of other efforts are integrated together in order to produce a product which can then be evaluated. Timeboxes thus combine with the activity objects to ensure quality and appropriate synchronization. They also provide a potential basis for outsourcing (see Chapter 4).

References

Booch G. (1994). *Object-Oriented Analysis and Design with Applications* 2nd edn. 589 pp. Redwood City, CA: Benjamin/Cummings

Booch G., Rumbaugh J. and Jacobson I. (1996). *The Unified Modeling Language for Object-Oriented Development*, Documentation set Vers 0.9 and 0.91 addenda

Daniels J. (1997). Object method: beyond the notations. *Object Expert*, **2**(2), 36–40

Firesmith D., Henderson-Sellers B. and Graham I. (1997). *OPEN Modeling Language (OML) Reference Manual.* 271 pp. New York: SIGS

Graham I. (1993a). Migrating to object technology. *Object Magazine*, **2**(5), 22–4

Graham I. (1993b). Interoperation: reusing existing software components and packages. *Object Magazine*, **2**(6), 25–6

Graham I. M. (1995). *Migrating to Object Technology.* 552 pp. Harlow, UK: Addison–Wesley

Graham I. (1997). Some problems with use cases ... and how to avoid them. In *OOIS'96* (Patel D., Sun Y. and Patel S., eds.), pp. 18–27. London: Springer

Henderson-Sellers B. and Edwards J. M. (1994a). *BOOKTWO of Object-Oriented Knowledge: The Working Object.* 594 pp. Sydney: Prentice-Hall

Henderson-Sellers B. and Edwards J. M. (1994b). Identifying three levels of OO methodologies. *Report on Object Analysis and Design,* **1**(2), 25–8

Henderson-Sellers B., Kreindler R. J. and Mickel S. (1994). Methodology choices – adapt or adopt? *Report on Object Analysis and Design,* **1**(4), 26–9

Hertha W. (1995). The architecture reference model, position paper to the Business Object Design and Implementation Workshop, OOPSLA '95, Austin, Texas, October 1995 (available from `http://www.tiac.net/users/oopsla/hertha.html`)

Highsmith J. (1997). Messy, exciting and anxiety-ridden: adaptive software development. *American Programmer,* **10**(4), 23–9

Humphrey W. S. (1989). *Managing the Software Process.* 494 pp. Reading, MA: Addison-Wesley

Jacobson I. (1994). Public communication on OOPSLA 94 panel: Methodology standards: help or hindrance?

Jacobson I., Christerson M., Jonsson P. and Övergaard G. (1992). *Object-Oriented Software Engineering: A Use Case Driven Approach.* 524 pp. Harlow, UK: Addison-Wesley

Low G., Henderson-Sellers B. and Han D. (1995). Comparison of object-oriented and traditional systems development issues in distributed environments. *Information Management,* **28**, 327–40

Meyer B. (1992). Applying 'design by contract'. *IEEE Computer,* **25**(10), 40–51

Pressman R. (1996). Software process perceptions. *IEEE Software,* **13**(6), 16, 18

Rational (1997). *Unified Modeling Language. Notation Guide. Version 1.0. 13 January 1997,* available from http://www.rational.com

Reenskaug T., Wold P. and Lehne O. A. (1996). *Working with Objects. The OOram Software Engineering Manual.* 366 pp. Greenwich, CT: Manning

Rumbaugh J., Blaha M., Premerlani W., Eddy, F. and Lorensen W. (1991). *Object-oriented Modeling and Design.* 500 pp. Englewood Cliffs, NJ: Prentice-Hall

Taylor D.A. (1995). *Business Engineering with Object Technology.* 188 pp. New York: Wiley

Unhelkar B. and Mamdapur G. (1995). Practical aspects of using a methodology: a road map approach. *Report on Object Analysis and Design,* **2**(2), 34–6, 54

Wasserman A. I. (1996). Towards a discipline of software engineering. *IEEE Software,* **13**(6), 23–31

Wirfs-Brock R.J., Wilkerson B. and Wiener L. (1990). *Designing Object-oriented Software.* 368 pp. Englewood Cliffs, NJ: Prentice-Hall

Additional referential sources related to Table 2.1

Booch G. (1991). *Object Oriented Design with Applications.* 580 pp. Menlo Park, CA: Benjamin/Cummings

Coad P. and Yourdon E. (1990). *Object-Oriented Analysis*, 1st edn. 232 pp. Englewood Cliffs, NJ: Prentice-Hall

Coad P., North D. and Mayfield M. (1995). *Object Models: Strategies, Patterns, and Applications.* 505 pp. Englewood Cliffs, NJ: Yourdon Press/Prentice-Hall

Coleman D., Arnold P., Bodoff S. et al. (1994). *Object-Oriented Development: the Fusion Method.* 313 pp. Englewood Cliffs, NJ: Prentice-Hall

Cook S. and Daniels J. (1994). *Designing Object Systems.* 389 pp. UK: Prentice-Hall

Embley D. W., Kurtz B. D. and Woodfield S. N. (1992). *Object-Oriented Systems Analysis. A Model-Driven Approach.* 302 pp. Englewood Cliffs, NJ: Yourdon Press/Prentice-Hall

Firesmith D. G. (1993). *Object-Oriented Requirements Analysis and Logical Design: A Software Engineering Approach.* 575 pp. New York: Wiley

Graham I. (1991). *Object-Oriented Methods.* 410 pp. Harlow, UK: Addison-Wesley

Martin J. and Odell J. J. (1992). *Object-Oriented Analysis and Design.* 513 pp. Englewood Cliffs, NJ: Prentice-Hall

Martin J. and Odell J. J. (1995). *Object-Oriented Methods. A Foundation.* 412 pp. Englewood Cliffs, NJ: PTR Prentice-Hall

Martin J. and Odell J. J. (1996). *Object-Oriented Methods. Pragmatic Considerations.* 560 pp. Englewood Cliffs, NJ: PTR Prentice-Hall

Object-Oriented Pty Ltd (1993). Documentation for MeNtOR, Sydney, NSW

Page-Jones M. (1991). Relationship between the structured and object-oriented worlds, TOOLS '91 tutorial notes, Paris, March 4–8, 1991

Rubin K. S. and Goldberg A. (1992). Object behavioral analysis. *Communication ACM*, **35**(9), 48–62

Selic B., Gullekson G. and Ward P. T. (1994). *Real-time Object-Oriented Modelling* 525 pp. New York: Wiley

Shlaer S. and Mellor S. J. (1988) *Object-Oriented Systems Analysis: Modeling the World in Data.* 144 pp. Yourdon Press Computing Series

Shlaer S. and Mellor S. J. (1991). *Object Lifecycles. Modeling the World in States.* 251 pp. Englewood Cliffs, NJ: Yourdon Press/Prentice-Hall

Waldén K. and Nerson J.-M. (1995). *Seamless Object-Oriented Architecture.* 301 pp. Englewood Cliffs, NJ: Prentice-Hall

Chapter 3
Seamlessness

3.1 The need for seamlessness

It has been forcefully argued by many authors that OT provides a seamless environment. While it is undoubtedly true that the extent of seamlessness in an OO development (done well) is significantly higher than in any other software development paradigm, it can also be argued that, by necessity, seamlessness can never be perfect. This follows from the fact that in early requirements analysis, a very-high-level view is taken of the system to be developed: a high-abstraction-level modeling approach is utilized. Finally, for the delivered system, the code reflects many design decisions to describe details at a much lower level of abstraction and, for some languages such as C++ and Ada 95, may be an imperfect match. These detailed, language-focused decisions cannot be modeled in the requirements stage; nor should they be. If they were, then we would in essence be using a programming language to do our user requirements analysis. While some programming languages, such as Eiffel, do in fact go a long way towards offering such a capability, semantic and modeling gaps must occur – at least for the foreseeable future.

What is undoubtedly true is that OT supports seamlessness to such a degree that these small gaps provide hardly any obstacle to a *smooth* and *reversible* progression, as emphasized in BON, from user requirements to an implemented and delivered system. Requirements documents, design documents and code are all easily kept synchronized in theory, although this can be difficult on large projects due to the relative immaturity of many tools. Furthermore, they may provide reusable elements at all stages of the OO lifecycle. In OPEN, this 'analysis to design to code' seamless transition is represented by the evolutionary development activity, closely linked to the user review (we find that although the number of major iterations is not prescribed in OPEN, three are often adequate: see Figure 2.5).

So what of the more traditional notions, represented in OPEN's evolutionary development activity as OOA, OOD and OOP? Figure 3.1 illustrates how the business object model (BOM) or the system object model (SOM) (in Chapter 4, a finer granularity will be developed and a BOM and SOM discussed separately) not only links smoothly with the implementation object model (IOM, the code)

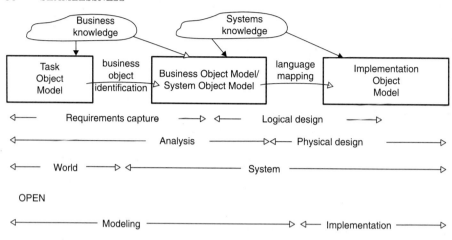

Figure 3.1. Process flow involving the TOM, the SOM and the IOM (after Graham, 1996).

Table 3.1. Mapping between models in OPEN's evolutionary development activity and the Architecture Reference Model shown in Figure 2.7 (Scheurer, 1997 personal communication).

ARM category	Business level	Evolutionary development
Business strategy	Mission and objectives	
Business process		TOM
Business components		BOM and SOM
Infrastructure		SOM and IOM

derived from SOMA but also backwards to the task object model (TOM), which represents the business knowledge to the SOM. This is described by an OOAD modeling language such as OML or UML. This structure is essentially equivalent to Syntropy's essential model, specification model and implementation model. It also maps well (Table 3.1) to the business process, business components and infrastructure of Figure 2.7 where, in addition, business strategy links to the ideas of mission and objectives. In this chapter we explore the nature of the seamlessness across the *full* lifecycle and how traditional terminology relates to this notion of full lifecycle seamlessness.

The technical side of software development has generally been regarded as falling into four major activities: analysis, design, coding and testing. Sometimes a clear distinction is made between logical design and physical design. In a traditional environment, these are seen as occurring sequentially. As can be seen in Figure 3.1, in an OO development environment there is considerable overlap. So, for instance, one might discriminate between

(1) requirements capture, which addresses both business-level requirements and systems-level requirements (thus overlapping the first two boxes in this figure)

(2) logical design, which addresses technical design issues as well as coding concerns.

On the other hand, it can be argued that design does not start until the language for programming has been chosen. Overlain on these might be the world versus the system perspective.

In many OO methodologies, the words analysis and design are retained. However, in doing so, it is sometimes not clear whether traditional definitions (analysis = breaking down, sometimes called discovery; design = building up or synthesis, sometimes called invention) are being used or not. Often it is the case that a distinction similar to the second one in Figure 3.1 is being used: the word analysis covers all activities through to the beginning of language-specific design details. This is generally the flavor, for instance, of MOSES (where the word analysis was replaced by the word specification to avoid confusion) and BON.

Whatever the words that are used, we can consider that:

(1) There is indeed a highly seamless transition across the lifecycle. The gaps between the three boxes of Figure 3.1 are minimal.

(2) There is a need to address the transitions between the TOM (business focus) to the SOM (software focus) and also from the SOM to the IOM model (the code). (Note that sometimes, confusingly, not only is the coding stage referred to as implementation but so too is the act of installing the software with the end-user.)

The second transition is the one most discussed. It is essentially the transition from logical design (OOPL-independent) to physical design, in which the nuances and capability of the chosen OOPL are utilized to their full. This stage of physical design thus incorporates true design (at the language level) as well as translation into code. For some OOPLs, this transition is so smooth as to be almost unnoticeable. For instance, using the language Eiffel supported by a methodology such as BON, MOSES or OPEN, the specification/logical design is a true two-way transition to and from code. For C++ the transition is not so smooth, but is well catered for by the detailed discussions of a methodology like Booch or a modeling language like UML.

The first transition, however, provides more challenge. Translating from the TOM requires significant skill. The OPEN approach is to ensure that this transition is as smooth as possible.

Figure 3.2 shows how this seamlessness is accomplished in SOMA and OPEN. From the mission, a set of objectives is derived. Each objective relates to a number of communication acts (messages) in the model. Each message has exactly one goal and one root task. The root tasks correspond to one or more atomic tasks; by analyzing the business objectives using hierarchical task analy-

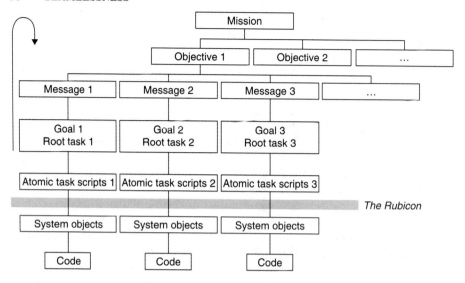

Figure 3.2. Crossing the Rubicon: from mission to atomic task scripts to system objects (after Graham, 1996).

sis (roughly a higher-level, business-focused type of use case), which gives a set of task scripts, the objectives can be represented by TOMs which can then be decomposed down to atomic tasks. Each of these atomic tasks may refer to one or more business objects and each business object may correspond to an object in the software domain.

We identify the system objects partly based on the nouns discovered in the scripts. We define classification, composition and association structures. For each class we find responsibilities and rules, partly based on the verbs found in the scripts. This is a creative process that cannot be automated. We have lost traceability; we have crossed the Rubicon.

However, we can at least validate the mutual consistency of the two models using a group of users and developers. They walk through with class cards (rôle-playing the classes) to prove that all tasks are correctly supported and that there are no processing or storage absurdities. The automatic linking of the two models described above amounts to finding a means to record and replay this dynamic scenario interaction.

How did we make the leap from the world model to the system model seamless? The trick is to notice that these task trees (i.e. each root task) constitute 'plans' for interaction during task performance and, thus, for system execution. Then each root task corresponds to *exactly one* system operation: in the class that initiates the plan. By making this link, we can generate event traces which correspond to aspects of the system functionality (what the user requires). This now gives us a seamless link from mission down to the specification (and maybe even to code when the specification is executable as in SOMATiK)

– *and back*! Because we can refine the SOM and generate a working code, we can trace changes to the code back to their effects on the TOM and even the mission.

The implications of this approach to software engineering for quality and testing are, we hope, obvious.

(1) The stored event traces constitute acceptance test scripts for later verification of the system built.

(2) The involvement of users in the creation of these traces (during the walk-through) proves that the SOM supports the TOM accurately and completely.

The second point is that we have a technique for proving the correctness of system specifications against the requirements model. Normally, the notion of provable correctness is only applied to proving that the implementation meets its specification. This suggests an approach that glues the two technologies together; but the demand for a Z specification generator for a tool like SOMATiK is, we suspect, quite limited at present.

3.2   Traditional OOAD terminology

It is also probably worth including a brief discussion on the terminology of analysis, design and other alternatives (e.g. specification, as in MOSES and Syntropy). Different OO methodologies approach the problem of overlapping OOA and OOD in different ways. The majority discuss OOA and OOD separately in the context of discovery/invention as outlined above and see the process as being an elaboration process. Others, such as Shlaer and Mellor's methodology see it more of a transformational process (discussion on the OOPSLA Panel, Portland, October 1995).

Traditionally, analysis provides the 'WHAT' and design the 'HOW'. Thus, in an OO methodology, OOA is applicable to the problem space of the customer/user; OOD to the solution space of the software. This means that there should be *no* computer influences in OOA and no language influences in OOD. In other words, the constructs used traditionally at the analysis activity should not represent computer constructs, such as files, programs, subroutines and the like, but should represent 'things' that appear in the problem domain. What these 'things' are depends upon the problem domain in question. However, unless a different metamodel for each domain is to exist, then a metamodel that is usable across domains is required; that is, a model that is sufficiently generic and basic in nature that it is able to capture the semantics of the wide range of domain problems. Object models (describing CIRTs and their static interrelationships) can *structurally* represent nearly everything (all knowledge) in the world.

Finally, many methodologists (including ourselves) make no distinction at the process level between analysis and design, but acknowledge the difference only at the micro level. Analysis and design, in the traditional sense, certainly occur as part of the human thought process – but they do so on timescales of minutes (or possibly seconds) and *not* on project management timescales (weeks or months) (see further discussion in Section 3.2.3). In such methodologies, a term such as 'specification' or 'modeling' (as in OPEN) is used to indicate the process by which the user requirements are turned into a fully fledged object model (static and dynamic) ready for implementation in a programming language. Thus a term such as 'modeling' (as in OPEN) encompasses what might otherwise be called analysis and logical design; deferring physical design plus coding to 'implementation.'

3.2.1 Analysis

A traditional definition is that 'OO analysis (OOA) models the problem domain by identifying and specifying a set of semantic objects that interact and behave accordingly to system requirements.' (Monarchi and Puhr, 1992) Analysis, then, is 'the process of creating a model of (the human perceptions of) the real system to be represented in the information system.'

During the activity of analysis a conceptual, or analysis, model of a universe of discourse (UoD) (in our case the business problem) is developed. The focus of the activity is to represent the UoD in as natural and concise a manner as possible. The user's problem can often be either intrinsically fuzzy or potentially internally inconsistent or both.

The analysis activity covers from the initiation of the project, throughout the user-needs analysis and the feasibility study and results in the production of a software requirements specification which is written in the language of the user. This can then be agreed upon by both the software engineer and the software user, and becomes a 'contract' between user and developer so forming a specification for the design.

3.2.2 Design

'OO design (OOD) models the solution domain, which includes the semantic classes (with possible additions) and interface, application, and base/utility classes identified during the design process. OOD should still be language independent, and precedes physical design.' (Monarchi and Puhr, 1992) Here physical design involves hardware-specific features (e.g. file structure, operating system) and constraints on efficiency, maximum allowable transaction time, storage restrictions, for example.

During design, a design model of the conceptual model is developed. The focus of the activity is to represent the conceptual model accurately and in a manner that satisfies a number of constraints such as cost, time to develop, efficiency and performance requirements. The concepts of the design model include classes, objects, client–supplier relationships, services, constraints and inheritance hierarchies. However, we should stress that the choice of modeling language should not be taken trivially. Kent (1978) notes that 'A model is a basic system of constructs used in describing reality ... [It] is more than a passive medium for recording our view of reality. It shapes our view, and limits our perceptions.'

The design activity is perhaps the most loosely defined of the object-oriented lifecycle activities since it is a broad phase of progressive decomposition toward more and more detail and is essentially a creative, not a mechanistic, process. The design activity of a methodology is concerned with developing a solution to an identified problem. Logical design is readily identified and merged with OOA and describes the conceptual level of design independent of implementation concerns (hardware and software concerns). Physical design then takes these hardware and software constraints into account. The problem may have been formally analyzed using an analysis technique, or it may simply be informally understood by a single person or a small group. The aim of design is to develop a computer solution to the real world/business problem that not only fulfills the problem requirements but does so in a way that produces a 'better' system than if the design method had not been applied.

The physical design activity explicitly introduces the computer and computer-related constructs, notably resource allocations and/or constraints. The goal of design is the representation of a problem domain model as a computer system model. A good design is one that represents the problem and also has a number of good software engineering traits. Physical design, then, 'is the process of creating a model of the information system (artifact) to be constructed based upon the model of the real system.' (Wand and Weber, 1989) Design should therefore have an emphasis upon the computer and the representation of problems on a computer. It should include constructs and guidelines that are known (or are argued) to produce good designs.

We should remember that the (physical) design model is not a model of the UoD but rather a model of the conceptual model. The purely logical or semantic object classes identified in analysis are now supplemented by 'physical' object classes, used to model entities which only occur in the solution domain and not in the problem domain. This also involves resource allocation, security checks, efficiency considerations, etc. Reuse should be even better supported than in design, both in terms of process (e.g. generalization and testing techniques) and in terms of quality control. Rôles should be converted to classes if a standard OOP language is to be used.

3.2.3   An alternative to 'analysis' and 'design'

In the alternative process view, OOA and OOD are not segregated at the macro scale. Instead, it is argued that software developers, while undertaking analysis and design in the sense described above, do so in a way in which they alternate between the two over a timescale of minutes or seconds. Analyzing the problem often leads rapidly to thoughts of a likely solution (design); discovery (analysis) immediately leads the human brain on to building a model of the discovered artifact which by its very nature is the design process. In other words, in methodologies such as MOSES, SOMA and OPEN which use this approach of merging OOA and OOD at the macro or activity level, the arguments discussed above remain valid but the timescale of their applicability is very much shortened (possibly by several orders of magnitude).

There is, however, some modification that now needs to be made in that it becomes useful to partition OOD between OO logical design and OO physical (or detailed) design (as discussed in Section 3.2.2) and only to incorporate the logical design portion into the 'merged OOAD.' This is seen also in SOMA, which created a strong distinction between logical and physical design but no distinction between analysis and logical design. This situation is retained in OPEN (Section 3.3) whereby we use the term 'modeling' to relate to analysis and logical design and the term 'implementation' is used to include not only OOP but also detailed design (or physical design).

Thus, in this approach, 'modeling' is an iterative, incremental and parallel activity combining both discovery ('analysis') and invention ('design') as well as both refinement and elaboration. The resulting artifact is a detailed design deliverable ready for coding – although of course OOP is also part of many of the iterations. 'Analysis' and 'design' activities thus occur concurrently, often on very short timescales; while the deliverables (on the timescale of weeks or months) are clearly delineated. They refer to the evolving detailed design documentation – there are no intermediate 'analysis diagrams.'

It is this notion of a merger of OOA and logical design – 'specification' (a term also used by Cook and Daniels for the same SDLC structuring) or 'modeling' (as preferred in OPEN) – which corresponds to the optimal support for a seamless transition; while acknowledging a slight gap between the language-independent SOM construction (created in 'modeling') and the detailed design and coding towards the implementation mode, as represented by the code itself (the focus of 'implementation').

3.2.4   Implementation and testing

Implementation is the part of the systems development lifecycle when the proposed solution, derived from a systems design, is implemented in a programming language. Traditionally, the constructs of the physical design are translated into the constructs of the programming language chosen for the implementation. The boundary between systems design and implementation in object-oriented systems is a blurred one, as noted above, although perhaps more identifiable than the OOA/OOD boundary in that design documentation is of a very different nature to implementation documentation (namely code). Although it could be argued that implementation is merely a continuation of design, just at a very detailed level, it is more realistic to differentiate design (actually logical design as we have just shown) and implementation as two different activities, design being at a level of abstraction above implementation. However, it may be that in some projects or organizations the design is actually undertaken in the implementation language and that it is consequently somewhat hard to distinguish between the two activities/phases. This may be especially true when the language provides a very close mapping to the model used at design. For example, the language Eiffel, or at least subsets of the language, could be used as a design language for developing OO systems.

In addition, decisions on algorithms and data structures, which are strictly implementation decisions regarding the way in which a particular feature is to be coded, may, in exceptional circumstances, need to be documented using structured techniques. So, for instance, the details of a particularly complicated algorithmic procedure in one class may require thought and documentation akin to design using DFDs, STDs or event models.

Once the system has been coded, then granularity has to be assessed and monitored at not only the class level, but also at the cluster (or as a subsystem) level. (A cluster (also known as a package in UML and Java or as a subsystem) is defined as a cohesive set of collaborating objects, classes, clusters and, optionally, non-OO software. It is typically developed as a unit by a small team.) Complexity management encompasses the concepts at design (discussed above) supplemented by code metrics for evaluating the 'goodness' of the programming style used, the code-level complexity and its implications for maintenance. Some statement is needed as to what types of metric collection are supported by the methodology and how these can be incorporated as feedbacks to the project management heuristics.

As part of quality control, a significant post-coding activity (at all granularities) must include testing techniques as well as procedures for verification and validation. The methodological metamodel needs to support both notions strongly. In current methods, neither are well described; in fact, generally being omitted totally in methodologies other than OPEN! However, testing procedures for object hierarchies are currently under development and V&V techniques increasingly stressed. These techniques must address both technical (software) competency and user satisfaction; the latter, especially, being relevant throughout the lifecycle. Methodologies should therefore support peer, expert and customer review, as well as consistency and completeness checking plus a mechanism to support auditability. Indeed, in OPEN, we go even further and mandate testing as part of the post-condition on *all* lifecycle activities.

Good, reusable classes require additional effort. The methodological metamodel supports reuse through generalization and class refinement specifically (as well as a higher-level class reuse mindset throughout the lifecycle). Such class reuse strategies should be seen both as part of the normal object-oriented lifecycle and as activities needed for modification, extension and maintenance.

3.3 'Analysis' and 'design' in OPEN

In the OPEN process lifecycle framework, the object model is constructed during the evolutionary development activity which is a process of gradual refinement, elaboration, discovery of business objects and then computer-specific objects but *not* in a constrictive way. Towards the end of each iteration, it is likely that the classes being discovered and refined will have more 'computer-specificity' – they may be newly demanded classes or themselves derived from concerns already present from the earlier requirements analysis. Flexibility is thus supported and the methodology acts as a road-map rather than a straightjacket for construction. This merging of 'analysis' and 'design' is also reflected in Taylor's (1995) 'analysis by design' whereby requirements are better understood after some design has been undertaken.

The evolutionary development activity encompasses 'modeling and implementation' (OOA/OOD/OOP) together with 'V&V.' Within this, we can group together OOA and the logical part of OOD as 'modeling' and the physical part of OOD and coding as 'implementation.' This follows the suggestions made in Section 3.2.3 of the alternative view of analysis and design. Thus the 'gaps' in seamlessness, small though they are, are only likely to appear between modeling and implementation (when the actual choice of specific OOPL is made and its features utilized) (Figure 3.1).

References

Graham I. (1996). Linking a system and its requirements. *Object Expert*, **1**(3), 62–4

Kent W. (1978). *Data and Reality: Basic Assumptions in Data Processing Reconsidered*. Amsterdam: North Holland

Monarchi D. E. and Puhr G. I. (1992). A research typology for object-oriented analysis and design, *Communications of the ACM*, **35**(9), 35–47

Taylor D. A. (1995). *Business Engineering with Object Technology*. 188 pp. New York: Wiley

Wand Y. and Weber R. (1989). An ontological evaluation of systems analysis and design methods. *Information Systems Concepts: An In-Depth Analysis* (Falkenberg E. and Lindgreen P., eds.), Amsterdam: Elsevier Science Publications/North Holland

Chapter 4
OPEN activities

On the left-hand side of Figure 4.1 (a slightly improved reproduction of Figure 2.5 – included again here for convenience) are activities which are associated with a single project; on the right-hand side, in the shaded box, are those activities which transcend a single project and are frequently associated more with strategic planning and implementation concerns across the whole programme; for example, resources across several projects, reuse strategies, delivery and maintenance aspects. OPEN includes both projects and organizational software strategies.

Activities also provide modularity and encapsulation – they are, after all, 'objects' themselves. They have pre- and post-conditions, the latter consisting of testing requirements and deliverables to be satisfied. As well as providing 'chunking' of the project, this approach also permits a mapping for a project that is to be wholly or partially outsourced. In this case, the company to which an activity is outsourced must meet the OPEN post-conditions which thus become part of the *business* contract between the two organizations. In addition, the use of a specified timebox structure permits quantitative evaluation on this contract and, if need be, penalty for late delivery.

The activities permit a large-scale structuring of the project management for an OO product development – a lifecycle pattern when fully fleshed out with appropriate tasks and techniques. What they do not do is identify things that have to be done at a low enough resolution to match those tasks that need to be done in order to meet the goals of each activity. For example, when the developer is focusing on an activity such as evolutionary development, there are a number of associated tasks which need to be undertaken successfully, one of which is: 'Construct the object model.' This is a clearly delineated goal for which someone can take responsibility (the delivery of a well-structured object model for the problem in hand). We should also note that for this particular activity, more than one task will be identified; for other activities there may be predominantly only one task required.

Each of the individual activities will be briefly described in the following 14 subsections preceded by a discussion on one interpretation of this model for project management control: timeboxes.

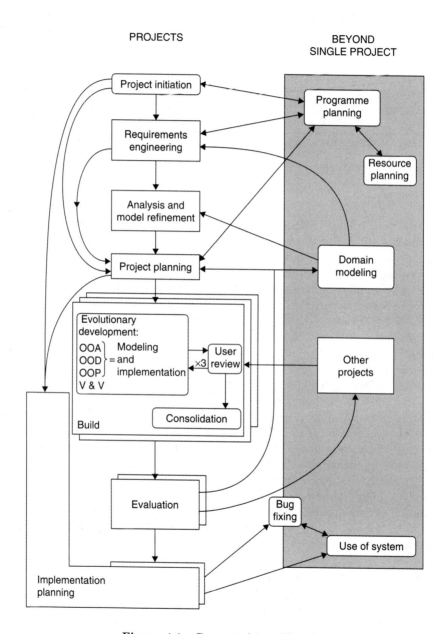

Figure 4.1   Contract-driven lifecycle.

4.1   Timeboxes

Timeboxing has been found to be an effective method for object technology by creating a set of mini-projects for each set of deliverables. The timebox technique offers the following benefits. It imposes management control over ripple effects and uncontrolled iteration. Control is achieved by setting a rigid elapsed-time limit on the prototyping cycle and using a small project team. Furthermore, it has a usable system as both the end-point of the process and its deliverable. There is no distinction between production, evolution and maintenance as there is with conventional approaches which usually ignore maintenance costs during project justification. Timeboxing is also a basic principle of the DSDM Consortium's (1995) standard for RAD projects.

The timebox tackles the following management issues.

- Wants versus needs – by forcing requirements to be prioritized by negotiation between users and developers. Users and the project team are forced to concentrate on the real needs of the business.

- Creeping functionality – in the traditional lifecycle the long delay between specification and delivery can lead to users requesting extra features. The use of a time limit reduces this tendency.

- Project team motivation – the developers can see a tangible result of their efforts emerging.

- The involvement of users at every stage reduces implementation shock.

The approach reduces time to market, not by a magic trick that makes hard things easy, but by delivering an important usable subset of the entire system in a shorter time than ordinarily expected.

It is absolutely critical to maintain credibility as well as to build on success and manage expectations during the application development process, which itself often uses rapid application development (RAD) or joint application development (JAD) techniques. This is achieved by several means. Users should be warned not to be deceived by the rapidity of developing a prototype because it may conceal a large amount of not-yet-implemented complexity. A working system will take time in proportion to the complexity of the tasks with which it assists. Equally, users should be stimulated by many small, incremental deliveries. Developers can often afford to accept reasonable changes to requirements, provided that existing, low-priority requirements can be eliminated by mutual agreement based on agreed priorities. This management of expectation is a key task for the project manager. If it is neglected, the project will usually fail.

The technique prevents 'analysis paralysis,' errors due to delay, spurious requirements and implementation shock. It usually motivates teams better than the waterfall approach – but some systems just cannot be built this way; for example, most of us would be uncomfortable about flying in an aircraft whose control systems were at the prototype stage or had only been partially delivered. This does not mean that RAD cannot be applied to real-time systems. In such cases, the techniques are applied to development on the test-bed but only fully tested systems are put into service.

One possible criticism of RAD is that its benefits may derive largely from the Hawthorne effect observed on many organization and management (O&M) studies, whereby merely paying more attention to users and developers makes them more productive regardless of the techniques used. It can also be argued that highly trained and motivated users and developers (two important rôles found in the software development process: Graham, 1995, p. 393) are the cause of the success, since many RAD-aware companies are also innovators with skilled staffs. We cannot disprove either of these assertions but remain confident of the utility of RAD nevertheless.

OPEN supports a synthesis of OT with JAD and RAD. In one company known to the authors, both RAD and OO programming had been introduced simultaneously but separately, with considerable and beneficial effects on productivity in each case. The RADs gave many of the benefits mentioned above but, unfortunately, they were run using structured techniques and typically produced normalized entity models and huge functional decompositions. The developers were prone to saying 'nice pictures,' filing them somewhere and then going off to find a user who could help them prototype something. The OPEN lifecycle model was developed as a generalization of the SOMA lifecycle model (Graham, 1995) which, in part, was aimed to help companies reconcile RAD with OOP. It also supports other instantiations, such as that of OPEN/Firesmith (Firesmith et al., 1997).

4.2 Project initiation

The development process starts with business planning and the organization's strategy plan. A request from part of the business, or even external legislation, can initiate the process by establishing the mission and the objectives of the work. These should be underscored by a list of priorities and associated measures to monitor progress and evaluate success. The product is a project proposal document, which should be short and to the point. It should contain a statement of the broad project mission together with costs and other constraints. The proposal should contain a problem definition in terms of business processes and commercial impact, the names of a sponsor, domain experts and key users, the broad scope of the project, a cost–benefit justification and the project completion criteria. It may also include cost–benefit, feasibility, risk and critical success factor appendices. These will be produced exactly when they are needed to obtain the sponsor's signature. A throwaway prototype may also be part of the proposal.

The project sponsor is a rôle played by an individual responsible for the project who has the authority to approve initial and continued expenditure on it as well as the authority to approve implementation of any changes to production systems. The sponsor pays the bills and is thus of key importance. He or she should be kept informed of all significant deliverables and be involved in all major review discussions. The sponsor will sign off on items such as the results of a

JAD/RAD workshop, the analysis document, the timebox deliverables and any changes in the overall plan.

A proposal, once agreed and approved, leads to user requirements elicitation as part of requirements engineering, often by running a RAD scoping workshop and usually a detailed RAD workshop immediately following. There is no definite assumption at this stage that the solution will be computerized and such a workshop is free to explore the possibilities of business process reengineering. Successful completion of this activity requires the completion of a number of tasks (Chapter 5 and Appendix A).

Prerequisites, completion criteria and time limits

Project initiation is an unbounded activity with no elapsed-time limits or prerequisites. The sole completion criterion is a project proposal signed by the sponsor. Supporting documentation may be needed before such a signature is obtained but this is not mandated and will be project and culture dependent.

4.3   Requirements engineering

Requirements engineering in OPEN will be described elsewhere in great detail (Swatman and Fowler, 1998). Here we note that we are working within a convergent engineering environment (Taylor, 1995) to bring together the technology and the business concerns in such a way that the technology does not merely support the business; rather the software reflects the reality of the business and becomes an integral part of the business. To do that, business users and technologists need to speak the same language: that of objects has been found to work well in many situations.

In OPEN using the term *requirements engineering* (a subset of which is requirements elicitation) seems more appropriate than either *requirements capture* or *requirements gathering*, since nothing is captured in the sense of imprisonment and it is wrong to give the impression that the requirements are just there to be gathered from the users. Object-oriented system building is about modeling and, as Bertrand Meyer has so aptly put it, is a process of negotiation (Meyer, 1995). Requirements engineering is no different; users often only realize the true nature of their requirement when they see the early prototypes.

Requirements may be classified (Thomsett, 1997) as:

- functional requirements
- quality requirements
- constraints
- added-value requirements.

Requirements engineering is best viewed as a form of knowledge elicitation because, in that discipline, it is usually recognized that much knowledge is latent or difficult to verbalize. In discussing OO requirements engineering there is much to write because, of approximately 50 published OO methods, only a handful have anything whatsoever to say about this topic. Arguably, only OOSE/Objectory (Jacobson et al., 1992) and SOMA (Graham, 1995) have addressed the issue at all, with most methods assuming that a written requirement specification exists at the start of the analysis. In practice, of course, the users of these methods have had to make do and mend in the absence of anything specific in their chosen method. We thus find practitioners like Cook and Daniels (1995) or Martin and Odell (1995) using a variant of the state and event modeling notations originally included in their methods to model the life histories of individual objects. These notations are, consciously or unconsciously, pressed into service as business process modeling techniques. Of course, this can be made to work but it may not be as effective as using a technique developed exactly for the purpose. Some academics (e.g. Gilligrand and Liu, 1995) and a few practitioners have proposed the use of variants of data-flow analysis for this purpose but there are evident dangers of ending up with functionally derived decompositions leading to problems with an OO implementation.

Information gathering can be accomplished by use of a RAD workshop that produces a report containing, for intance, a user TOM, task scripts and a preliminary, but tested, BOM consisting of completed class cards and event traces. The people participating in a RAD workshop may play several rôles. As well as a scribe, an experienced analyst or systems architect, the sponsor of the project should take part under the direction of the facilitator. This person should be an experienced business analyst who will be responsible for overseeing the RAD session, ensuring that the requirements are captured in a structured way, so that they are complete and consistent, and for ensuring that the correct level of detail is achieved. Further details are given in Graham (1995) and Henderson-Sellers and Younessi (1997).

The review of business processes should be complete by this stage. Each goal in the scoping environment model is resolved into the tasks that users expect to be performed in order that it be accomplished. This includes examination of system internals as well as mere interface behavior though not details of how these internals may be implemented. This is an important extension over and above recent suggestions that tend to restrict the tasks (generic use cases) ascribed to those of the actors. The tasks are organized into a full object model and the report should contain task cards (Figure 4.2) showing all four structures of such a model.

In building the TOM, there is a need first for a (business process) context model. (If using COMN, the context model is one of the semantic nets, as described by Firesmith et al. (1997).) This addresses issues of:

- stakeholders (described by external objects)
- actors
- support systems
- semiotic (communication) acts (interpreted here as messages).

Task Name	
	Abstract/Concrete
Task body	
Supertasks	
Component tasks	
Associated or analogous tasks	
Task attributes	
Time taken	
Complexity	
Exceptions	Side-scripts
Rules:	

Figure 4.2 A task card (after Graham, 1995).

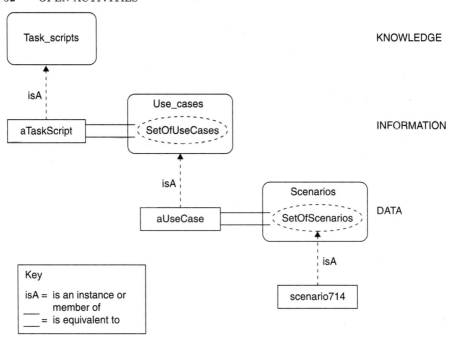

Figure 4.3   Scenarios, use cases and task scripts (after Graham, 1997).

Having derived this business-focused model, then the goal for each message has to be derived. Use of task scripts and a high degree of interaction with the business users are found to be valuable here. The relationship of task scripts to use cases is shown in Figure 4.3. Task scripts document business processes, whereas use cases document the interactions between a user (actually a rôle of a user) and the proposed software system viewed as a blackbox.

4.4   Analysis and model refinement

The developers must now review the model for completeness and consistency and discover any logical dependencies or unrealistic features. The models in the requirements document are thus refined into a systems analysis report, which also should include project plans and estimates.

During requirements engineering, a business focus has been maintained and, often, task analysis utilized. This creates a TOM, perhaps documented by context diagrams and task cards. During the analysis and model refinement activity that diagram is modified from reified business processes of the TOM into objects that, while retaining a business terminology and focus, are structured in a way that is amenable to ready translation to a SOM in the technical domain.

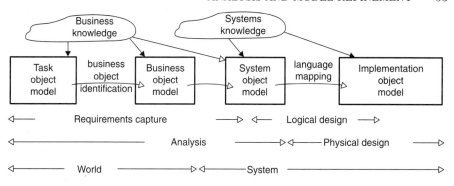

Figure 4.4 Process flow involving the TOM, the BOM, the SOM and the IOM.

Thus we produce here a BOM which is more akin to the mindset of use cases (as opposed to task scripts) and, since retaining a real-world focus (Figure 4.4), can act as a contract between the users and the developers since it provides the bridge between the business and the technical viewpoints. Addition of systems knowledge permits it to become smoothly transformed into the SOM during later activities.

The analysis report will thus contain both a TOM and a BOM. These will include a message table/context model (Figure 4.5), task scripts, use cases, class cards, event traces, a task/objectives matrix, an objects/objectives matrix, priorities for layers and most of the other material that appeared in the requirements document. Additionally, definitions based on a thorough and technically informed analysis of the problem are included that the hurly burly of the frequently used RAD workshop does not always allow the time for. The task scripts and event traces are important as they form the basis of test scripts. During the preparation of the systems analysis report, preliminary decisions concerning reuse of repository objects ('with reuse') will be made and these should be reported.

Message name	Trigger event	Source	Target	Information sent/received	Expected result	Goal

Figure 4.5. Message table in which each message now pertains to one interaction on the context diagram – all such interactions must be shown in the table (after Graham, 1995).

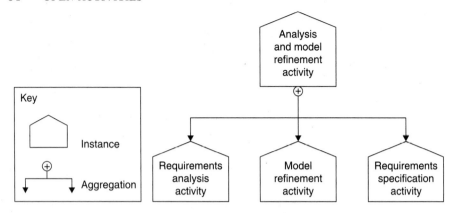

Figure 4.6. The analysis and model refinement activity may be broken down into three subactivities. The notation used is COMN.

It is useful to base the analysis report on a standard document template. The advantages of using a template are that it supports faster document creation and should result in a better quality document because the information is presented once, and in the right context. It should speed and ease reviewing – the inspection of such a document (e.g. using Fagan's inspection technique) will be easier, as the reviewers will have a better idea of what should be contained in each section and ease information retrieval for future developers of the system. Ease of review of system documentation by external auditors is also enhanced.

The objectives of this activity are to confirm that the TOM is valid, to produce a BOM in sufficient detail to confirm the technical approach and to identify critical areas of system performance and revise development and implementation plans.

While this analysis and model refinement activity is represented in Figure 4.1 as a single activity, the name belies the truth and in fact it may be more realistic and useful to describe this activity as an aggregate of three separate activities (or subactivities if you prefer). While such a breakdown may vary from organization to organization, a typical breakdown, as shown in Figure 4.6, may be: requirements analysis, model refinement, and requirements specification. Requirements analysis aims to understand the user's requirements statement (in the language of the user), assisted by feedback from the user which leads to model refinement. Out of the iterative cycles between analyst and user, an agreed requirements specification is developed which forms the contractual basis between customer and developer and also states the implementation requirements that must be adhered to by the following technical development process. It is this document which provides the measure by which the final product will be evaluated. While small changes to the requirements specification are readily accommodated, others may need, by agreement between user and developer, to be deferred until a later version as a future enhancement and costed separately.

The capability of OO to fully support an iterative development style (at the technical level) should not blind the business decision makers to the real possibility of feature bloat if these enhancements are not properly managed.

Prerequisites, completion criteria and time limits

Project initiation and *initial* requirements capture activities must be completed prior to model refinement. The systems analysis report should contain a review of the impact of change on production systems, a development plan, including a projected end date and an estimate of the metrics of the system including non-development costs. The formal time limits are from one day to two weeks. There are overall limits on RAD workshops and project planning activities which, combined, should be of between one day and four weeks elapsed duration. A one-week minimum may be expected for the combined activities. Time used in this activity is to be deducted from the overall maximum of six months to implementation.

4.5   Project planning

Project planning starts when the project proposal has been signed off by the user sponsor and the project manager responsible. The proposal should be submitted to the appropriate management for prioritization. Metrics should be updated at every phase of the project. A cut-over plan will also be prepared for use during the implementation planning activity. Also necessary are plans for quality control and assessment, disaster recovery, security, configuration and version management and testing.

The project manager is responsible for ensuring that initial user training is performed, because it has a direct impact on the success of the implementation. She or he will be in the best position to determine who actually does the training, which may well be one of the full-time users seconded to the project team or the supplier if it is a package solution. The project manager should decide.

However, users also have an interest in ensuring that training is done, so they are not absolved of all responsibility. Users also have responsibility for ensuring that their requirement is defined in terms of content and attendance. They are also required to release the staff at the appropriate time. This should be *before* implementation. Post-implementation training is the responsibility of the user group.

Prerequisites, completion criteria and time limits

Project planning is a continuous, unbounded activity with no specific time limits. However, within each timebox iteration it is clearly bounded in time (as shown in Figure 4.1) since its completion is a prerequisite for the commencement of the build activity.

4.6   Build

The build activity, as borrowed from MOSES and SOMA, is illustrated here in OPEN by the constrained build box in Figure 4.1 of the OPEN contract-driven lifecycle. It has embedded within it, in an iterative and flexible fashion, three unbounded (sub)activities: evolutionary development, user review and consolidation. In some senses, these correspond to the five phases of the original MOSES fountain lifecycle (Figure 2.2) in that they represent the technical (as opposed to management and project control) aspects of software development. Across these three activities there is arguably a seamless transition which allows the iterative and incremental delivery style of software development much espoused by OO gurus. Since this is a central tenet of the OO paradigm, it becomes necessary for us to evaluate the validity of such a claim – this we have done in Chapter 3.

4.6.1   Evolutionary development

The OOD activity may follow completion of the OOA activity or overlap it, normally within a timebox. Both may precede or follow programming. During this activity, computer system design is carried out to produce a computer solution in terms of program, database, interface and file specifications.

Only limited user participation will be required in this activity, although the user should take part in the review/test process at its completion.

The objectives for OOD are:

- To produce a technical design which meets the business objectives as simply as possible while taking account of performance, security and control requirements and system-based risks, quality, flexibility, ease of use and reuse.

- To specify technical details of how the system will operate in terms of program modules, files and database usage.

- To finalize the physical formats of input and output for all types of systems, including the conversation structure of interactive transactions for online systems, if appropriate.

- To estimate the likely utilization of hardware and software resources, identifying likely requirements for change.

These will typically be documented by a mixture of graphical (e.g. COMN) and textual 'design' models, including static diagrams (particularly semantic nets), dynamic diagrams (interaction diagrams and state transition diagrams) and use cases/task scripts (scenario class diagrams in COMN) to describe the functional aspects of the system. These are cataloged and described in Chapter 7.

OOP converts the model as designed into a working system, prototype or fragment of a system. The first prototype will generally be broad and shallow, covering the whole range. Subsequent prototypes will extend earlier ones and treat all or part of the system in depth. Narrow and deep prototypes will be used to identify reusable components for subsequent iterations.

During this activity (OOP), individual programs are designed, coded and tested. These programs are then linked and their interfaces tested. Formal OOD may precede or (rarely) follow coding. Users will have little input to programming and the associated testing processes but they will be required to specify the acceptance test plan, construct test cases and review the results.

The developers should be required to provide an environment that is as close as possible to the production environment. Acceptance testing is designed for users to determine that the system works as originally specified and satisfies the business requirement, using actual terms and procedures.

The objectives (for OOP) are:

(1) To physically design, code and test each application.

(2) To produce the necessary documentation for subsequent program maintenance and operational running.

(3) To ensure that objects, classes and clusters (e.g. layers) collaborate together properly.

(4) To ensure that the system performs as specified, and meets the business requirement.

(5) To establish that any conversion programs are working as specified and can be implemented.

(6) To verify that the system works within hardware operating requirements.

(7) To establish that the completed system can be released to users for acceptance testing.

Use of testing aids is recommended during this activity wherever possible. The objective of this activity is to design, code and unit test each object, class or cluster individually before testing the system (or iterative build or release version) as a whole.

The detailed OOD tasks (see Chapter 5) depend on the method selected, the timebox iteration reached and the type of project. The major deliverables from the OOD part of the evolutionary development activity are a system design report, unit test plan, integration test plan and acceptance test plan.

The major deliverables from the OOP part of the activity are the prototype itself (source code) with system test report and technical documentation, including metrics.

Prerequisites, completion criteria and time limits

The prerequisites for rapid OOD are the completion of a system analysis report and an OOA confirmation of it within the current timebox iteration. The timebox has to have started, the project infrastructure must be in place and user reviews planned.

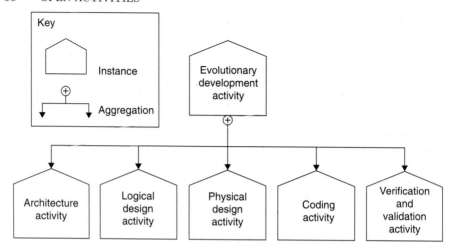

Figure 4.7.   The evolutionary development activity may be broken down into five subactivities – expressed using COMN.

A design review confirms that the documentation is adequate for maintenance in addition to its primary purpose of establishing the viability of the system. Test the system design to ensure that the business and technical needs are met, that it is secure but not over complex, that the design is still justified in terms of costs and benefits and that all functions have been addressed, including hardware/operating software requirements.

The team should review the test plans and reports to ensure completeness. Available techniques for this include informal walkthroughs or inspections (such as Fagan's inspections) for larger systems.

For the code, confirm that the test results are adequate and that both the product and the documentation conform to standards.

Evolutionary development at a finer grain

While for many purposes the evolutionary development activity is the most appropriate granularity in which a truly iterative and incremental delivery technical lifecycle can exist and flourish, since these are objects, we can also consider the evolutionary development activity to be an aggregate object (Figure 4.7). The component parts are probably five in total: architecture, logical design, physical design, coding, V&V. The danger of course (as discussed in Chapter 3) is that the identification of such names (as in the MOSES five phases of the process lifecycle) can lead to the impression that these are disjoint activities – whereas in reality, as has been commonly known since at least 1990, there is significant overlap (see the fountain model in Chapter 2, particularly Figure 2.2). As we discussed earlier, we do not deny that these activities are real and distinct. What is in question is the timescale. If this is short then identification of the component parts (such as those in Figure 4.7) may be impractical for project management. If the timescale is lengthy, then it is of more use in managing the projects but may have deleterious effects on the seamlessness of the whole process.

Architecture includes not only 'analysis' but also large-scale distribution design and layering design (e.g. using COMN's semantic nets e.g. layer and configuration diagrams). Logical design includes tasks such as undertaking domain design, user interface design and database design, whereas V&V focuses on testing/model evaluation.

4.6.2   User review

This activity involves both developers and users. The tested prototype is demonstrated to the users and, if possible, exercised by them. Every user review contains some acceptance testing (confirmed in the evaluation activity). Thus, traditional acceptance, as in non-OO systems, does not occur until after the software is delivered to the customer, but does occur incrementally throughout the build activity.

Prerequisites, completion criteria and time limits

Before starting, the coded prototype must have been produced, all OOD/OOP criteria satisfied and the users must be available. On completion, confirm that all relevant event traces can be handled correctly and that the usability checks are satisfactory.

4.6.3   Consolidation

This activity takes place after a number of iterations through OOA/OOD/OOP/ V&V (evolutionary development activity) and user review. It consolidates the products of this timebox with those of earlier timeboxes or other projects and systems. It confirms the candidate classes identified as potentially reusable and consolidates user and technical documentation. In addition, plans for implementation and system conversion are influenced, although these may have been triggered earlier by messages from other activities such as requirements engineering.

Prerequisites, completion criteria and time limits

As a prerequisite, the results of prototype iterations must be signed off for consolidation and delivery by the users on the timebox team.

All mandatory and recommended tasks listed in this subsection must be complete at the end of this activity. There must be a justification for any recommended tasks not included. Check that:

- the system runs in the target environment
- test results are accepted by users

- the product and its documentation are complete and conform to standards
- metrics are within acceptable ranges (to detect collection errors)
- all relevant event traces can be handled correctly
- usability checks are satisfactory
- timebox team user sign-off is complete
- documentation is complete and conforms to standards
- conversion plans are satisfactory.

4.7   Evaluation

The final evaluation activity is the formal review of the system and documentation of the lessons learned. It is a simple matter to just demonstrate the system or current increment but to do so is a one-way process – the most vital element in the whole 'prototyping' approach is obtaining and exploiting user feedback. It is therefore very important that users recognize the need and plan for enough time to review the results properly. Thus the review process needs to be highly organized and may, though rarely, become a major logistical exercise. The review should primarily allow the project sponsor to agree that the deliverables have been produced according to the requirements definition, analysis and timebox planning documentation. However, representatives from all the users who may be affected by the system need to be present, so that all aspects of the system can be reviewed and feedback obtained.

This activity is, consequently, very important. Here it is decided whether the deliverables are adequate and whether implementation should proceed or the work need be redone or even abandoned as impracticable. The evaluation team must involve the sponsor and personnel not on the project team, preferably representatives from the end-user community. Reference to the quality plan should be made during evaluation. This plan should contain a statement of what elements of the method would be used and what deliverables mandated. There should be reference back to existing architectures, networks, operations and hardware. Suitably knowledgeable people should be co-opted if necessary. Evaluation should merely confirm that all tests mandated earlier in the user review activities have been done.

The Fagan's inspection technique may be used where appropriate and coding standards reviewed. A more refined version of the Fagan inspection technique due to Gilb and Graham (1993) is recommended, but either technique may be used. Inspections may be applied to all deliverables – not just software. The team will need to be assured that the testing was adequate by reference to both the task scripts/use cases and normal system test plans.

Evaluation for each timebox produces an evaluation report, including reuse recommendations, reuse candidates approved, a quality report and an outline implementation plan. The report should confirm the results of the tests against task scripts and consolidate all metrics from this and earlier timeboxes (if used). The objectives of an evaluation are:

- To authorize the project to continue, or not.
- To authorize delivery of the product of a timebox, or not.
- To confirm potential reusability of components identified as reusable within the timebox.
- To review stage tolerances, security issues and provide data for audit.
- To act as a collection point for project metrics.
- To review progress on both the current activity and the whole project against plan.
- To review and approve any exception plans.
- To review the plan for the next stage.
- To identify the effect of both current and potential problems and plan remedial action if necessary.

Efficiency will be enhanced by the reuse of software. Some organizations have made designers responsible for packaging the code so that it can be reused as many times as possible in subsequent projects. The problem with this is that well-constructed, reusable classes take time and care to produce; and this presents a contradiction to the philosophy of rapid development within a timebox. Developers should be required to consider code reuse specifically for each project but only insofar as they identify reuse potential. The evaluations have the task of confirming candidate classes for reuse. These should be passed to a specialist class developer for refinement, generalization and testing, then be reissued to projects. Class developers could be evaluated on the number of times their classes are reused, the number of defects in them reported, or on productivity improvements resulting from their reuse.

As part of the evaluation process, defect analysis takes place. The volume of defects identified should be compared with industry standards and past performance in order to track improvements in quality and accuracy in specifying and coding systems. Object-oriented software metrics should be used to measure changes and trends in productivity levels. The number of atomic tasks supported is taken as the equivalent of traditional logical business transactions. Usability metrics should also be collected where possible; for example, time to complete a task, time to forget, and so on. Comparisons of reliability (mean time-to-failure), cost and programming efficiency (task points per person-month development time) will be made, amongst others. Reuse metrics will also be collected where appropriate; including number of classes reused, number of (candidate) reusable classes created. Metrics for each project must be completed before the project goes live, and must be maintained at each stage of the lifecycle.

The project plan and quality plan should be made available. A nominated scribe should record the project name, the stage being assessed and the date of the meeting.

Prerequisites, completion criteria and time limits

This activity takes place after the end of a timebox or other planned iteration. All mandatory and recommended tasks listed in this subsection must be complete. There must be a justification for any recommended tasks not included. The completion criteria for earlier activities should have been met. All parties must agree that the review is complete or decide by a simple majority in any case of dispute. In the latter case, senior management and the project sponsor must give their approval.

The iteration or timebox products must be reviewed to ensure that:

- The program documentation is complete and the program test plan has been executed correctly.

- Completion criteria have been achieved for both unit and program testing and the programs are now ready for acceptance testing.

- The programs are maintainable.

- Operation of the system has been successfully demonstrated.

- The techniques used and the documentation conform to standards.

- All required metrics information is complete.

- Reuse candidates are acceptable.

- The justification from the project proposal remains valid.

- There are no decisions or items pending.

- All security policies have been adhered to.

- The relevant legislation has been adhered to.

This activity should never take more than two weeks and should typically last less than a day.

4.8 Implementation planning

Implementation issues include the following:

- training
- education
- change management (through the sponsor)
- hardware and software resources
- environment/locations
- support.

The objective of this activity is to ensure that all necessary activities are completed prior to the system starting live operation. It involves three groups of tasks concerned with implementation planning, training and installation.

The implementation planning activity really begins within the JAD/RAD workshop activity. Implementation planning is concerned with ensuring that all necessary activities are complete prior to going live.

The objectives are:

- To ensure that the production environment has been set up.
- To provide for, and ensure, complete and accurate file conversion and take-on.
- To convert to the new system.
- To provide support and assistance at and beyond changeover to the new system.
- To obtain formal acceptance of successful system implementation.
- To ensure that the change management organization has been informed of the impact of proposed changes.

Prerequisites, completion criteria and time limits

Sign-off from the evaluation stage is a prerequisite for delivery, although much planning may have been completed earlier.

On completion, review the implementation of the system and ensure that:

- The system has been accepted by both the users and the IT organization.
- The appropriate hardware/software has been installed.
- The network has been installed (if required).
- Production libraries have been set up.
- All special stationery has been approved and obtained.
- All required system documentation is available and conforms to standards.

This activity is constrained by the overall limit to the project timebox, often six months.

4.9   Programme planning

Planning comprises two types of activity: the detailed planning of an individual timebox, which was dealt with separately in Section 4.5, and the planning of a whole programme composed of several projects and/or timeboxes. This latter activity cannot be separated from the need to balance the resource requirements of the development department as a whole. Where there is only one timebox, these activities are combined. This section considers the planning activity as one that starts from global and site considerations and apportions work to various timeboxes given the discoveries and imperatives of the earlier activities: project initiation, RADs, OOA and other timeboxes and their plans. In parallel with this activity, the identification of potentially reusable classes from the repository is conducted.

Programme planning focuses on working out the implications of this project on other projects in the organization and resolving issues of interaction. The second issue is closely related to domain modeling. The project manager must plan checkpoints for integration with other projects, infrastructural services, etc.

It has been suggested that OO modeling could be used to take distributed and concurrent models further. Centralized sequential development corresponds to the waterfall model. Its disadvantages have been discussed already. Since it may also be hard to install large numbers of developers in just one office, there can be a distributed version that introduces additional problems of collecting and disseminating information among distributed teams. Concurrent development shortens time to market drastically but creates new problems of coordinating multiple, concurrent activities. When the development is also distributed, the complexity may be double that of centralized, sequential developments. However, this is the ultimate model for downsizing the development organization and its processes: Figure 4.8 shows the four possibilities.

We have in fact a simpler problem than the one described above because (1) we have a single point of initial requirements capture and (2) there is no notion of maintenance or enhancement as distinct from a project as such. We do still, however, have to coordinate across projects and timeboxes. The problem is to ensure that integration of timebox products is adequately planned for and that timebox synchronization is accomplished. The model we recommend is shown in Figure 4.9.

Figure 4.9 shows how the consolidation activity within each timebox integrates the results of other efforts to produce a product which is then subjected to evaluation. In some cases, the timeboxes communicate directly and informally; in others only after evaluation. If the products of the two final timeboxes interact, there would have to be a combined evaluation.

A useful rule of thumb is that estimates should be doubled when there are concurrent timeboxes that must be evaluated together; this is to allow for the inevitable reworking that will sometimes arise. To make it work and to maintain consistent levels of quality, everyone involved must speak the same development language and that language must be sufficiently expressive, or semantically rich. OPEN is offered as just such a basis for an OO development *lingua franca*.

4.10   Resource planning

Project management focuses on planning the allocation of time, money, people, range, tools and techniques (collectively 'resources') and quality. Resource planning thus involves the identification of:

- temporal constraints and temporal orderings
- units of work (tasks), deliverables and milestones

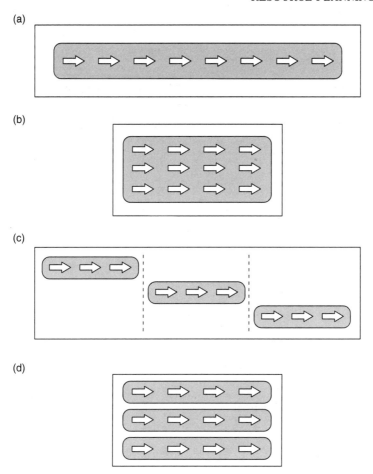

Figure 4.8. Four approaches to development: (a) centralized, sequential, (b) centralized, concurrent, (c) distributed sequential and (d) distributed concurrent (after Graham, 1995).

- team structure
- choice of hardware and software
- the development of an education and training plan
- use of resources in terms of an appropriate iteration plan and subsystem coordination
- the rôle of reuse
- the implementation of an appropriate metrics programme.

Each becomes a prime focus of a task or technique in OPEN (Chapters 5 and 6).

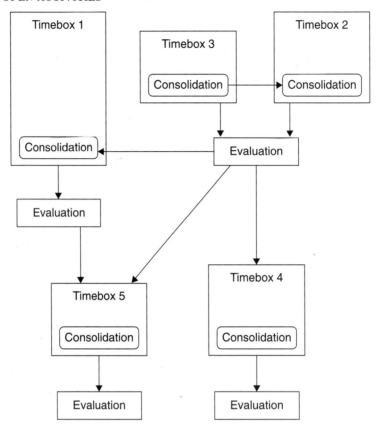

Figure 4.9   Coordinating concurrent development in OPEN (after Graham, 1995).

4.11   Domain modeling

Interviews and workshops may lead to the discovery of new domain objects and
it must be decided whether the extra expense of preparing them for inclusion in
the library is justified. This applies to specifications as well as code modules.
On the other hand, the domain model may already include components that
can be used in the timebox to enhance the quality of the deliverables and speed
up the process. Domain analysis is best separated from application systems
analysis because development pressures make it hard to abstract from immediate concerns to truly flexible, complete and application-independent components.
Furthermore, it is hard for a development team to see the broader issues within
the organization and, of course, producing reusable components often requires
more effort and may slow down projects unacceptably. Ways must be found
to inform teams regularly about the contents of the domain model and advise
them on what could be profitably used. The solution is to create a separate
team of domain modelers, class librarians and component 'salesmen' or 'reuse

consultants.' The individuals on this team must be committed to the OO viewpoint, have first-class analysis skills, be very familiar with the business and know what is in the existing library and how to use it well. Often development team training can be made the responsibility of this team, especially in the areas of software architecture and reusability. They are also a potential source of quality reviews to estimate whether reuse principles have been applied properly and as fully as practicable. Domain models may also form the basis of business process re-engineering efforts.

Domain modeling is the continuous activity of defining and refining the objects that represent the business regardless of the particularities of applications. It is closely related to the issue of repository management and the development of reusable assets.

4.11.1   Hairies and conscripts: making reuse work in the organization

Most development departments have infrastructure support for such services as networks precisely because they can reuse them across many different systems. Why should code, design patterns, specifications or requirements be treated any differently? Surely they are, in a reuse-aware culture, a major part of the infrastructure of IT?

For any reasonably large IT organization, having some developers not involved in directly productive development work systems will be more than offset by the savings gained from developers being able to use a set of well-documented, fully supported objects. One recommended model is the establishment of a small, full-time domain modeling and reuse team to produce, collect and maintain reusable codes. This is effectively a software infrastructure team. It is not just a matter of objects; there are usually also libraries of conventional code, database scripts and so on, all of which can be reused. It would be a capital error to underestimate the complexity of this task. It is the boring matters of documentation, configuration management and version control that are the key determinants of its success. A reuse or software infrastructure team focuses effort in the right place at the right time.

Domain modeling plays an important rôle in component management and reuse. In this respect a key personality in the domain team is the *class librarian*. A key task of analysis, following initial requirements elicitation, is the identification of classes suitable for reuse that have emerged from the requirements and the discovery of existing components which can be used within the new development. The criteria that make an object reusable need to be established carefully since the costs of creating a reusable component are usually much higher than those for an application-specific one. The class librarian will provide valuable input to this process. Another key rôle is that of the *reuse engineer* or *toolsmith*. Such a person is devoted *inter alia* to quality, efficiency, reliability and maintainability. However, these characteristics are not always found together with deep application knowledge or the social skills of the business analyst. Thus, a third rôle needs to be catered for: that of the *application conscript*; a developer who works on the reuse team for short fixed periods. Reuse engineers have the same skill and dedication as systems programmers, though they are fully immersed in the OO philosophy. However, they may not communicate well with users nor know much of the business at first. Colloquially they are sometimes referred to as 'hairies,' after the stereotypical systems programmer with full beard, jeans, anorak and sandals. This gives us a mnemonic for the management approach: the 'hairies and conscripts' model (HCM). Some organizations use their annual intake of new graduate trainees to staff reuse teams. We would be wary of entrusting the creation of important business objects that are likely to be extensively used in critical applications to such neophytes. This approach therefore requires that the new talent is embedded within an existing skilled team.

Code libraries and domain analysis must be managed as an integrated activity. The librarian, or reuse administrator, is ideally placed to advise projects on existing, relevant parts of the domain model, suggest candidates for generalization and incorporate them seamlessly into the library.

Organizationally, there is a danger that, given immediate pressure to deliver, developers or their managers may abuse a relatively loosely defined resource. Creating a separate software infrastructure group is one solution to this problem, having it report directly to senior management is another. There is insufficient experience to pontificate on which approach is best and organizations will differ. A priori, it appears that the group needs to be separated from project teams so that personnel are not pirated by specific project managers.

For the purposes of this argument, we assume that some OO repository tool (like SOMATiK or Simply Objects) is in use. The software infrastructure team, a technology-focused group, is responsible for maintaining and supporting this tool (where used). The team should maintain the repository tool for use in RAD workshops and publish information on reusable classes to project teams at both code and specification levels. Also at these levels, the team should collect and generalize classes as they are produced in RAD workshops and projects. The group should work closely with every new project, initially through the offices of the RAD facilitator, capturing and generalizing every new class specification as it arises. A good, practical suggestion is that the librarian should meet with project teams on a regular basis, say at project meetings, to discuss reuse based on a walkthrough – or tool-based animation session when available. The rôles involved are as follows:

- management of the repository and the team
- facilitation services for RAD workshops, BPR workshops, brainstorming and inspections
- generalization of candidate classes originating from projects or RAD workshops
- testing these classes against technical and business criteria
- maintaining the repository

- publishing the reusable classes to projects
- supporting the tool being used (e.g. SOMATiK)
- freeing other developers to get on with the job.

This group should take ownership of the key objects that are used throughout the organization's systems and productize them. It should act as a center of technical expertise, perhaps conducting one-day library awareness sessions for other developers who want to know what is available. It should be seen as a distributor of objects and seek general purpose commercial objects. The rôle of the team could also encompass methods and reuse awareness training though the skill profiles are then slightly different.

Other key tasks include:

- cross-project coordination
- change management
- ownership
- version control and configuration management
- control and ownership of reusable items (at whatever level)
- documentation and examples.

The repository software will mandate that there be an owner for everything in it. The approach should also evolve as the new team matures and gains experience. It would be wrong to fix it at too early a stage.

It is critical that the reuse team does not become an 'empire' with its own agenda. It must stay close to its interim customers; that is, the developers of projects and thereby close to the demands of users. The hairy/conscript model helps this by bringing a constant stream of new business awareness to the work. However, the reward structure has to be treated with great care.

4.12   Other projects

Other projects benefit from reusable components. Concerns are many, including managing updates and releasing updates to the repository. Here we give only a brief overview of some management issues for reuse which are appropriate to this activity.

Four different models of reuse coordination can be described. In the end-lifecycle model the generalization activity is carried out after projects are completed. Our observation has been that there is a severe danger that this activity is omitted due to the demands of new projects for the newly released human resources who are the ones expected to carry out the generalization. Even if these resources are made available, it is unlikely that the customer will be altruistic enough to fund the apparent extension to his or her project after delivery of a satisfactory end-product. The obvious alternative is to make developers responsible for creating reusable classes during the project. This is called the G-C1 model (Menzies et al., 1992) or the constant-creation model. The arguments for this approach are strong. The costs can be attributed to the customer during development. Furthermore, good developers have a tendency to produce reusable code 'as a silk worm produces silk'; as a by-product of what they are doing anyway. However, in practice this increases costs and increases time to market and is often the victim of time pressures within projects. Obviously, nothing should be done to discourage the production of high-quality, reusable classes during projects but it cannot be enforced in practice. When this régime is in place we tend to observe a lot of source-code copying and improvement rather than subclassing. To overcome problems with both these approaches, two models have been suggested which may be appropriate for small to average and very large companies respectively: the two-library model and the alternative cost-center model. The OPEN version of the two-library model is illustrated schematically in Figure 4.10. Here there is a library of potentially reusable classes identified during projects and another of fully generalized and adopted classes maintained by the domain team. How an object's potential for reuse can be determined is almost impossible to legislate for. Business knowledge and development skills combine to determine the result in concrete circumstances. Developers will typically ask if the concept is important to the business, likely to be used in other systems, fundamental to technical components of applications and so on.

The only additional effort specific to the project in this approach is the recognition of potentially reusable classes and the extra cost is almost nil. As we have seen, early on in projects, from RAD workshops to prototyping in the timebox, library components are scanned. If the classes identified in this way happen to reside in library 1 then an additional generalization cost is incurred by the project, but this is entirely as it should be and the costs can be happily borne by the sponsor. The two-library model directly addresses the danger of over-generalization.

The alternative cost-center model involves creating and funding a separate cost-center centrally. It is not funded by projects and initially runs at a loss, costs being recovered by selling classes to projects long term. This model is only considered appropriate for very large organizations. OPEN is compatible with this approach also.

4.12.1   Rewarding reuse

One of the most vexed questions of OT management is that of how best to reward people in the reuse culture. Traditionally, according to theory at least, programmers have been rewarded on the basis of productivity as measured by the number of source lines of code (SLOCs) or function points they can churn out per annum. This militates against reuse, where the idea is to write as little code as possible. Of course, we can start to measure the number of SLOCs or function points reused and the ratio of this to new code and reward the developers on the

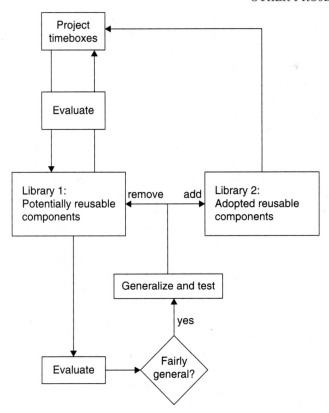

Figure 4.10. The two-library model of reuse (after Henderson-Sellers and Pant, 1993).

basis of this ratio. This would give the biggest rewards to those people who solely assemble systems but penalize those who write the new, creative stuff. Obviously, this type of approach is most unlikely ever to work in practice, as the correct balance could never be fixed. In practice, even in the presence of formal appraisal schemes, developers are rewarded on the basis of a number of highly subjective judgments made by their managers and colleagues; how well they did at the initial interview, whether the organization feels it wants to keep them, the state of the job market, the perception of their overall contribution to projects and so on.

It is easier to see that project teams as a whole can be rewarded on the basis of productivity, speed and quality. A team that understands and utilizes reuse is helped by finding fewer defects in the library code but should be measured by defects in custom code *and* defects overall. Reusing classes reduces development time and increases quality. In this sense, reuse is its own reward and every successful project that has reused a code will further encourage reuse.

In an OO organization there are two kinds of developer; the ones that build applications and the ones that generalize and refine classes for the library.

For the former, informal evaluations based on overall project work, subjective evaluations, time to market and defect levels are probably the only rational basis for reward. For the toolsmiths or reuse engineers, a common suggestion is that they be rewarded on the basis of quality (reported defects) and the number of times that their objects are reused. A problem with this approach is that a developer could produce a very simple object, such as a date object, that is reused in every project henceforth and that saves a very small amount of effort in each case. Another developer might create a complex reusable framework that is reused only once but thereby gives massive savings. The first developer could retire on the proceeds while the second would have to struggle along to the next creative effort. Weighting the rewards according to the complexity metrics discussed in Graham (1995) or Henderson-Sellers (1996) goes some way to addressing this conundrum but it is probably still too early to legislate exactly on how to reward toolsmiths. They will be judged informally in practice anyway.

Reward systems should be team and project based and remain flexible.

In summary, reuse at the code level is important and beneficial but does not scale up. Informal reuse too only works on a small scale. The cost of centralized code reuse management soon outstrips its benefits. The solution is to build a repository of business object specifications and link them back to the source code. Current repository and CASE tools offer no suitable facilities and new tools like SOMATiK are needed. The HCM model (Section 4.11.1) helps ensure that the software infrastructure group is infused with up-to-date business knowledge and focused on business requirements while maintaining a commitment to investment in high-quality, reusable objects (both specifications and code). It also helps disseminate an understanding of the library to development teams.

4.13   Bug fixing

Identification of errors in code – bug fixing – can be somewhat alleviated in an OO environment as a result of the finer granularity of classes and subsystems. Modularity and a contract-driven design assist in constraining the impact on the rest of the system of an error in one module. Historically, maintenance, a large percentage of lifecycle costs, consisted of bug fixing and extensions – weighted heavily to the former. Using OT, those weightings can be effectively regarded as having been reversed. This activity may occur both within a single project and beyond it – thus it is shown straddling the boundary in Figure 4.1.

4.14   Use of system

System use focuses on the end-user: the non-technical person who has often had little or no involvement with the software package as it was being developed. For some organizations, there will be a need for a user acceptance subactivity. In good OO developments, users will have been intimately involved *throughout* the development, thus rendering unnecessary a user YES/NO acceptance activity. In other words, every user review contains some acceptance testing, confirmed in the evaluation activity. Users need training, experience and are often likely to bring to the system different prejudices about how it should work. A key issue here is good usability design.

References

Cook S. and Daniels J. (1995). *Designing Object Systems.* Englewood Cliffs, NJ: Prentice-Hall

DSDM Consortium (1995). *Dynamic Systems Development Method – Version 2.* Farnham: Tesseract

Firesmith D., Henderson-Sellers B. and Graham I. (1997). *OPEN Modeling Language (OML) Reference Manual.* 271 pp. New York: SIGS

Gilb T. and Graham D. (1993). *Software Inspection: Effective Method for Software Project Management.* Reading, MA: Addison-Wesley

Gilligrand D. and Liu K. C. (1995). Specification of the dynamics of object behaviour. *Report on Object Analysis and Design,* **1**(6), 28–32, 43

Graham I. M. (1995). *Migrating to Object Technology.* 552 pp. Harlow, UK: Addison-Wesley

Graham I. (1997). Some problems with use cases . . . and how to avoid them. In *OOIS '96 Proceedings* (Patel D., Sun Y. and Patel S., eds.), pp. 18–27. London: Springer-Verlag

Henderson-Sellers B. (1996). *Object-Oriented Metrics: Measures of Complexity.* 234 pp. Englewood Cliffs, NJ: Prentice-Hall

Henderson-Sellers B. and Pant Y. R. (1993). When should we generalize classes to make them reusable? *Object Magazine,* **3**(4), 73–5

Henderson-Sellers B. and Younessi M. (1997). *OPEN's Toolbox of Techniques.* Harlow, UK: Addison-Wesley

Jacobson I., Christerson M., Jonsson P. and Övergaard G. (1992). *Object-Oriented Software Engineering: A Use Case Driven Approach.* Addison-Wesley

Martin J. and Odell J. J. (1995). *Object-Oriented Methods: A Foundation.* Englewood Cliffs, NJ: Prentice-Hall

Menzies T., Edwards J. M. and Ng K. (1992). The case of the mysterious missing reusable libraries. *Technology of Object-Oriented Languages and Systems: TOOLS12&9* (Mingins C., Haebich B., Potter J. and Meyer B., eds.). Sydney: Prentice-Hall

Meyer B. (1995). *Object Success: A Manager's Guide to Object-Orientation, its impact on the Corporation and its Use for Re-engineering the Software Process.* Englewood Cliffs, NJ: Prentice-Hall

Swatman P. A. and Fowler D. (1998). *Requirements Engineering for High-Quality Information Systems. The FOOM Approach.* Addison-Wesley (in preparation)

Taylor D. A. (1995). *Business Engineering with Object Technology.* 188 pp. New York: Wiley

Thomsett R. (1997). It's the expectations, stupid! *American Programmer,* **10**(4), 30–3

Chapter 5
OPEN tasks

As we noted earlier, a fully OO lifecycle modeling framework can provide a set of activities which can themselves be regarded as objects with pre- and post-conditions on their methods (tasks). OPEN's tasks are statements of things that need to be done. They are described as the 'smallest unit of work on a schedule which contributes to a milestone.' Tasks are either completed or not completed. From OBA, we can also delineate the information associated with a task (Table 5.1). The generic information suggested here by Goldberg and Rubin (1995) is essentially that given for the OPEN tasks in their definitions and descriptions in Appendix A. The figure of merit is between 0 and 1 and is assigned by the project manager. It indicates the importance of the task in meeting the associated milestone, where a milestone may be an activity post-condition or a timebox deadline, for example. For each individual milestone, the sum of all the associated tasks should be unity. Risks and likelihood factors can be allocated on a per project basis, although some generic values may also be possible. Likelihood values, ranging from 0 to 1, indicate belief as to whether the task will be completed on schedule. In addition, project tasks have allocated to them values for the remaining aspects (Table 5.1): duration, start and stop dates and required resources.

Moving from activity to activity is governed by these constraints which express the contract between the activity objects via their tasks (hence the name of the lifecycle model: the contract-driven lifecycle). These activities thus provide a large-scale structuring in time and an architecture amenable to outsourcing if deemed desirable. Different configurations, that is different lifecycle patterns, chosen to reflect the needs of different problems and different organizations, can be constructed from this flexible framework. Each combination of activities and interconnecting paths defines a SEP within the overall OPEN architectural framework (SEPA). Once chosen, the lifecycle process is fixed – although, at least in an OO project, it is still highly iterative, flexible and with a high degree of seamlessness.

For each activity there may be one or several tasks. Then, secondly, for each task the developer may have to choose between several possible techniques,

Table 5.1. Information associated with a task (adapted from Goldberg and Rubin, 1995).

Aspect	Definition
1. *Generic*	
Name	Unique identifier for the task, often intended to be informative
Description	High-level description of the task's goal
Purpose	Why the task deliverable is required
Capabilities	System capabilities (external or internal) created by the task
Process model activity	Process model activity supported by the task
Subtasks	List of subtasks, if applicable
Techniques usable	Identification of techniques likely to be useful for accomplishing the task
2. *Project-specific or project-influenced*	
Figure of merit	A number between 0 and 1 which indicates the importance of the task in meeting its associated milestone
Risks	Description of risks associated with a task that contribute to determining the likelihood factor
Likelihood factor	A number between 0 and 1, where 1 indicates that the task can definitely be done, and 0 that it cannot be done
Deliverable(s)	Description of the deliverable(s). The overall activity deliverables are specified generically and built up incrementally by the output of the tasks. Here, in the context of tasks, these outputs will have some project specificity
Planned start date	Specific date the task should start, which defines the start date for any subtask
Expected duration	The amount of time required to complete the task, which reflects the time by which all subtasks will have been completed
Required resources	People and material assigned to do this task and all of the subtasks
Actual start and finish dates	Actual dates on which work on the task started and finished
Actual resources	Actual resources that were required to carry out the task
Deviations	Description of any deviations from the planned task

Table 5.2   OPEN tasks can be loosely grouped.

User interaction and business issues
Large-scale architectural issues
Project management issues
Database issues
Distribution issues
Modeling/building the system
Reuse issues

---

some of which may be always useful, some may be sometimes useful and others should be avoided altogether. We can thus think of these links (tasks to activities) in one of two ways: in a probabilistic manner or in a purer OO fashion by allocating tasks as methods of the activity objects. At a future time, we assign, in very general terms and in more specific terms for any one, highly specific project, probabilities or, to be more accurate, deontic certainty factors, for each of these task/activity links. (Deontic logic is the logic of duty or obligation. It adds extra operators such as MAY, MUST and OUGHT, to ordinary first-order predicate calculus.) As the lifecycle is increasingly tailored to a specific domain, the values of the deontic factors change to a bimodal distribution (0 or 1) and thus allocate, with certainty, which tasks are needed for which activities. These tasks can now be more usefully modeled as responsibilities or methods of the activities. Thus the deontic matrix between tasks and activities of Henderson-Sellers et al. (1996) turns out to be only an unstable, transient modeling artifact.

Like the activities of one of its predecessors, MOSES, the OPEN tasks are not all equal. Some occur typically earlier in the lifecycle; others group around a particular domain such as distributed computing systems (DCS) or database management (DBM), occurring in clusters; while others occur almost exclusively at a particular stage in the software development lifecycle (e.g. planning the iterations, identification of subsystems).

OPEN tasks can thus be grouped. In this section only an overview of some of the more important task groups is given, gathered into seven loose groupings (Table 5.2).

The full detailed descriptions of all the OPEN tasks are given in Appendix A presented in the form of a reference guide (ordered alphabetically as an easily searched reference section) and listed here in Table 5.3.

In the following seven sections, we illustrate some of the tasks that you might wish to use in your tailored lifecycle process model of OPEN. (Application of OPEN to projects then requires accessing these detailed descriptions, as in the style of using a reference manual; that is, reading in detail in the early learning cycle and then, when more skills and experience have been gained, using them only as a reference when more unusual or more difficult situations

Table 5.3   OPEN tasks (with subtasks) in alphabetical order.

Analyze user requirements
Code
Construct the object model
Create and/or identify reusable components ('for reuse')
    Construct frameworks
    Optimize for reuse
Deliver product to customer
Design and implement physical database
    Distribution/replication design
    Operational and performance design
    Performance evaluation
Design user interface
Develop and implement resource allocation plan
    Choose hardware
    Choose project team
    Choose toolset
    Decompose programmes into project
    Develop education and training plan
    Develop iteration plan
    Develop timebox plan
    Identify project rôles and responsibilities
    Manage subsystems
    Set up metrics collection programme
    Specify individual goals
    Specify quality goals
    Use dependencies in the BOM to generate first-cut project plan
Develop BOM
Develop software development context plans and strategies
    Develop capacity plan
    Develop contingency plan
    Develop security plan
    Establish change management strategy
    Establish data take-on strategy
    Integrate with existing, non-OO systems
    Tailor the lifecycle process
Evaluate quality
    Analyze metrics data
    Evaluate usability
    Review documentation
Identify CIRTs
    Determine initial class list
    Identify persistent classes
    Identify rôles
    Refine class list
Identify context

Table 5.3   (Continued)

Identify source(s) of requirements
Identify user requirements
    Define problem and establish mission and objectives
    Establish user requirements for distributed systems
    Establish user DB requirements
Maintain trace between requirements and design
Manage library of reusable components
Map logical database schema
Map rôles on to classes
Model and re-engineer business process(es)
    Build context (i.e. business process) model
    Build TOM
    Convert TOM to BOM
    Do user training
    Prepare ITT
Obtain business approval
Optimize reuse ('with reuse')
Optimize the design
Test
    Perform acceptance testing
    Perform class testing
    Perform cluster testing
    Perform regression testing
Undertake architectural design
    Develop layer design
    Establish distributed systems strategy
    Select database/storage strategy
Undertake feasibility study
Undertake in-process review
Undertake post-implementation review
Undertake usability design
Write manual(s) and prepare other documentation

are encountered.) While the tasks are grouped under seven headings (Table 5.4), many span two or more such loose groupings. These sections are intended to give an overall, non-verbose summary so that the overall picture can be viewed.

Full descriptions will be found in Appendix A which acts as reference material for, and the formal definition of, each task.

Table 5.4   OPEN tasks in logical/temporal groupings.

(i) *User interactions and business issues*
Identify context
Identify source(s) of requirements
Identify user requirements
 Define problem and establish mission and objectives
 Establish user requirements for distributed systems
 Establish user DB requirements
Analyze user requirements
Model and re-engineer business process(es)
 Build context (i.e. business process) model
 Build TOM
 Convert TOM to BOM
 Do user training
 Prepare ITT
Undertake feasibility study
Obtain business approval
Develop BOM
Write manuals and prepare other documentation
Deliver product to customer

(ii) *Large-scale architectural issues*
Undertake architectural design
 Develop layer design
 Establish distributed systems strategy
 Select database/storage strategy
Construct frameworks (subtask)
Optimize the design

(iii) *Project management issues*
Develop software development context plans and strategies
 Tailor the lifecycle process
 Develop capacity plan
 Develop security plan
 Establish change management strategy
 Develop contingency plan
 Establish data take-on strategy
 Integrate with existing, non-OO systems
Undertake feasibility study
Develop and implement resource allocation plans
 Choose project team
 Identify project rôles and responsibilities
 Choose toolset
 Choose hardware
 Specify quality goals
 Specify individual goals

Table 5.4   (Continued)

Decompose programme into project
Use dependencies in the BOM to generate first-cut project plan (Gantt chart)
Develop timebox plan
Develop iteration plan
Set up metrics collection programme
Manage subsystems
Develop education and training plan

Quality issues
Test
Perform class testing
Perform cluster testing
Perform regression testing
Perform acceptance testing
Write manuals and prepare other documentation
Evaluate quality
Analyze metrics data
Evaluate usability
Review documentation
Maintain trace between requirements and design
Undertake in-process review
Undertake post-implementation review

(iv) *Database issues*
Identify user database requirements (subtask)
Select database/storage strategy (subtask)
Identify persistent classes (subtask)
Map logical database schema
Design and implement physical database
Distribution/replication design
Operational and performance design
Performance evaluation

(v) *Distribution issues*
Identify user requirements for DCS (subtask)
Establish distributed systems strategy (subtask)
Develop security plan (subtask)

(vi) *Modeling/building the system*
Analyze user requirements
Identify CIRTs
Determine initial class list
Identify persistent classes
Identify rôles
Refine class list
Construct the object model

Table 5.4   (Continued)

Design user interface
Map rôles on to classes
Optimize the design
Undertake usability design
Code
Write manuals and other documentation

(vii) *Reuse issues*
Optimize reuse ('with reuse')
Create and/or identify reusable components ('for reuse')
　　　Construct frameworks
　　　Optimize for reuse
Manage library of reusable components

5.1   User interactions and business issues

This group of tasks occurs relatively early in the lifecycle (but may also persist over larger parts of it). They tend to focus on business issues (Taylor, 1995; Graham, 1995 and, in less detail, Henderson-Sellers and Edwards, 1994; also Waldén and Nerson, 1995; Goldberg and Rubin, 1995; Meyer, 1995; these are only summarized here, for full details, please see the cited texts) and on user requirements. The relevant tasks are:

(1) identify context
(2) identify source(s) of requirements
(3) identify user requirements

　　　(a) define problem and establish mission and objectives
　　　(b) establish user requirements for distributed systems
　　　(c) establish user DB requirements

(4) analyze user requirements
(5) model and re-engineer business process(es)

　　　(a) build context (i.e. business process) model
　　　(b) build TOM
　　　(c) convert TOM to BOM
　　　(d) do user training
　　　(e) prepare ITT

(6) undertake feasibility study
(7) obtain business approval

(8) develop BOM

(9) write manuals and other documentation

(10) deliver product to customer.

Problem definition and user requirements

The beginning of a project is the identification of a problem within the business domain and within the context of the overall mission and company objectives. The problem may pre-exist or need to be set here – possibly using RAD techniques similar to those used later in requirements engineering. Here, however, it is senior organizational personnel who must be involved, rather than the end-user.

It is too easy to see the current problem as 'automate the accounting system' or 'give the customer a faster turn-round.' The first statement does nothing to define the problem (which is more likely to be something along the lines of creating an efficient means to manage the accounts) and the second leaves us wondering who the customer is. Do we mean *all* customers or just the majority (say 90%)? What does faster mean? Should it be measured for all customers? Should it be a relative or percentage change? and so on.

The problem-solving literature is highly relevant here (e.g. Polya, 1957; Starfield et al., 1990). What is the problem that requires a solution? What is the system to which this all applies? Where are the system borderlines? BON advises that the system borderline allows us to focus not only on the problem area to be modeled at the highest level, but also on the communication mode between the system model (of interest) and the external world (of no interest other than as a boundary condition). Good use of scenarios, use cases and task scripts can help by drawing a box around the system (i.e. the business system in the first instance) that is of relevance. Items inside the box require our further consideration; items outside do not, unless BPR is being undertaken. Thus we identify the problem and its context. COMN's context diagrams are a useful documentation tool here.

It should be stressed that, at this stage, there is no supposition at all that, first, the identification of a problem will automatically lead to a project to solve the problem (it may be too expensive, too risky, dangerous etc.) or, secondly, that if a solution is sought, it will necessarily be a computer solution. Of course, in this book we are only really interested in those solutions that involve computers. Nevertheless, all tasks in this section are equally applicable to non-computer solution domains. Indeed, it is this computer-independence which marks out this group of tasks as belonging together.

For the purposes of describing OPEN we will assume that a decision to proceed (this decision will be made as part of the process) will in fact belong to the software domain.

Identifying and formalizing user requirements, although initially undertaken early in the lifecycle, should not be seen as a one-off procedure. Indeed, with an iterative lifecycle as commonly advocated in the use of OT, there are many opportunities to keep the customer/user 'in the loop' throughout the whole lifecycle of the development process. This is a significant advantage gained from developing using an OO software development approach (compared to more traditional methods).

The first task is often to identify the source or sources of information pertaining to the requirements. This may be documents and people (users, managers). Identification of the relative weights of the inputs to be provided by the different 'interested parties' is important to avoid a bloated requirements specification that demands a 'kitchen sink' of functionality to address every whim of every likely (current and future) user. Capturing user requirements in OPEN derives largely from the techniques advocated in MOSES and in SOMA; in particular, the contribution from SOMA of interviewing techniques and OO RAD workshops is considered to be significant. Other useful SOMA techniques include brainstorming, rôle play, user-focused questionnaires and videotaping. Interviewers should be trained both in interview techniques and in OT. Interviews should be arranged with the end-users regarding business requirements. However, it is important to note that the user/customer is not interested in the use/non-use of OT in providing them with their demanded quality product. The final product will be independent of its method of production. Quality, particularly reliability, usability and maintainability, will be one of the manifestations of OT which the end-user will perceive. Commitment of top executives is particularly needed for the successful adoption of new technologies – and OT is no exception. Hence, interviews with senior management may also be useful. Information from the interviews and user workshops is documented using task scripts. Difficult areas may be simulated in a throwaway prototyping environment.

Analysis of user requirements

Once the source or sources of requirements have been identified and an idea of the overall requirements obtained, the analyst starts the analysis activity by trying to understand, validate and reconcile these requirements. One good way of doing this is for the architect/analyst to probe for, and try to understand, the central issue of concern to each stakeholder (the current interviewee). Asking several questions starting with 'why' usually proves useful. Be tactful and helpful but assertive, as at times stakeholders do not wish to disclose these deeply held 'secrets,' or may genuinely have not thought about the matter or at least not deeply enough. Possibly it is so deeply embedded in the psyche as not to be consciously recognized as part of the problem (or its answer). This is one potential area where the old adage 'the customer always knows best' may not apply.

Once this recognition is made, the analyst will be in a position to discuss with the stakeholder the *purpose* of the system as they view it. Once agreement is reached as to this 'purpose,' the analyst must review and reconcile the compatibility and consistency of this 'purpose' for the system, together with those identified by other stakeholders, obtained through the same mechanism. This is important because this separation of concerns allows the analyst to appreciate the various potential interactions, uses or aspirations held in connection with the system to be developed. This separation of concerns is also important because, although a single requirements set which represents the views of many stakeholders may be inconsistent (simply because it reflects differing views of different stakeholders having different aims, objectives and purposes for the system), system views described by a single individual *are* usually consistent (individuals can also have conflicting requircments, but this is much less prevalent and much more easily resolved by appealing to their rationality).

In addition, it often helps during analysis to categorize stakeholders into distinct groups. We recommend at least a top-level categorization that recognizes the roles of various stakeholders to include:

(1) Clients: those stakeholders who will be the beneficiaries or 'victims' of the system concerned.

(2) Actors: those stakeholders who will cause the human-based internal transformations of the system.

(3) Owners: those stakeholders with the power to abolish the system.

It is important, however, to recognize that, in various views of a particular problem situation, these rôles may be played by different individuals or groups of individuals, depending on the 'purpose' that they see for the system. The rôles are also not necessarily orthogonal. As such, one individual may play a number of these rôles. Categorization of stakeholders into these groupings assists the analyst in formulating a conflict resolution strategy.

This rich environment of concerns, purposes, views, approaches and interactions opened to the analyst is a complex one. The task of the analyst is now to capture this complexity and richness in such a sufficiently loss-less way as to make its retention, its future communication (to the analyst at a later time, or to others) and its likely further investigation (further analysis) a practical task. Concepts such as objects, types, mappings, inheritance, messages, and so on, being natural constructs for expressing the natural world and our knowledge about it, become some of the tools to be gainfully used to this end. An OO model can thus be created.

Once a composite, reconciled and stable model representing the consensus or near-consensus views of all important stakeholders has been arrived at, the analyst must then check back with all involved parties with regard to this understanding.

Business process engineering

Business process engineering has evolved recently and is often focused upon the notion of business process re-engineering with the well-known acronym of BPR. However, since most business processes have not been engineered in the first place (more a case of slow evolution), the 're-' of BPR may well be inappropriate. Business process engineering, on the other hand, does reflect the need to consider the business from a systematic perspective. Typical BPR issues are given in Taylor (1995) which discusses the concept of convergent engineering. Material in that book is not repeated here but will be incorporated into the OPEN methodology as appropriate. Fingar et al. (1997) also note the support for this notion of convergent engineering implicit in the OMG's Common Business Objects and Business Object Facility.

Context modeling is a business process modeling technique in which the business processes and business strategy are analyzed for the purpose of, it is to be hoped, improvement. Hammer and Champy (1993) advocate dramatic restructuring and redesign of business processes in order for the desired level of improvement to be achieved. BPR suggests the context for good modeling is no longer the task but the business process. As part of this, technology (such as OT) is quite reasonably seen as an enabler not a prime focus.

The issue is really one of optimization. Businesses exist to make a profit, which are earned when the money made from sales exceeds the money spent on producing and marketing the goods or services. To increase profits either (a) sales must go up, (b) costs must come down, or (c) both. For sales to go up, the business must be customer focused as, in the final analysis, it is the happy customer who comes back and brings new potential customers with him or her. Consequently, a customer focus must be a central tenet of business engineering. This means that the system boundary of the business must be expanded to include those concerns that lead to such a customer focus. It also means that business engineers must model the internals of the business to support this requirement. To do this effectively, a process approach to, or view of, the business should be taken. This allows modeling the system using systematic and robust modeling tools as used in engineering process design: tools such as OT.

Also, to lower costs, once again the business must look at its operation in terms of a process. Only when a stable and well-defined model of the business is at hand can the business engineer decide on the course of action to be taken towards orienting the internal business processes to the lowering of costs. Again, OT will prove effective as a powerful modeling tool.

Once a rich model of the business process is obtained, the business engineer will turn his or her attention to the problem of bringing these internal processes towards lower costs; two options are available.

(1) Distinguish the common causes from special causes and redesign that aspect of the system (the business process) that is responsible for the special causes. This is called process improvement (à la TQM).

(2) Distinguish that there is sufficient common-cause perturbation or, conversely sufficient process stability such that the present process will not (no matter how much we fiddle with it) produce the results we require. This is when a brand new process must be designed. This is at the heart of BPR.

If the new system is designed using systematic process engineering principles, is customer focused and targeted towards the *real* aims of the business, then it has a good chance of contributing to a lowering of costs *and* to customer satisfaction and hence to an increase in sales. Once these two aims are achieved, higher profits will inevitably follow.

Most BPR methods also incorporate process modeling techniques borrowed from old-fashioned structured methods. Typically, the process models are arrived at using functional decomposition, flow charting and data flow techniques. In these methods, processes are viewed as being composed of activities disembodied from the agents responsible for their performance. These activities are linked by so-called 'logical flows' that represent information (data actually), materials or controls. The semantics of such links is sometimes unclear. This approach evades what is actually the key stumbling block in BPR projects: responsibility. Furthermore, much of the semantic content of real business processes is lost by the representation. To solve both problems, we must adopt an OO, responsibility-driven approach to business process modeling based on semiotics of communication (messages).

What is needed is a truly OO requirements engineering technique. In our view it should enable developers and users, working together, to build a model of the business processes that a system will support. It should do this while applying the basic principles of object orientation in a thoroughgoing manner. It must be easy to use and easy to understand. The results should provide a model that is readily accessible and understandable by users as well as developers so that it provides the basis for communication and negotiation between these two groups and their managers. Its models should be small and tractable while capturing all the essential details of a project. In other words, it must capture all the information about the processes and the business objects that they entail. It must allow the processes to be described from both an internal and external viewpoint and its modeling constructs should not multiply beyond manageable proportions, even for complex systems. The requirements engineering and business process modeling techniques of OPEN meet all these objectives.

A key part of the SOMA approach to system development (on which this part of OPEN is based) is the use of RAD workshops for requirements capture and analysis. The RAD technique, of course, predates OT and was used long before there were any methods for OO analysis available. Running RAD workshops, it is found that data-centered or static modeling approaches to object modeling are not a good place to start with users. Obtaining an entity model takes quite a long time if attempted at the start of a RAD workshop. Many people with similar experience have observed that users respond better to a process-oriented approach. However, if we want to extract an OO model from the activity, constructing data-flow diagrams is really worse than useless and likely first to be ignored by real OO programmers and secondly to lead to a horrid functional decomposition that poorer programmers can use as an excuse to write functionally oriented code. Our experience has shown that all these problems can be overcome by basing the requirements model on business processes using a modeling technique that is strictly OO and is a generalization of the

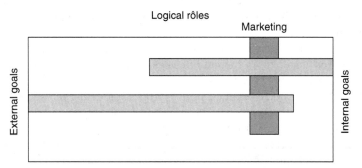

Figure 5.1   Activity grid (after Graham, 1997).

data-flow approach and the use-case approach. As a side effect of the approach, it turns out that if an entity model view is required it can be extracted from the object model and agreed with users in a matter of moments.

Both requirements engineering and BPR must start with a model of the communications and contracts among the participants in the business and the other stakeholders, customers, suppliers and so on. But first we need to model the whole organization and decide what business it is or should be in. In conformity with the principles of OPEN we should build an object model of the entire business to address this problem. As it turns out most businesses are far too large and complex to make such an approach viable and we need first to apply a simple decomposition technique, inspired by the spreadsheet metaphor, and known as an activity grid.

We start business process modeling by asking who its customers and stakeholders are. These latter could include regulators, suppliers, shareholders, sister companies and so on. We then work to define the goals that the organization shares with the stakeholders and especially with its customers. These are essentially *external* goals that represent value propositions shared between the organization and the stakeholders, such as 'provide reliable product promptly' or 'give accurate advice.' These shared goals are written along one edge of a grid; in Figure 5.1 the left edge has been chosen. Of course, a company always has goals that it may not share with customers, such as keeping the executives out of jail on charges of false accounting and the like. To represent this we write such *internal* goals on the facing edge of the grid.

For both internal and external goals we now ask: What has to be done to support each goal? In other words we establish the processes required to support the goals. We can now compare these with the processes currently in place and produce grids representing the situation *before* and *after* re-engineering. At this point we must decide whether to go for a radical restructuring or minor changes. OPEN has little to say on this, essentially creative, activity but does provide the essential modeling tools to establish which processes contribute to the goals so that rational decisions about both the processes and process automation can be made.

The next step is to identify logical rôles representing abstract job descriptions for the people who will conduct the processes. The grid is then reorganized iteratively to minimize illogical role and task assignments. Once the processes are assigned to the rôles we only need to discover the dependencies between any linked processes to complete the high-level business process model represented by the grid. The text of each cell now describes the essential mission of each process area (or business area) along with any linkages to related processes and ordering and time constraints.

This technique has decomposed the business into chunks that are small enough to be modeled in detail using an OO style.

Business object modeling

Business object modeling can be best undertaken using hierarchical task analysis and provides a solid underpinning for OPEN's system object modeling.

Task scripts are primarily used to discover business objects and are retained for testing purposes. However, they are objects in their own right, albeit in a different domain. Because of this, task scripts may be organized into composition, classification and usage structures. The components of a script are arrived at by using hierarchical task analysis and are called *component scripts*. This is where the hierarchical decomposition takes place down to the level of atomic tasks (Figure 3.2) that refer directly to objects and their operations. (Atomic tasks permit the collection of the task point metric, currently being evaluated by the International OO Metrics Club.) Classifying scripts into more specialized versions gives rise to *subscripts*. When exceptions require the flow of control to be redirected to a script dealing with a special case, the latter is dealt with by a *side-script*. It is important to emphasize that task scripts deal with business processes and not business functions in order to avoid the danger of capturing the requirements in the form of narrow functional specializations which are often present in the existing organization.

Each script states what the system is *normally* expected to do. However, to emphasize exceptions it is advisable to record the side-scripts corresponding to exceptional conditions. To reduce the number of scripts we have to deal with, we classify them and link them to associated task scripts. An exception, or side-script, is also useful. For example, the 'settle trade' script might read 'on receipt of ticket, match trade and record data.' When the match fails, a side-script such as 'alert exception manager and print letter' must be added. These scripts focus on business objects which are, themselves, incipient system objects – an important aspect of OPEN's 'seamlessness.' Figure 5.2 shows a side-script for what to do when you have sold something that you do not possess. Component scripts form a recursive hierarchy while side-scripts define a usage structure and help to discover event traces.

Task scripts may be classified just like objects. For example, a script for 'capture equity trade' may inherit features from 'capture trade' and add extra features specific to equities, as illustrated in Figure 5.2. Subclassifications of this sort are subscripts.

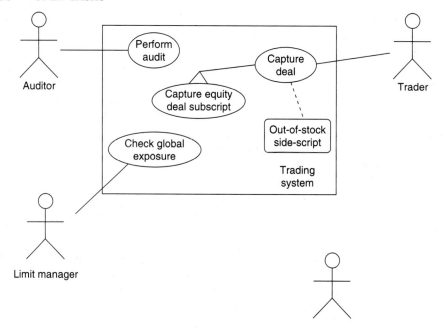

Figure 5.2.   Context model for a trading system with task scripts added (after Graham, 1995).

In short

- task scripts may be one sentence or an essay
- task analysis should be used to decompose complex scripts into component scripts
- atomic scripts should be in subject–verb–direct.object–[preposition–indirect.object]. (SVDPI) format ideally
- there may be subscripts
- there may be side-scripts dealing with exceptions
- textual analysis can be used to find objects and operations
- task attributes and associations should be recorded, if known.

Other useful techniques for business object modeling, such as rôle playing, are also available in OPEN.

Feasibility study

An OO feasibility study is little different from a traditional IS approach. This study evaluates options ranging over, for instance

- do nothing
- modify current system
- implement new computer system
- implement new manual system.

Feasibility studies and their outcomes are closely related to business engineering activities and must be done within a defined context and to fulfill a vision or purpose.

Approval to proceed

However good a *technical* case may appear to be, the final arbitration is undertaken on business grounds. OT is a supporting technology to help businesses, and their information infrastructure, to succeed in obtaining the goals that they have set for themselves. Just because a software system can be built, and built very successfully, does not mean that anybody needs it in a business sense – either internally to support other business functions or externally as a viable product. Consequently, approval to proceed is necessary before any further investment in resources (time and money) is justifiable.

Develop BOM

The TOM focuses on business processes and is at the high level that can be best described by tasks, task scripts, task cards and so on. Although tasks can be regarded as objects, they are reified processes and need to be translated (smoothly as it happens) into business objects. Business objects can be considered to be at the same level of abstraction as system objects but in the business, not the technical, domain. Business objects thus have a technical flavor while retaining a nomenclature immediately recognizable as belonging to the business domain. Once agreed with management and users, the BOM is the starting point for the technical development and from this can be derived cost estimates and a first cut at the project planning, perhaps using Gantt charts (see below).

Prepare documentation

An important task is that of writing manuals and documenting the process and the product. Good documentation can turn an average product into a highly usable one – however, it should be noted that users find much of the documentation currently supporting software to be intractable and arcane. A good development team employs a technical writer and is strict on its control of the quality of both internal and external documentation.

Deliver product to customer

A major task following successful in-house testing is the delivery of the product to the customer. The task is not that of pure delivery but also needs to take into account the customer need for education and training on the new product, customer site testing (often with larger databases than it has been possible to trial) and, finally, customer acceptance.

5.2 Large-scale architectural issues

This group of tasks deal with early lifecycle or larger-scale issues, such as architecture, including hardware allocation, database design strategy and decisions regarding whether or not to use a DCS. The relevant tasks here are:

(1) undertake architectural design

    (a) develop layer design
    (b) establish distributed systems strategy
    (c) select database/storage strategy

(2) construct frameworks (subtask)

(3) optimize the design.

Architecture

Architectural issues deal with large-scale disposition, style, hardware support, database design strategy, division into subsystems, extent of distribution – all important issues.

Domain analysis is the basis for building so-called application frameworks and many class libraries. Domain modeling is especially important for an OO approach. This is because of the importance of reuse in motivating the adoption of OT. Domains include graphical user interfaces, decision support systems, financial trading systems, and so on. McNicoll (quoted by Berard) defines domain analysis as 'an investigation of a specific application area that seeks to identify the operations, objects and structures that commonly occur in software systems within this area.'

There are three specific subtasks here which address the architecture by layering and that are imposed by the use of a distributed and/or database-inclusive strategy. The architectural layer is best represented in terms of standard two- or three-tier client–server applications (Figure 5.3). Layers may address the application model, the domain, the server interface, the relational database wrapper, and so on (Figure 5.4). Layers are essentially large 'horizontal' clusters used as a strategic architectural unit of design (Firesmith et al., 1997, p. 44) and thus correspond to the layers in a traditional three-layer architecture (Figure 5.3). Each main cluster (represented in COMN as a dotted, rounded-corner rectangle) within the layer represents the software allocated to the associated hardware. In the example shown (Figure 5.4) of a two-layer client–server architecture the lower layer in the client software is connected to the top layer in the server software by an observer linkage (see Firesmith et al., 1997 for discussion on how

Figure 5.3   Typical three-tier architecture (supplied by P. Haynes, 1997).

this important pattern is realized in COMN). Two allied subtasks are the establishment of an appropriate strategy for distribution (one answer has just been discussed – see also Rasmussen et al., 1996) which includes full consideration of the underlying (hardware) technology, and an appropriate storage strategy, which might use an objectbase or a relational database which may or may not be a distributed database.

Framework construction

Frameworks offer architectural scope support for reuse. Frameworks thus span reuse concerns and architectural issues. A framework provides a set of predefined subsystems with clearly specified responsibilities which are the skeleton for future applications. Business objects proffer reuse at the modeling level (ex-OOA/OOD) where greater benefits can be anticipated compared to design or code reuse. OPEN 'objects' can be represented at all these levels.

   A framework also expresses, at the architectural level, a fundamental structural organization for software systems by providing a set of predefined clusters (or subsystems) with specified responsibilities and including a set of rules and guidelines for organizing the relationships between them (Buschmann, 1995). An application using a framework will then instantiate all the abstract classes in the framework by adding concrete subclasses – which in effect creates the application. It is widely reusable through synthesis and is often available as a packaged product. The framework thus predefines a set of design parameters so that the application developer can concentrate on the specifics of the application itself. Since the framework captures the design decisions common across a whole application domain, it can be considered to be *design reuse* (Johnson and Foote, 1988).

Optimization

When computing resources are scarce and/or the problem demands are high, the design may require optimizing. This may lead to redesign at an architectural level as well as optimization at the method or algorithm level. For example, facilities supplied by the particular hardware and software support configuration may be used – for example paging considerations, loop minimization. The database component may have extra relationships added primarily to accelerate searching

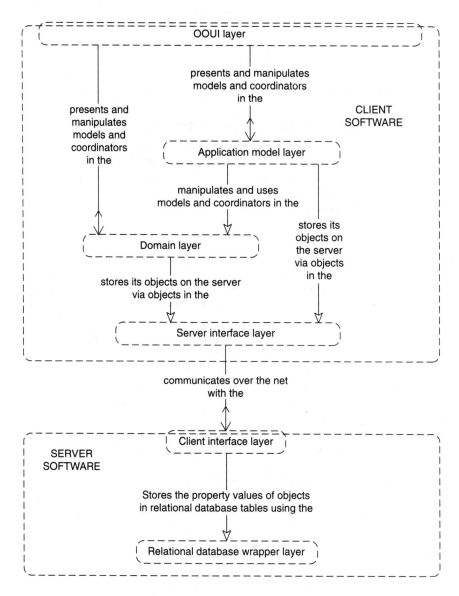

Figure 5.4.   COMN layer diagram for a two-tier client–server application (after Firesmith et al., 1997).

along the navigation paths. Finally, it should be stressed that tests should precede optimization; these tests being used to identify bottlenecks and problem areas. There is no point in, for example, optimizing a code that contributes an insignificant percentage to the overall run time.

5.3 Project management issues

This group of tasks tends to span the whole lifecycle being focused on project-management and personnel issues as well as technical issues such as testing and quality evaluation. The relevant tasks are:

(1) develop software development context plans and strategies

    (a) tailor lifecycle process
    (b) develop capacity plan
    (c) develop security plan
    (d) establish change management strategy
    (e) develop contingency plans
    (f) establish data take-on strategy
    (g) integrate with existing, non-OO systems

(2) undertake feasibility study

(3) develop and implement resource allocation plan

    (a) choose project team
    (b) identify project rôles and responsibilities
    (c) choose toolset
    (d) choose hardware
    (e) specify quality goals
    (f) specify individual goals
    (g) decompose programme into projects
    (h) use dependencies in the BOM to generate the first-cut project plan (Gantt chart) – this can be automated by products such as SOMATiK
    (i) develop timebox plan
    (j) develop iteration plan
    (k) set up metrics collection programme
    (l) manage subsystems
    (m) develop education and training plan

Quality issues

(1) Test

    (a) perform class testing
    (b) perform cluster testing
    (c) perform regression testing
    (d) perform acceptance testing

(2) write manuals and other documentation

(3) evaluate quality

    (a) analyze metrics data
    (b) evaluate usability
    (c) review documentation

(4) maintain trace between requirements and design

(5) undertake in-process review

(6) undertake post-implementation reviews – these are in fact optional, since the need for post-implementation reviews is obviated to a large degree by testing everything earlier.

5.3.1 Business and large-scale project planning

Large-scale software planning must depend upon business decision making. Decision making is a complex procedure, a critical element of which is estimation of risks. It is a sobering thought that of 8000 software projects from over 350 companies investigated (Standish Group, 1994, 1995) only 16% could be classed as successes, the remainder either being canceled before completion or incurring massive time and budget over-runs. Five of the most highly ranked causes of failure were identified to be related to requirements, the other three being managerial – but none related to technical areas. In other words, problems focus on poor requirements and inadequate risk analysis (Stevens and Putlock, 1997).

Business and large-scale project planning tasks focus on those organizational-level (as opposed to project-level) decisions which define the organizational culture and the software development paradigm within which all the technical software development must exist (and, one would hope, flourish).

Planning at this level must also take into account the existing culture. A culture epitomizes the 'normal behavior' expected of a member in an organization, embodied in rituals, symbols, folklore and a shared language (Hohmann, 1997). Constantine and Lockwood (1994) describe four stereotypical organizational cultures: closed, random, open and synchronous. They argue that unless such organizational self-assessment is undertaken, project management – and also change management (from traditional to OO) – will likely be unsuccessful. Indeed, the project manager is a key player in the software development process. He or she has responsibility for day-to-day management of the project and must therefore have technical knowledge as well as managerial/people skills.

There are seven subtasks to this task:

- tailor the lifecycle process
- develop capacity plan
- develop security plan
- establish change management strategy

- develop contingency plan
- establish data take-on strategy
- integrate with existing non-OO systems.

Tailor the lifecycle process

OPEN is a methodology that contains many options from which to choose so that when that choice has been made the resulting method, tailored to your organization and your project, is readily learnable and becomes your organizational standard; yet 'your own methodology' is completely compatible with the published (and larger, more comprehensive) OPEN methodological framework, as described in this book.

The OPEN lifecycle model, the contract model, offers an overall number of activities and some likely connection paths (Figure 4.1). In this subtask, you choose which of those paths are appropriate; which tasks should be used to support those activities. Which techniques should be used can be left as less prescriptive since the way you accomplish the result (the outcome of the task) has less impact on project management. So long as the choice is one from several, all being equally efficient and effective techniques, the choice can be merely that of personal taste, past experience and so on. In this way, the methodology description can be likened to a salad bar: the chef prepares a number of dishes for your delectation, but it is up to you the customer (read developer) to choose what delights your palate and avoid those items you find unpalatable.

Develop capacity plan

Capacity planning for OO systems is no different than for non-OO ones. There are basically two techniques: simulation or queuing theory approaches. A standard text may be consulted.

Develop security plan

Security should be considered for a variety of vulnerable areas. User security and authorities should be considered to protect the system against unauthorized access to information through firewalls, system screens and reports.

Establish change management strategy

Managing the change to OT is non-trivial. People and technology and their capabilities and restrictions should be analyzed carefully, particularly the organizational culture or mindset. Is it compatible with iteration, incremental delivery and reuse? Are the required skills available? Will consultants and/or contractors be needed? Will the local job pool be able to provide people for the various rôles required? There are many pitfalls on the way (Webster, 1995).

Develop contingency plan

It is vital for an organization to develop contingency plans so that the business itself does not fail in the event of some unlikely catastrophe. Contingency plans might include, in the context of OT, a plan for unavailability or unforeseen failure of the selected compiler or CASE tool. What is the back-up strategy? What contingency exists for the case of a delay in delivery of the software to the organization when work is outsourced?

Establish data take-on strategy

There is nothing different here about OO systems. There is the usual choice between big-bang and phased approaches – and the usual cost and ennui.

Integrate with existing non-OO systems

There are a number of scenarios in which an OO application should interoperate with existing non-OO systems. These include:

- the evolutionary migration of an existing system to a future OO implementation where parts of the old system will remain temporarily in use
- the evolution of systems which already exist and are important and too large or complex to rewrite at a stroke and where part or all of the old system may continue to exist indefinitely
- the reuse of highly specialized or optimized routines, embedded expert systems and hardware-specific software
- exploiting the best of existing relational databases for one part of an application in concert with the use of an OO programming language and/or OO databases for another part
- the construction of graphical front-ends to existing systems
- the need to build on existing 'package' solutions
- cooperative processing and blackboard architectures may involve existing agents working with newly defined objects
- the need to cooperate with existing systems across telecommunications and local area networks.

The first issue is how to tackle the migration of vast systems, systems that are almost invariably very costly and tricky to maintain. The recommended strategy is to build what is known as an object wrapper. Wrappers are a technique to add encapsulation and information hiding to existing, or legacy, components or systems. Thus, for example, a whole COBOL program could be given a wrapper to make it appear as a single object to the rest of the OO system (Figure 5.5). It must also appear to the outside as an object, offering the same functionality as the original code. Effectively the wrapper is a large object whose

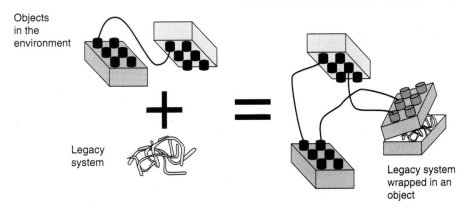

Objects
in the
environment

Legacy
system

Legacy system
wrapped in an
object

Figure 5.5. Retaining a legacy system by adding an object wrapper (after Goldberg and Rubin, 1995).

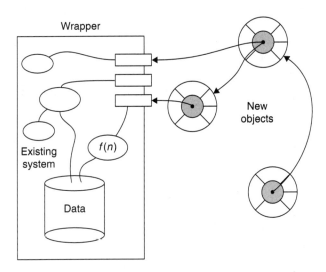

Wrapper

New
objects

$f(n)$

Existing
system

Data

Figure 5.6   Object wrappers (after Graham, 1995).

methods are the menu options of the old system (Figure 5.6). Although wrappers may be large or small, in the context of interoperability, they tend to be of quite coarse granularity.

These issues are of major importance and, although not directly pertinent to our current discussion, are discussed in detail in Appendix D.

Undertake feasibility study

An OO feasibility study is little different from a traditional IS approach. This study evaluates options ranging over, for instance:

- do nothing
- modify current system
- implement new computer system
- implement new manual system.

5.3.2 Project management

Once the large-scale planning has been done, the specific project must be managed. Project management focuses on planning, control and measurement of the allocations of time, money, people, range, tools and techniques, and quality. Here, we need to discuss resource allocation in terms of the choice of project team members; choice of toolset; iterative plans; subsystem management; education and training. At the project level, a schedule needs to be developed. This identifies temporal constraints, possibly temporal orderings (particularly of deliverables), units of work (tasks) and milestones by which to measure progress.

A good project manager realizes what is known and what are the unknowns; what needs to be done to eliminate the uncertainties and unknowns; what needs to be done to ensure milestones are technically (as well as politically) feasible; and needs to be able to replan as the plan unfolds and needs correction mid-course. It is also worth noting that a winning strategy delivers results incrementally (which builds management trust and retains customer interest), if possible on a one to six month time basis – or shorter. Timeboxes (Chapter 2) can be usefully deployed here.

In OPEN, there are thirteen subtasks:

- choose project team
- identify project rôles and responsibilities
- choose toolset
- choose hardware
- specify quality goals
- specify individual goals
- decompose programmes into projects
- use dependencies in the BOM to generate the first-cut project plan (often in the form of a Gantt chart)
- develop timebox plan
- develop iteration plan
- set up metrics collection programme
- manage subsystems
- develop education and training plan

Supportive project management techniques include PERT charts, CPM charts, Gantt charts, risk analysis, cost estimation and workflow analysis. Priorities need setting and timescales for deliverables need to be carefully planned.

Project team structure

Selection of team structure and then the members of that team can be critical to the success of the project. A team consists of a few individuals, each playing one or more rôles. Success is determined both by leadership and by interteam member communication skills – more important determinants of success than language.

Team structure can vary – from hierarchical (layered) to fully cooperative (flat). Teams may also have different foci – from application production to reuse. Rôles within the team may also vary, depending upon organizational culture, type of project and available resources. All should be chosen carefully in order to optimize the possibility of success. For initial projects, the best team members should be selected and they should be given every opportunity to succeed, for example adequate training, time to investigate and understand the new paradigm (i.e. protection from unrelated interruptions) and sufficient and timely resources.

Tools

One of the difficult tasks, often for the project manager, is the choice of the tools to be used on the project. Sometimes there are organizational standards; yet often a specific project will need specially selected tools. An organization needs to retain a balance between an internal standard and the inflexibility that it brings. It is often a mistake to use, say, C++ for *all* projects simply because you are 'a C++ shop.' Choose the appropriate tools for each new project; watch as technology changes and matures, do not get locked in to a single vendor. Defer the language choice; most languages can be used effectively. However, if there are no supporting tools for browsing, debugging, documentation, then other choices should be considered. In addition, more important determinants to success than language are (in no particular order)

- organizational culture
- project management style
- effective lifecycle development method
- knowledge of the object paradigm.

Hardware

Although hardware these days is seldom the main constraint on a project, there are times when sophisticated OO tools may be pushing the limits of your current equipment. Consequently an analysis of whether to adopt different tools or upgrade the hardware will be needed. As well as costs and capacity, there will likely be compatibility concerns, particularly in a modern intranet environment. Other systems may demand a client–server environment, perhaps based on a mid-sized server or a mainframe. For example, in a banking environment, workstations, while increasingly powerful, may not be adequate for main database interactions. Selection of hardware may thus simply be from what is currently available or may require a commissioning process.

Goal setting

Goals need to be set both for the personal developer and for the overall project team, the latter usually framed as a set of quality goals.

Decompose programme into projects

Programmes span many projects and thus need to be split into those projects in such a way that there is in general a one-to-one correspondence between projects and project teams.

Develop the first-cut project plan

Project plans in the form of PERT, CPM or Gantt charts are still useful in an OO environment although the iterative and incremental delivery nature of the environment adds an additional overlay. Iterations should be carefully planned. Typically three will be needed within a project's lifetime.

Develop timebox plan

Timeboxes need to be very carefully planned, in terms of both their number and their duration. The degree of completion per timebox iteration should also be clearly specified.

Planning for an iterative development

An iteration plan needs not only to plan the number of iterations but also the associated documentation so that it is available for reviewing the results of the project in comparison with the planned/anticipated results. The purpose of this task is to develop a project plan detailing the required resources, objectives and timeframe for the next iteration. A number of subtasks have been defined which include:

- identify and prioritize system requirements
- document external dependencies and deliverables
- establish a schedule.

Quality assessment (metrics)

A good quality assessment programme needs to be both initiated and actioned. Metrics need to be carefully considered (see Section 5.3.3 below) – thresholds rather than absolute values should be selected.

Subsystems

Subsystem (or clusters) in a software development need to be identified and also coordinated. The project manager is responsible for identification of the most appropriate subsystems – an architecture decision (see Technique: Subsystem identification). Subsystems are needed particularly in large systems as a tool by which to manage technical complexity. It is also necessary to coordinate the development of subsystems. Often, one team is responsible for each subsystem; however, someone needs to be responsible for ensuring compatibility between subsystems. This could be a linchpin person or a member of the cross-project team (see Technique: Subsystem coordination and Subtask: Choose project team).

Education and training

Training and education must go hand in hand throughout a person's lifetime. Required life skills change rapidly and an ongoing education, whether personal or organizational, is demanded for success in business and in life. It is therefore important to set up and put into action an education and training plan that will take into account both advances in technology and the skills level (current and desired) of the team members.

Training formats vary. On-the-job experience, seminars and other training courses are all highly valuable but need to be followed up by opportunities to try out these new ideas (the combination of education in the seminars – often mistakenly called 'training courses' – and training on the job). Mentoring at this stage, by external consultants or by the internal object coach, is usually highly beneficial.

User training is also an important component of any training and education programme. Although most software should indeed be 'user-friendly,' even the most educated user often has problems understanding the full capability of a piece of today's sophisticated software. Training of these users can thus often ensure that the software will actually be used. Then it will be acclaimed a success. Frustration with glitches, even if small, can sometimes lead to the total abandonment of software that is otherwise fairly usable and useful.

5.3.3   Testing and quality

Quality is much more than end-phase testing. Quality needs to be built in *throughout* the development process, not as a one-off quality assessment test of

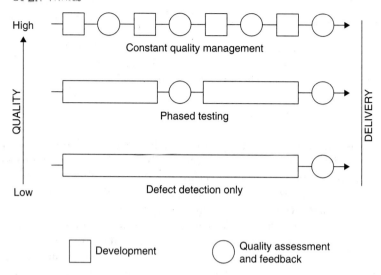

Figure 5.7.   The evolution towards constant quality management (after Adams, 1992) ©1992, SIGS.

the final product. Short cycle times have been advocated in a 'constant quality management' framework (Figure 5.7). Metrics provide the tool to accomplish this quality goal.

Testing

Software artifacts must undergo testing (verification and validation). However, testing and quality assessment must be distributed across the whole lifecycle. In OPEN, testing is part of the post-condition on each activity. The basis for testing is closely linked to the task scripts and use cases of the system. Testing is performed at various levels of granularity. The basic unit of OO being the class, much of the 'unit testing' is done at that level. As well as class testing, cluster testing is important in OPEN. Regression testing is also advocated and finally, when the product is delivered to the customer, some form of acceptance testing is permissible, but should be unnecessary because of constant user involvement and rigorous evaluation procedures.

Testing was discussed previously in MOSES, SOMA and in the OOSE methodology. In addition, unpublished work by Firesmith and Berard is pertinent. Since few of these ideas have been published in a coherent fashion, a full discussion of testing of OO systems will be deferred to the OPEN testing book, currently in preparation by Don Firesmith.

Metrics for quality

The only significant inclusion of metrics into an OO software development to date has been from MOSES Version 2.1 and SOMA. Indeed, many of the SOMA metrics were borrowed from MOSES, augmented by the original proposition for the 'task point' as an early lifecycle estimate of business benefit and, possibly when combined with other metrics, design complexity. It is proposed that task points are the OO equivalent of function points. An international project, under the auspices of the International OO Metrics Club (IOMeC), was initiated in mid-1995 to investigate this empirically. Results are anticipated by 1998/9.

In addition to the small set of metrics advocated in MOSES and SOMA, a full description of OO product measures for static complexity is to be found in the text by Henderson-Sellers (1996). These results are integrated into the OPEN metrics suite. Process metrics typically attempt to relate estimates of the product metrics, made relatively early in the lifecycle, to overall effort required in order to produce costing estimates.

Usability

The effectiveness with which a user can utilize the facilities offered by the applications software is becoming increasingly important – and not before time, in our opinion. Too many software systems satisfy the developers' needs but not those of the user. Usability evaluation adds significant quality to a piece of software and should be undertaken carefully and seriously.

Documentation quality

If the documentation (printed or online) is not of high quality, then either the product will not be used or else the distributors' help desk will be besieged by phone calls, leading to significant overheads and eroding profits. Documentation review should be carried out at regular intervals (i.e. weekly, monthly) or at predetermined 'breakpoints' in the development process – for example, at the end of each activity. In particular, the evaluation activity should have documentation assessment as a prime focus.

All documents should therefore be reviewed in the contexts of:

(1) Existence – a check can be made for mandatory and optional documents. These could be mandatory because of the lifecycle being used or mandated by the organization. As noted earlier, the separate techniques of Fagan, Gilb and Graham are recommended.

(2) Accuracy and consistency checks.

This task is essentially a check on the deliverables before final presentation.

5.3.4   The ongoing review process

While some of these topics are discussed above, the coherence of the three review tasks makes it worthwhile to collate them here. In early OOAD methods, the focus was on the technical build and the idea of planning and *reviewing* was lost. It is important, in any process, to review the results and compare them with the plan. In this way, and only in this way, can developers and managers learn what works, derive quantitative data about times and costs and optimize future project plans. Review should, however, not simply be something that is done at the end of the lifecycle (as in a waterfall). Inevitably schedules get squeezed and the review process (sometimes euphemistically known as 'quality assurance') is dropped. Quality is not something that can be added by inspection at the end of the lifecycle but has to be built in throughout. One way of facilitating this and encouraging a quality mindset in developers and management is to have repeated reviews throughout the lifecycle (in process), at the end of the lifecycle and after the product has been put into service with the customer.

Document preparation

Documents need to be created throughout the software development process. These include the user requirements specification, increasingly detailed analyses and designs, code, test reports, product and process metrics, and so on. These documents should be carefully planned and be an integral (and unavoidable) part of the tailored lifecycle process.

In-process review

Review points should be scheduled not just at the end of development but at significant points within the development. In-process reviews, carried out by similar techniques to other reviews, can catch errors early in the development and identify any misunderstandings with customers since the 'current working demo' is available for their inspection and evaluation as part of the in-process review.

Post-implementation review

Once the software has been deployed on site and end-users have had time to get to grips with the new program(s), a review between the developers and the actual end-users (as opposed to those users chosen for small-scale trials) *working under actual operating conditions* of the industry in question is vital not only for remedying any problems with the current product but also in understanding the likely context for any enhancements that might be requested in the future.

5.4   Database issues

This group of tasks focuses on the interface to a database, either relational or OO. The relevant tasks are:

(1) identify user database requirements (subtask)
(2) select database/storage strategy (subtask)
(3) identify persistent classes (subtask)
(4) map logical database schema
(5) design and implement physical database

    (a) distribution/replication design
    (b) operational and performance design
    (c) performance evaluation

Current OOAD methodologies do not, in general, include complete consideration of database issues. A proposal has recently been made for a generic or metamethodology which extends OOAD concerns into the database arena. Those suggestions provide very general guidelines which were implemented in terms of MOSES (Case et al., 1995). These authors identified four new MOSES activities and two new subactivities for the MOSES activity: O/C identification (O/C in MOSES stood for object or class and has become CIRT in OPEN). These new findings have been incorporated into the tasks and techniques of OPEN.

Quantitative information on the volume of the objects stored, the ways in which the objects are accessed, the frequency of the accesses, and so on, is required from the users when designing a database for an OO system for the same reasons as when designing a traditional system, since one must ensure that the final physical design of the database maximizes all the criteria of the database system being developed, that is, time and storage requirements as well as the functional requirements. Performance issues are important.

Selection of database (i.e. storage strategy) requires the selection of both DBMS style (OB or RDB) and the actual product selection. The first of these can be performed at any point up until the first iteration in which the CIRT model is mapped on to the logical database schema in the Task: Map logical database schema. The second technique is appropriate at any point until the first iteration of the Task: Design and implement physical database.

Mapping of the static model (e.g. as described by a semantic net or other class diagram) to the database schema can only be carried out when the database model has been selected. The mapping to an objectbase is straightforward; only when a relational, hierarchical or network database is being used does this stage require any significant effort.

When a relational database is in use, the behavioral aspects of the interaction diagram are not supported directly by the database management system. Some developers may prefer to convert the object model to an ER model, on the basis of familiarity. Undertaking such a mapping, while throwing away behavioral information, should nevertheless be fairly straightforward. Rules have already been presented for mapping the properties and relationships depicted in an object (structure) diagram into third normal form relations. More recently, the OOram composition system (Reenskaug et al., 1996) has been proposed as a smooth translation technique to a relational database.

Loomis (1991) identifies three problems and three approaches to object-relational interoperation across object and relational databases. The three problems are to:

(1) Build OO applications that access relational databases.
(2) Run existing relationally written applications against an OO database.
(3) Use an SQL-like query language in an OO environment.

The three approaches are to:

(1) Convert the applications and databases completely to OO ones.
(2) Use standard import–export facilities.
(3) Access the relational databases from the OO programming languages.

The first of these approaches is complicated and expensive, and works badly if some old system functions are to be reused or migration is gradual. The same problem referred to earlier arises, in that coordinating updates across heterogeneous databases is problematical. However, if you can do periodic downloads of data to the new system, the approach can be tolerated. This is exactly what is often done when migrating from IMS to DB2 and building MIS extensions. The second approach relies on standards having been defined, which will depend on the application; for example, standards exist in the CAD and VLSI design worlds but not in general. The best variant of this approach is to use an OO database which supports SQL gateways to your relational databases, as does GemStone for example. Here though, the application must provide a mapping between table and object views of data and, except for the simplest cases, this can be complicated. The third approach implies adopting Object SQL or SQL3.

Conventional databases let relations such as 'all the children who like toys' be stored in a table, but not the rule that 'all children like toys'; nor do they store the fact that when one field is updated another may have to be. Both of these kinds of relationship are easy to express in Prolog, say, or in any knowledge-based systems shell. For some time now relational database vendors have extended the relational model to allow database triggers to capture the latter kind of rule. In AI frame-based systems the support for rules is more general and less procedural in style, but there is undoubtedly a trend to enriching the semantic abilities of databases in this way. Object-relational databases, in addition, now offer facilities for defining abstract data types so that they can deal with complex data types exactly in the manner of an OO database. At present no OO database product known to the authors offers explicit support for declarative rules.

One way to enhance interoperability, we are told, is to place system syntax and semantics in enterprise repositories. These days, nearly all new repositories are based on OO database technology. In some cases a mixture of I-CASE and expert systems technology is used. See, for example, Martin and Odell (1992) for the arguments for this approach. Such repositories will store an interface library and this will help systems to locate and utilize existing objects.

The output associated with this task is a logical database schema. If an objectbase is being used, the schema consists of a definition for each class of its properties and operations and its inheritance, aggregation and association relationships with other classes. For a relational database, the database schema consists of a list of relations and their attributes.

Design of the physical database involves mapping the logical data schema to the physical DBMS taking into account the issues raised in the database-specific user requirements report. In undertaking the design, consideration needs to be given to the DBMS product specifics such as recovery, security, concurrency control, versioning, distribution and query optimization.

The fragmentation design is determined using the database specification component of the object storage requirements document created as a delivery to the Task: Identify user requirements (DB).

Objects may be partitioned horizontally by assigning groups of objects from the same class or associated classes to different fragments in an objectbase or by making groups of tuples of a relation into fragments in an RDB. On the other hand, objects may be partitioned vertically by assigning properties or attributes in objects or relations to separate fragments. Horizontal fragmentation may improve efficiency if a class has many objects of which only a few are referenced regularly at a given site. Vertical fragmentation may improve efficiency if a class has properties with different access patterns.

Operational considerations include recovery, concurrency control, security control and versioning. An implementation plan should be developed for each of these items to ensure the desired functionality as outlined in the database-specific user requirements report.

Performance is impacted by the operational considerations, distribution design and issues such as indexing, clustering, object replication, storage of derived properties, and classes that can be collapsed (see companion volume on OPEN techniques: Henderson-Sellers and Younessi, 1997).

An analysis of performance is required for each identified event in order to assess whether the user-stated performance requirements have indeed been met.

5.5   Distribution issues

This group of tasks only comes into play when a DCS is being built. While it is recognized that a DCS seems to be almost a standard way of building systems in the mid-90s, better advice would be only to build a distributed system *if it is the only option*. Indeed, many industry leaders in OT strongly advise that a distributed environment should only be entered after specific consideration. Simply taking a large database and splitting it across several servers does nothing practical to alleviate the size problems of such a data store and, indeed, adds problems which occur as a result of running the application over a network. The relevant tasks are:

(1) identify user requirements for DCS (subtask)

(2) establish distributed systems strategy (subtask)

(3) develop security plan (subtask).

Distributed systems development may include development work in different cities or even countries. In this case, the development team may need to be split to allow for geographical distribution of its members. Leadership, planning, standards, skills and support need to be planned in cognizance of this split. DCS issues, hardware and business requirements are likely to place constraints on the alternative configurations and system designs that may be considered in the feasibility study. Furthermore, hardware, DCS, impact on users and team planning issues will also have direct impacts on the technical, economic and operational feasibility of the distributed system alternatives. When considering economic feasibility, the future value of experience with DCS design and the cost of the extra risk should both be considered.

However, before discussing partitioning and allocation decisions in distributed systems, physical issues such as the communications semantics and concurrency control should be shown by dynamic models. Active objects may be identified as those objects that require their own thread of control because they monitor other objects or because they are a source of events. These are identified as such in the CIRT model (for example, using COMN this would be in one or more of the semantic net diagrams; in UML notation it would be the class diagram). Once the dynamic models and the appropriate semantic nets have been updated with these details, the Task: DCS architecture specification (partitioning and allocation) may be performed. Database distribution would also be considered at the same time.

Partitioning and allocation are of vital importance in the development of a distributed information system. There are several approaches that may be taken to the partitioning and allocation decisions – two possible techniques are described in the Task: DCS architecture specification (partitioning and allocation). They are not mutually exclusive.

A client–server topology approach which divides the application into several layers of presentation logic, business logic and data management logic. Standard templates are then used for the partitioning and allocation decisions where different templates simply place the layers on the clients or servers. For an organization that has limited experience of DCS development, this approach reduces complexity and therefore risk.

A subsystems approach where the original object model is decomposed into subsystems. These subsystems should have high internal cohesion and low internal coupling with other subsystems. Each subsystem may be further decomposed into other subsystems and/or partitioned by any other of the techniques described here. The resultant subsystems and/or object models are then allocated to physical nodes.

A distributed systems approach where the object model is partitioned into cohesive and independent components based on requirements for concurrency and communications. These are then allocated to one or more processors with the actual allocation being dependent on issues such as interprocess communication cost, execution cost, load balancing, reliability and scalability.

A layered approach where objects from the logical design are assigned to the generated, configured and relation layers. Objects in the configured layer are active or passive and are allocated to their own virtual nodes. Objects in the relation layer are active and allocated to their own virtual nodes. The generated objects reside in one or more database server virtual nodes, or migrate between the configured objects. These virtual nodes are then allocated to one or more processors with the actual allocation being dependent on issues such as interprocess communications cost, execution cost, load balancing, reliability and scalability.

None of these issues are well discussed in the antecedent methodologies of MOSES, SOMA or Firesmith. Consequently a full description of how to specify, implement and represent a distributed system will be the focus of a future OPEN book.

5.6   Modeling/building the system

This group of tasks has a technical, model-building focus. In some ways, these are the core 'analysis/design' techniques which build the SOM of Figure 4.4. Between them, they advise the developer on how to build a model of the problem space and the system to be developed. The techniques start with the user requirements (elicited within other OPEN activities) and end with the delivery of a design sufficiently detailed that it can be implemented. Indeed, we might also include, in this group, those specific tasks which address implementation issues; while noting that a good 'breakpoint' between modeling and implementation is the point at which language-specific design decisions are taken and the code written (see Section 3.3). While many of these tasks are concentrated in modeling, some will also be found useful in earlier stages (for example, to help build a prototype that will assist in eliciting user requirements) or in later stages (for example, some classes may be identified or modified as a result of testing and quality metrics assessment later in the lifecycle). The relevant tasks are:

(1) analyze user requirements

(2) identify CIRTs

    (a) determine initial class list
    (b) identify persistent classes
    (c) identify rôles
    (d) refine class list

(3) construct the object model

(4) design user interface

(5) map rôles on to classes

(6) optimize the design

(7) undertake usability design

(8) code

(9) write manuals and other documentation.

Modeling is central to software engineering practice and especially to OO development. A model is a representation of some thing or system of things with all or some of the following properties.

- It is always *different* from the thing or system being modeled (the original) in scale, implementation or behavior.
- It has the shape or appearance of the original (an iconic model).
- It can be manipulated or exercised in such a way that its behavior or properties can be used to predict the behavior or properties of the original (a simulation model).
- There is always some correspondence between the model and the original.

Examples of models abound throughout daily life: mock-ups of aircraft in wind tunnels; architectural scale models; models of network traffic using compressed air in tubes or electrical circuits; software models of gas combustion in engines. Of course all software is a model of something, just as all mathematical equations are (analytic) models.

5.6.1 Analysis of user requirements

This is one of the tasks that appear in several of our 'loose groupings.' Understanding the requirements is at the interface between the user and their requirements and the mandate to commence system construction (see also Section 5.1).

5.6.2 CIRT identification

A core task in an OO systems development is the identification of likely or candidate CIRTs. Early in the process of deriving a model, the task will essentially be one of discovery, whereas later in the process it will be more one of refinement and invention. Refinement will never result in a 'perfect' model but will, after a few iterations, lead to a stable and sufficient model. Newly discovered CIRTs should be documented in the CIRT model (COMN semantic nets or UML class diagrams primarily) and in the class specification and will be refined as the development proceeds.

Identification of object types is well described in the base methodology texts. Particular emphasis should be placed on the contribution from the Martin/Odell methodology of power types. Other useful techniques include textual analysis, task scripts, use cases, event modeling, CRC cards, Kelly grids, rôle playing, hierarchical task analysis, analysis of judgments and simulation.

5.6.3   Building the object model

Building the object model is the prime *technical* focus of any OO methodology. Based on the stated requirements, an 'object model' is built which reflects these requirements and the software solution in increasing detail. In that sense, OPEN is an elaborational methodology. The focus of the activity is the addition of more and more detail, managing that detail by using abstraction techniques supplied in OPEN. The activity spans the traditional stages of analysis and logical design.

The object model to be built is best represented by a set of model diagrams which each emphasize different attributes of the whole system. The first model is that of the static architecture, sometimes known as a class diagram. In COMN, these are classified into one of six kinds of semantic nets:

- context diagrams
- layer diagrams
- configuration diagrams
- cluster diagrams
- inheritance diagrams
- deployment diagrams

One of these is a class diagram but not so named because it also contains objects, types and clusters. Semantic nets are used, in OPEN's notation, COMN, to describe different views and different abstraction levels – less well supported in the current (Ver 1.0) UML notation.

Context diagrams document the scope of the application, treating each layer, or subdomain, as a blackbox. It may set the context for the whole system (including people, hardware, etc.) (Figure 5.8) or just for the software. (The COMN notation used in these diagrams is given in Figure 5.9.)

Layer diagrams document the software architecture and the allocation to resulting processors (especially in a DCS) – Figure 5.4.

Configuration diagrams document the overall structure, visibility and semantically important relationships (Figure 5.10).

Cluster diagrams document the static structure of a set of clusters or mechanisms of collaborating objects or rôles in terms of semantically meaningful relationships (Figure 5.11).

Inheritance diagrams separately describe inheritance structures. For small models, inheritance can be shown on the other semantic net diagrams, but for realistically large systems this can lead to unnecessary repetition and complexity.

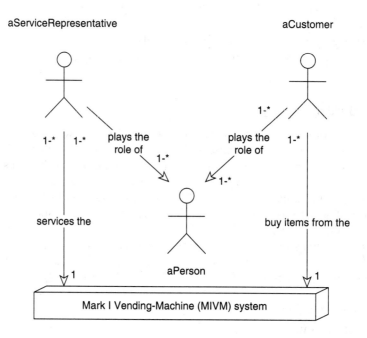

Figure 5.8.   Example COMN system-level context diagram for a vending-machine application (after Firesmith et al., 1997).

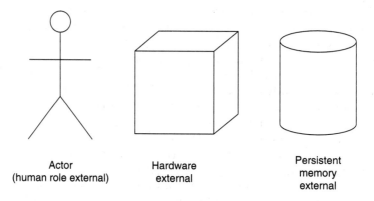

Figure 5.9   Icons for externals (after Firesmith et al., 1997).

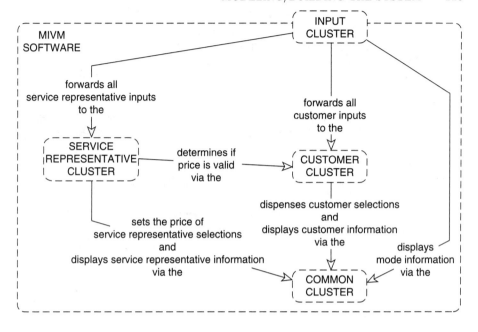

Figure 5.10   Example COMN configuration diagram.

Deployment diagrams document the structure of the hardware and the allocation of software components to that hardware, particularly relevant in a distributed system (Figure 5.12).

The second model in OPEN's COMN is the scenario class diagram which documents the three types of scenario class supported:

- mechanism (a mid-sized pattern of collaborating rôles)

- a task script (for business processes) – essentially a generic use case

- a use case, which describes interactions between externals (actors) and the application viewed as a blackbox.

An oval is used as the standard icon for these various scenario classes with a dotted line to represent the 'uses' dependency (between actor and use case) and a solid line to represent the 'invokes' dependency (between use case and use case). Examples are shown in Figure 5.13 using COMN notation as explained in Figure 5.14.

Sequencing is shown in interaction diagrams (UML and COMN) as either a collaboration diagram, which is similar to a semantic net but with a focus on the messages and their ordering, together with exception handling (Figure 5.15) or a sequence diagram – the 'fence diagram' of OOSE. In COMN, this may either be of blackbox (Figure 5.16(a)) or of whitebox (Figure 5.16(b)) persuasion – for a notational explanation see Figure 5.17.

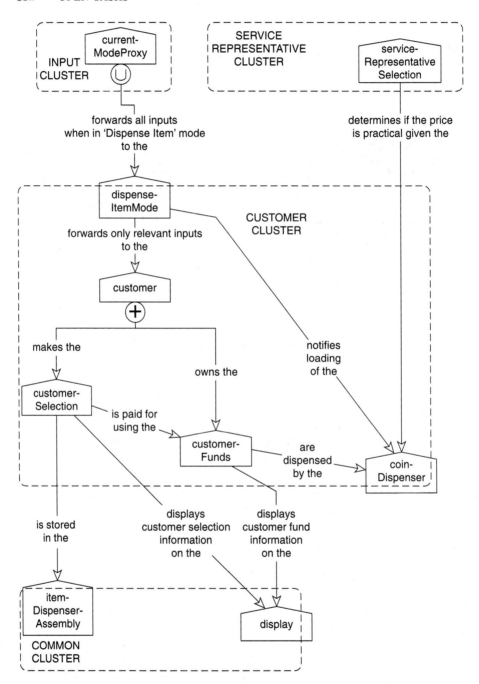

Figure 5.11 Example COMN cluster diagram.

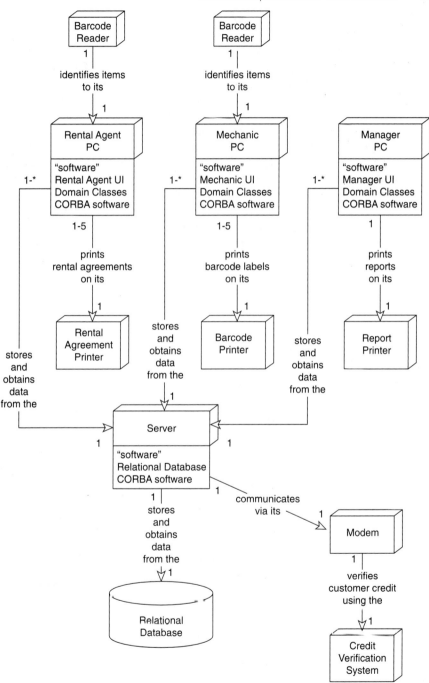

Figure 5.12. Example COMN deployment diagram for an order entry and processing application (after Firesmith et al., 1997).

State transition diagrams depict the states (a rounded-corner rectangle icon) and the transitions between states (a thin arrow indicates a normal transition – there are other, more advanced transition styles). STDs typically focus on a single CIRT. The state represents any equivalence set of property values used for state representation – this includes associations and attributes. The transition is simply a change of state which is normally considered to be of so short a duration, compared with the length of time an object exists in the state itself, that it can be considered to be instantaneous.

Following the construction of the object model, we have a fairly detailed design (documented in the object class specification deliverable), but not one that yet accommodates the nuances or facilities of any programming language. That conversion is made during the coding activity (OOP within the evolutionary development activity). At that stage we might draw an analogy with the transformational school of thought (of Steve Mellor and Sally Shlaer) that translates the analysis (actually in OPEN one smooth 'phase' encompassing analysis and logical design as noted above) into code.

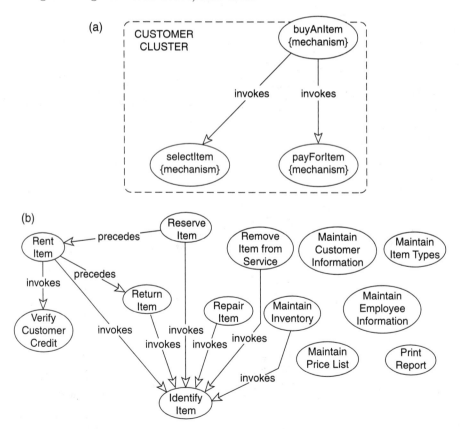

Figure 5.13. Example COMN scenario class diagrams: (a) mechanism diagram; (b) task script diagram; and (c) [overleaf]

(c)

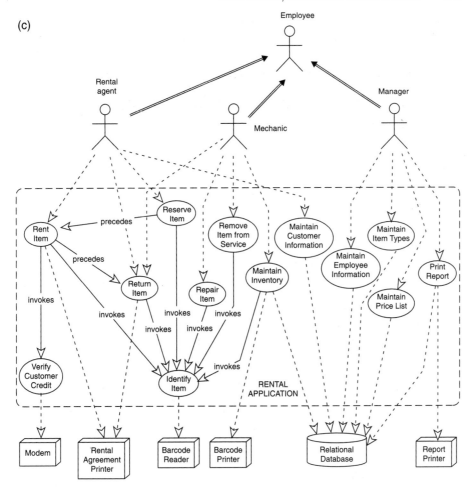

Figure 5.13   (c) use case diagram (after Firesmith et al., 1997).

Building the object model thus relies on object modeling techniques. There are a wide variety of these, many of which are well known. The more important of these are listed in Chapter 6 and fully documented in an accompanying volume (Henderson-Sellers and Younessi, 1997). These techniques assist in accomplishing tasks which are then documented by a selected notation set such as UML or COMN. For OPEN, we recommend COMN, which is 100% compatible with the concepts and philosophy of OPEN. The Light version of this is shown in Appendix B and the full version in a book by Firesmith et al. (1997).

5.6.4   User interface design

User interface design is seldom addressed in OO methodologies. SOMA has some guidelines on this topic; as does the IBM Visual Modeling Technique (Tkach

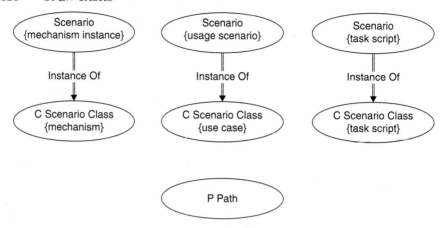

Figure 5.14. Icons for scenarios, scenario classes and paths (after Firesmith et al., 1997).

and Puttick, 1994) method and the GUIDE method (Redmond-Pyle and Moore, 1995). Since this is a crucial component of building an effective system, the full OPEN guidelines also include this critical element.

HCI design involves the following issues:

- functionality: How does the interface help users carry out tasks and how does it impede them? Does the interface itself make something possible or impossible?
- usability, covering:
    - learnability
    - memorability
    - productivity
    - propensity to errors
    - support for tasks (task analysis)
    - safety
    - range of users
    - suitability for different locations and conditions

- aesthetics
- acceptability
- structure
- reliability
- efficiency
- maintainability
- extensibility
- cost.

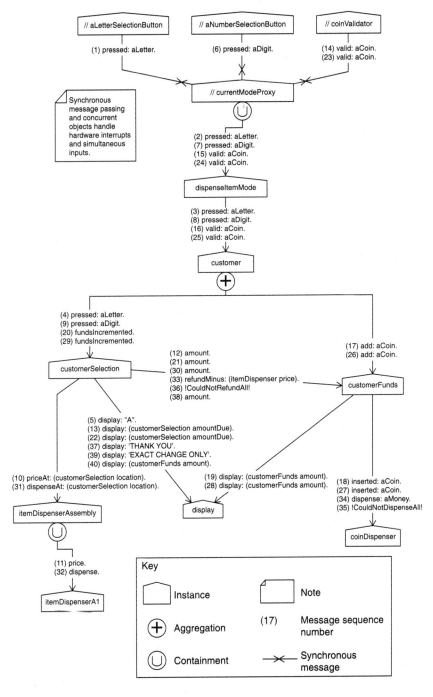

Figure 5.15.   Example COMN scenario collaboration diagram for a vending-machine application (after Firesmith et al., 1997).

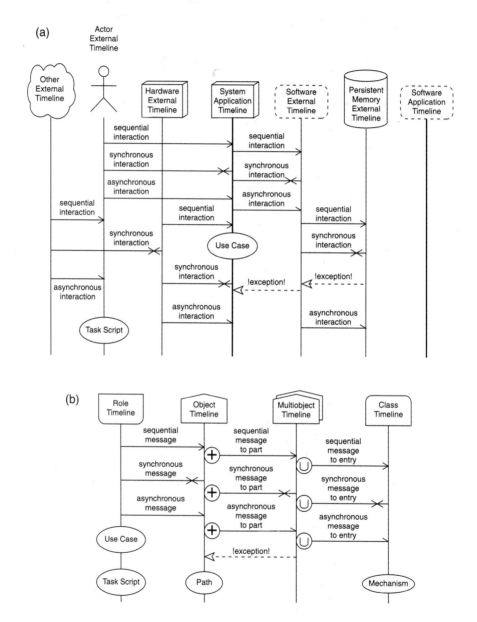

Figure 5.16.   Example COMN sequence diagrams: (a) blackbox and (b) whitebox (after Firesmith et al., 1997).

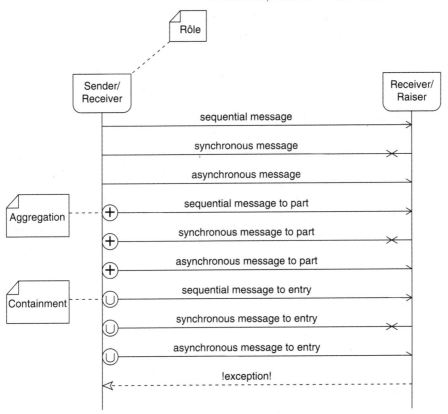

Figure 5.17.   Messages and exceptions on sequence diagrams (after Firesmith et al., 1997).

Designers should remember that there are considerable variations among users. Users come to the system with different backgrounds and knowledge levels. Psychology tells us that during skill acquisition, knowledge is first stored as declarative knowledge, often in the form of rules and objects to which those rules apply, and can be directly recalled as such. Practice helps people store associations between items and form chunks based on these associations; this is associative knowledge. More practice compiles the rules into procedural knowledge by which stage it is often inaccessible to consciousness; as with the knowledge of how to ride a bicycle or read a sentence. On this basis, designers should design for the knowledge level of the users they anticipate using the systems and preferably provide both novice and expert modes. Remember that documentation, training and the user's knowledge are all part of the user interface.

It is also crucial that the interface designer, like the software engineer, does not stop at merely analyzing and automating existing practices. Computers can, and should, change the tasks they were designed to assist with and this is often their largest contribution. Word processing, for example, has largely changed the nature of document preparation work in offices and groupware and hypermedia systems and the global internet are continuing the trend.

5.6.5 Rôle modeling

Rôles are a lesser-known, highly useful modeling concept. They represent dynamic classification, that is when an object temporarily assumes an additional type. For example, an instance of PERSON class may, during the hours of nine and five, take on the rôle of EMPLOYEE. Later he/she may actively play the rôle of PARENT and, possibly at the same time, CHAUFFEUR.

Rôles are used in OOAD (in OPEN and OOram) but not really supported in OOPLs. Thus, at present, they must be mapped to classes or objects in the language of choice, that is of implementation concern.

5.6.6 Design optimization

Optimizing the design may be required in terms of database access paths, perhaps involving the removal of classes and relationships or adding design classes to store information. In the OMT methodology, a number of guidelines are given for optimizing the object model based on the 'hit' rate of queries in the search for objects. They suggest the use of indexes to reduce the search and traversal requirements of the model. Alternatively, redundant relationships may be added to reduce traversal paths and message sends. Other optimizing techniques may require violation of the pure OO model, for example violating encapsulation or the use of friend mechanisms which can lead to reduced overheads albeit at the expense of flexibility and reuse. Such optimizations and redesign are largely system specific including a reworking and prototyping iteration to ensure the performance criteria are met.

5.6.7 Usability design

Usability is a key element in creating high-quality software. While usability can be tested *post facto*, it is more important to adopt a user-centered focus throughout the design and *design in* the usability from the commencement of the project. One way of assisting is to involve the user throughout the project, as well as inculcating in individual designers a mindset which moves away from 'gee-whizzery' at the technical level to a more considered and client-focused approach to designing software.

5.6.8   OOPLs

The task of coding is often seen as the most important in the whole lifecycle since, as it is often said, 'bubbles and arrows can't crash; code can.' However, if the design is of high quality, then the translation to code should be relatively straightforward (as discussed above), particularly if the object model of the method and the programming language are close, as for instance in the case of BON or OPEN coded into Eiffel. Desfray (1994) notes that in coding 'the description of the model entities is adapted and all elements not yet described in the model are developed.' This definition stresses, quite correctly, the twin notions of (a) a smooth translation of the design into code yet (b) the need to take further, low-level implementation/coding decisions which cannot and should not be shown in the logical design. In OPEN, we include the notion of coding those final, low-level design decisions; in other words, detailed design and coding are often indistinguishable.

While many of the detailed coding-level designs will be taken late in 'design,' we can consider these to be part of the coding-task. Some of these are readily represented in the normal notational sets as used in OOAD; others require the use of the coding level extensions. These include parameterized or generic classes (Technique: Genericity), export controls (public, private and protected in C++), static/virtual/friend properties, and possibly class utilities, metaclasses, modules and/or processes.

Indeed the choice of language will dictate to some degree how well this SOM–IOM interface (Figure 4.4) is handled. It must be harder for a language like C++, which is very near the machine, than for a language like Smalltalk, Eiffel or possibly even Java, which embodies the full object paradigm just as well as does the OOAD method.

Purposely, none of the base methodologies offered full support for detailed design – by which we mean design which relies on the syntax of a specific programming language. Extensions under the OPEN banner are anticipated.

5.6.9   Documentation

Documentation pervades OPEN. Without documentation, it is difficult to explain artifacts to new developers, to developers several months down the track, to users and to management. Documentation is needed not only for the technical aspects of the analysis and detailed design models, but also for the management decisions taken (decision taken *plus* rationale for the decision), user requirements, test results and other quality and process metrics.

5.7   Reuse issues

The reuse tasks in OPEN encompass both technical and managerial/cultural issues. While it may be considered that reuse is a late lifecycle concern, it is more appropriate that a reuse mindset be adopted *throughout* the lifecycle. Inculcating such a reuse mindset into an organization is discussed in detail by McGibbon (1997) who advises that a 12-month timescale is needed, as it is for introducing a metrics programme (see, e.g., Henderson-Sellers, 1995). Organizations most successful in reuse are those for which reuse is an integral part of their development environment; where credit is given for writing reusable classes (perhaps assessed by how many times other people use them); and where credit is given for building a system by writing the minimum of new code. The relevant tasks are:

(1) optimize reuse ('with reuse')
(2) create and/or identify reusable components ('for reuse')

    (a) construct frameworks
    (b) optimize for reuse

(3) manage library of reusable components.

5.7.1   Optimize reuse ('with reuse')

The objective of this task is to maximize the reuse of library components that already exist. OO development emphasizes the importance of reuse in the development process and, as we have already discussed, the successful outcome of this methodology is a software base of reusable components. The fountain model as found in MOSES (Figure 2.2) or in OOram (Figure 5.18) graphically represents this.

Surprisingly, most methodologies do not provide support for optimizing the reuse of software assets (exceptions being MOSES, SOMA and OOram as well as OPEN). They note it is insufficient to make statements such as: 'Now you are ready to pick a design – see if one already exists to handle the event.' Techniques and guidelines are needed; for instance ensuring there is a common vocabulary of object names and messages. OBA recommends as a step the explicit searching for architecture design models and then utilizing the existing rôles and responsibilities by folding them into the current model. In OPEN, these OBA directives are supported by a range of techniques (Henderson-Sellers and Younessi, 1997).

Integrating and reusing the corporate class library in a new development is an important part of the process. During the evolutionary development activity, the developer should be examining the library of components in order to maximize reuse of already existing classes (the 'reuse mindset'), which encourages more of a bottom-up approach. This is particularly useful during coding, whereas in OOAD there is initially an emphasis on the top-down refinement

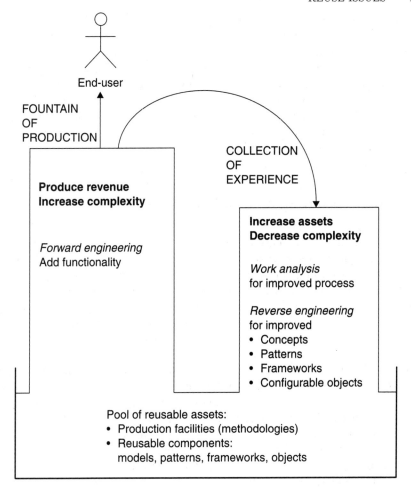

Figure 5.18 The OOram fountain model (after Reenskaug et al., 1996).

process. This mixing of approaches appears 'fuzzy' and undisciplined but in fact more closely reflects the way many designers operate.

Reuse of classes can be achieved in a number of ways:

- by instantiation
- by composition
- by class hierarchies
- by abstract-level reuse.

An important point is that reuse can occur at all levels of the development process – it is not confined to the coding task. The reuse of specifications from previous projects is an important element. Reuse by composition will lead to new aggregation, association and client–server relationships in the build activity.

An evaluation of the extent to which classes from a library have been incorporated into the design can be made within the consolidation activity where the development team can stand back from the design and undertake a design review. Design reviews should aim to be critical and try to identify classes that can be reused from the corporate library although, ideally, design review and the identification of reusable components have occurred much earlier – from requirements engineering onward.

5.7.2   Create new reusable components ('for reuse')

Effective reuse involves not only using classes from a library but also adding new classes to the library for reuse in later projects. The objective of this task is to improve the quality of the project classes so they can be used outside the project, and consequently to maximize the reusability of classes. This task can initially represent a significant investment of time and effort on top of the normal system development process. It may begin at the end of the basic system development where further work is necessary to guarantee reusability for future projects – although if the goal of reusability is borne in mind throughout the process the task actually should be actioned throughout the whole development lifecycle. This is unlikely in the first few OO projects, but as more OT skills are acquired so generalization will become integrated into the overall development process.

The additional work during generalization may be simply a 'honing' or refinement of existing classes or it may require the introduction of additional classes (possibly of a deferred or abstract nature, namely ones which cannot be instantiated) at intermediate levels in the inheritance hierarchy. Furthermore, overly complex classes may require splitting into a larger number of smaller classes. The underlying guideline here is to consider whether a class developed in the current project really represents a single concept of the domain (an object type or rôle) or whether it encompasses two (or more) concepts. This refinement work is needed to ensure classes are really reusable and augments any project-specific refinement of the inheritance hierarchy. Such refinements may, of course, lead to iteration and a reconsideration of the class model describing the system.

Domain analysis is a useful technique here. Creating reusable components often requires lateral thinking coupled with careful documentation, stating assumptions, limitations, expected ways for the artifact to be used (e.g. inheritance, aggregation). Reuse producers (as here) and reuse consumers ('with reuse') should work in an interleaved fashion. Two-way feedback should be strongly encouraged.

It should also be remembered that increasing refinement of inheritance hierarchies is likely not only to lead to deeper hierarchies and more multiple inheritance but also to the introduction of abstract (or deferred) classes. It is generally recommended that abstract classes should not inherit from concrete classes; although exceptions to this rule do exist. Another heuristic is to construct an

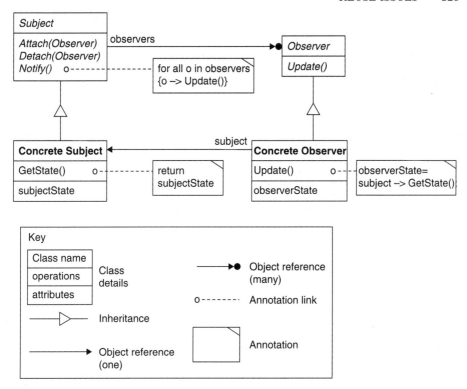

Figure 5.19   The observer pattern (after Gamma et al., 1995).

inheritance hierarchy using the rule that no concrete classes should have sub-classes. This last rule is, of course, not applicable for prototypes or subsystems where subsequent addition of detail is envisaged. For example, in a hierarchy of CAR (the superclass) with subclasses of FORD_CAR, TOYOTA_CAR and so on, there may be no subclass for TRABANT_CAR. Until such a subclass is created, any Trabant instances must be instances of the superclass *only* – which is therefore a concrete class.

Components are not only classes (or object types) but also include patterns, clusters and frameworks. These are increasingly being recognized as providing a more powerful basis for reuse. A pattern is a recurring theme as exemplified by a tightly interrelated group of concepts. These are collected together in a number of books – an example (the 'observer' pattern) is shown in Figure 5.19. They typically involve a relatively small number of classes. At the other extreme is the proactive development of a framework which is, typically, of a larger size, composed of a number of interacting abstract classes. The framework might be that of a GUI, an accounting system etc. Instantiations (by adding concrete subclasses) can then be created for specific applications. Somewhere in between, in scale, other terms are used. OPEN supports clusters (or subsystems). Even the word component is often used to indicate a 'mid-sized chunk.' In this context, a component is the least well defined in terms of current (1997) common usage and the more general notion of reusable components (patterns, clusters, frameworks etc.) as used here may turn out ultimately to be the most useful. All component types provide reusability.

The 'hairies and conscripts' model introduced by SOMA (Section 4.11.1) ensures that knowledge is exchanged effectively between projects and the reuse team. Business knowledge flows from projects to domain modeling with the conscript who is seconded to domain modeling for a period as the project is wound down. Incidentally, this helps to optimize human resource utilization compared with retaining all project staff until the project is formally closed. Others typically will be transferred to bug fixing. In the reverse direction, when the neophyte returns to a new project, knowledge of the repository goes with him/her.

5.7.3   Manage library of reusable components

Once library components have been created, they need to be archived in such a way that future users have easy access to them. The main concerns relate to

- classification of CIRTs
- indexing and cataloging
- the need for browsing and retrieval tools and techniques.

The ways in which components are tagged with sufficient information to ensure efficient retrieval include faceted classifications together with sufficient indexing data. For instance, the future user may seek particular functionality, perhaps constrained by a specific industry domain, possibly (if at the class level) written in a selected OOPL. Many of these techniques for cataloging and retrieval are still experimental (e.g. Freeman and Henderson-Sellers, 1991; Thorne, 1997) and are not supported by commercially available browsing and retrieval tools.

The goals of a library management scheme include

- reducing redundancy
- avoiding inconsistency
- allowing multiple users access
- ensuring all users are aware of what is available.

The politics and chargeback of a library can be accomplished in several ways. The most likely is that of the two-library model (Henderson-Sellers and Pant, 1993): a library of potentially reusable components (LPRC) and a library of adopted reusable components (LARC). Components are identified as 'potentially reusable' in the current project but are not generalized for future use (at a cost of possibly several hundred percent of the development cost) until their use is perceived in a later project. Only after refinement and testing by their use in (preferably) at least three projects can they be considered to be of high enough quality to be moved into the LARC (see further details in Section 4.12).

References

Adams S. (1992). Constant quality management (part 4 of a series). *Hotline on Object-Oriented Technology*, **4**(1), 5–8

Buschmann F. (1995). Pattern-oriented software architecture, *Conf. Proc. Object Expo Europe* 25–29 September, 1995, pp. 57–66. London: SIGS

Case T., Henderson-Sellers B. and Low G. (1995). Extending the MOSES Object-Oriented analysis and design methodology to include database applications. *Journal of Object-Oriented Programming*, **8**(7), 28–34, 56

Desfray P. (1994). Object Engineering. The Fourth Dimension. 342 pp. Paris: Addison-Wesley

Fingar P., Clarke J. and Stikeleather J. (1997). The business of distributed object computing. *Object Magazine*, **7**(2), 29–33

Firesmith D., Henderson-Sellers B. and Graham I. (1997). *OPEN Modeling Language (OML) Reference Manual*. 271 pp. New York: SIGS

Freeman C. and Henderson-Sellers B. (1991). OLMS: the Object Library Management System. In *TOOLS 6* (Potter J., Tokoro M. and Meyer B., eds.), pp. 175–80. Sydney: Prentice-Hall

Gamma E., Helm R., Johnson R. and Vlissides J. (1995). *Design Patterns: Elements of Reusable Object-oriented Design*. 395 pp. Reading, MA: Addison-Wesley

Goldberg A. and Rubin K. S. (1995). *Succeeding with Objects. Decision Frameworks for Project Management*. 542 pp. Reading, MA: Addison-Wesley

Graham I. M. (1995). *Migrating to Object Technology*. 552 pp. Harlow, UK: Addison-Wesley

Graham I. (1997). Some problems with use cases . . . and how to avoid them. *OOIS'96* (Patel D., Sun Y. and Patel S., eds.), pp. 18–27. London: Springer

Henderson-Sellers B. and Younessi H. (1997). *OPEN's Toolbox of Techniques*. Harlow, UK: Addison-Wesley

Hammer M. and Champy J. (1993). *Re-engineering the Corporation: A Manifesto for the Business Revolution*. New York: Harper Collins

Henderson-Sellers B. (1995). The goals of an OO metrics program. *Object Magazine*, **5**(6) 72–9, 95

Henderson-Sellers B. (1996). *Object-Oriented Metrics. Measures of Complexity*. New York: Prentice-Hall

Henderson-Sellers B. and Edwards J. M. (1994). *BOOKTWO of Object-Oriented Knowledge: The Working Object*. 594 pp. Sydney: Prentice-Hall

Henderson-Sellers B. and Pant Y. R. (1993). When should we generalize classes to make them reusable? *Object Magazine*, **3**(4), 73–5

Henderson-Sellers B., Graham I. M., Firesmith D., Reenskaug T., Swatman P.

and Winder R. (1996). The OPEN heart. In *TOOLS 21* (Mingins C., Duke R. and Meyer B., eds.), pp. 187–96. TOOLS/ISE, Melbourne

Hohmann L. (1997). Changing your development culture. *Object Magazine*, **7**(2), 59–61

Johnson R. E. and Foote B. (1988). Designing reusable classes. *Journal of Object-Oriented Programming*, **1**(2), 22–35

Loomis M. E. S. (1991). Objects and SQL. *Object Magazine*, **1**(3), 68–78

McGibbon B. (1997). Reuse strategy for large-scale legacy systems. *Object Magazine*, **7**(2), 70–73

Martin J. and Odell J. J. (1992). *Object-Oriented Analysis and Design*. Englewood Cliffs, NJ: Prentice-Hall

Meyer B. (1995). *Object Success*. 192 pp. London: Prentice-Hall

Polya G. (1957). *How to Solve It: A New Aspect of Mathematical Method*. Princeton, NJ: Princeton University Press

Rasmussen G., Henderson-Sellers B. and Low G. (1996). Extending the MOSES methodology to distributed systems. *Journal of Object-Oriented Programming*, **9**(4), 39–46, 100

Redmond-Pyle D. and Moore A. (1995). *Graphical User Interface Design and Evaluation (GUIDE): A Practical Process*. Englewood Cliffs, NJ: Prentice-Hall

Reenskaug T., Wold P. and Lehne O. A. (1996). *Working with Objects. The OOram Software Engineering Manual*. 366 pp. Greenwich, CT: Manning

Standish Group (1994). *The CHAOS Report*. Dennis, MA: The Standish Group

Standish Group (1995). *The Scope of Software Development Project Failures*. Dennis, MA: The Standish Group

Starfield A. M., Smith K. A. and Bleloch A. L. (1990). *How to Model It. Problem Solving for the Computer Age*. 206 pp. New York: McGraw-Hill

Stevens R. and Putlock G. (1997). Improving the industrial application of requirements management. *American Programmer*, **10**(4), 17–22

Taylor D.A. (1995). *Business Engineering with Object Technology*. 188 pp. New York: Wiley

Thorne F. (1997). A software classification scheme for reuse. *MSc Thesis* University of Technology, Sydney (unpubl.)

Tkach D. and Puttick R. (1994). *Object Technology in Application Development*. 212 pp. Redwood City, CA: Benjamin/Cummings

Waldén K. and Nerson J.-M. (1995). *Seamless Object-Oriented Architecture*. 301 pp. Hemel Hempstead, UK: Prentice-Hall

Webster B.F. (1995) *Pitfalls of Object-Oriented Development*. 256 pp. New York: M & T

Williams J.D. (1995). *What Every Software Manager MUST KNOW TO SUCCEED With Object Technology*. 273 pp. New York: SIGS

Chapter 6
OPEN techniques

Knowing that the Task: Construct the object model, is one (of several) task(s) that the developer can undertake in order to complete the build activity does not, however, tell the developer *how* to accomplish that task(s). The task is the statement of the unit of work required, the what; the how is described by one or more techniques. This is similar to saying that I want to hang a picture on my living room wall. This is today's task. But how do I do that? I use some technique – but often I have a choice between techniques; and furthermore I may use not just one but several techniques to accomplish my task. In this case I have a choice between using (a) a hammer to knock a nail into the wall or (b) a screwdriver[†] and a screw, *together with* (for either option) a piece of string and knowledge of how to tie an appropriate (reef) knot.

Similarly, in OPEN tasks are accomplished by techniques. Techniques are thus ways of doing things. They include ways that have been tried and tested over the last four decades; but also may include new techniques that are more experimental. Some indication on the level of maturity of the individual technique is thus given as part of its full specification, in terms of a 'star rating' – see Appendix A.

Remember, the techniques you use are your choice – within the constraints of being effective and efficient in accomplishing the task. In other words, the developer chooses the appropriate technique(s) from those described in OPEN or from their own experience, sometimes selecting between two competing alternatives Thus, for example, in order to find objects, the choice may be between, say, using use cases, using noun analysis, identifying concepts and their responsibilities, using CRC cards, etc. In reality, many tasks are best accomplished by a mixture of techniques rather than just one. There are too many cases of the use of a single technique being taken to an extreme. For example, at one conference, a story of noun analysis being used for a 300-page requirements specification rightly created disbelief in the audience at such a gross misapplication of the technique.

---

† We would prefer a power screwdriver; or a hook for the picture rail (reuse!).

Our own recommendations are based on both theory and practice; although we fully realize the need to permit individual managers and project team members not to feel bound in a straitjacket – we therefore recommend, we do not mandate. Our own 'toolbox' collection of techniques, which you are free to borrow, will be described in detail in other OPEN publications (e.g. Henderson-Sellers and Younessi, 1997). For your assistance, we will also publish details of some pretailored SEPs appropriate for specific domains such as MIS, finance, client–server. These are combinations of tasks and techniques found to be useful in practice. They may serve you well just as they are – if you are in these particular domains; or may just give you ideas for your own tailoring process. OPEN's techniques number well over 100 and are listed in Table 6.1.

Choice of techniques is assisted by a deontic matrix linking techniques to tasks (Chapter 1, Figure 1.6). In OPEN we give our overall recommendations in terms of M (= mandatory), R (= recommended) O (= optional), D (= discouraged) and F (= forbidden). For instance, some tasks are clearly best accomplished with a single, specific technique – a technique applicable to that task and nothing else (for example, implementation of services which support the coding task). Other techniques will be found useful in a range of tasks (for example, contract specification). Finally for some tasks there may be a choice that the project manager has to make. For example, there are many ways of identifying classes, objects and types. These include interactive techniques such as the use of CRC cards to identify responsibilities; scenarios/task models/scripts/use cases to focus on functionality delivered as a prelude to finding CIRTs within these scripts; textual analysis, in which nouns in the requirements analysis have the potential to be realized as CIRTs; simulation which focuses on the objects within the modeling exercise; and even (for some skilled[†] people), the use of ER diagrams as a basis for a CIRT structure diagram.

However, it should be remembered that these levels of enforcement are assigned from study across a large number of contrasting projects. For your own project, you will be able to tailor the OPEN lifecycle process: one significant element of this is refining these probabilities – preferably until they (almost) all fall into either the M or F categories.

We describe these deontic links first in a visual representation as a two-dimensional matrix which links together each task with each technique and allocates to that linkage a measure of its likelihood of occurrence. Once again we stress that these are only global guidelines (that is as if averaged over a large number of disparate projects) and for any given project the actual pattern of M/R/O/D/F should be determined as part of the initial planning activity, usually the responsibility of the project manager.

This two-dimensional matrix also offers the project manager significant flexibility. If new tasks and techniques are developed in a particular context, then

---

† We say skilled not to disparage ER but rather to stress that it is our experience that good OO designers can make good use of ER since they have the OO mindset; but that novices or poor designers use ER as a crutch to stay within the procedural paradigm while fooling themselves, and probably their managers, that they are doing OO design.

Table 6.1   OPEN techniques in alphabetical order.

Abstract classes
Abstraction
Acceptance testing
Access analysis
Access path optimization
Action research
Active listening
Activity grids
Agents – see Intelligent agents
Aggregation – see Composition structures
Analysis of judgments
Approval gaining
Assertion language
Associations
Audit requirements
Beta testing
Blackboarding
BNF
Brainstorming
CD-ROM technology
CIRT indexing
Classification
Class internal design
Class naming
Clustering (DB)
Clusters
Code generation
Code/document inspections
Cohesion measures
Collaborations
Collapsing of classes
Color in UIs
Completion of abstractions
Complex adaptive systems (CAS) theory
Complexity measures
Composition structures – or Aggregation
Computer-based assessment (CBA)
Configuration management
Connascence
Containment
Context modeling (BPR)
Contract specification
Cost–benefit analysis (CBA)
Cost estimation
CPM charts

Table 6.1   (Continued)

CRC cards
Critical success factors (CSFs)
Customer (on-site) training
Database authorization
Data-flow modeling (dangerous)
DBMS product selection
DBMS type selection
DCS architecture specification (partitioning and allocation)
DCS optimization
Defect detection
Delegation
Dependency-based testing
Descoping
Dialog design in UI
Discriminant
Domain analysis
Early prototype to exercise DCS
Encapsulation/Information hiding
ER modeling (but take care)
Event charts
Event modeling
Exception handling
Expected value analysis
Fagan's inspections
Formal methods
Frameworks
Function points
Fuzzy logic and fuzzy modeling
Games
Gantt charts
Generalization (contrast with Classification)
Generalization for reuse (see Refinement of inheritance hierarchies)
Genericity specification
GQM
Group problem solving
Hierarchical task analysis
Hypergenericity
Idioms
Impact analysis
Impact estimation table
Implementation inheritance
Implementation of distributed aspects of system
Implementation of rules
Implementation of services
Implementation of structure

Table 6.1   (Continued)

Indexing
Information engineering (but take care)
Inspections – see Code/document inspections and Fagan's inspections
Integration testing
Intelligent agents
Interaction modeling
Internet and web technology
Interviewing
Kelly grids
Law of Demeter
Lectures
Library class incorporation
Literate programming
Mapping to RDB
Mechanisms
Mentoring
Metrics collection
Mixins
Multiple inheritance (see subsections in Generalization and in
      Implementation inheritance)
MVC analysis
Normalization
Object lifecycle histories
Object replication
Object request brokers (ORBs)
Object retention requirements
Ownership modeling
Partitions
Password protection
Path navigation
Pattern recognition
PERT charts
Petri nets
Physical security
Pistols at dawn
PLanguage
Polymorphlsm
Power analysis (political systems analysis)
Power types
Priority setting
Process modeling
Project planning
Protocol analysis
Prototyping
PSP

Table 6.1   (Continued)

PS–PPS
Quality templates
Questionnaires
RAD
RAD workshops
Record and playback
Redundant associations
Refinement
Refinement of inheritance hierarchies
Regression testing
Relational DBMS interface specification
Reliability requirements
Repeated inheritance
Responsibilities
Reuse metrics
Reverse engineering
Rich pictures
Risk analysis
Rôle assignment
Rôle modeling
Rôle play
Rule modeling
Scenario classes
Screen painting and scraping
Scripting
Security requirements
Self-paced exercises
Semiotic modeling
Service identification
Simulation
SMART goals
Social systems analysis
Soft systems analysis
Specialization inheritance
Specification inheritance
Standards compliance
State machines
Static analysis
Statistical analysis
Stereotypes
Storage of derived properties
Storyboarding
Subsystem coordination
Subsystem identification
Subsystem testing

Table 6.1   (Continued)

Task cards
Task decomposition
Task points
Task scripts
Team structuring
Textual analysis
Throwaway prototyping
Time-threads
TQM
Traceability
Train the trainer
Traits
Transformations of the object model
Tuning of database
Unit testing
Usability testing
Usage
Use cases
Variant analysis
Versioning
Videotaping
Viewpoints
Visibility
Visioning (for BPR)
Visualization techniques (OO notations, Petri nets, STDs, fishbone diagrams,
     histograms and so on)
Volume analysis
Walkthroughs
Workflow analysis
Workshops
Wrappers
Zachman frameworks

Incorporating them into this framework is extremely easy. It only requires the addition of a single line in the matrix and the identification of the M/R/O/D/F nature of the interaction between this new technique and the tasks of the chosen lifecycle process model. The actual choice of tasks and techniques to support activities can be tailored for your individual project (Task: Tailor the lifecycle process), for example during program planning. It is this flexibility in creating an organization-specific or project-specific lifecycle process that is a major advantage of using a development method such as OPEN. This approach is useful at the more generic, almost meta-level of the process description.

In this way, techniques are intrinsically orthogonal to the notion of tasks.

Table 6.2   OPEN techniques in logical/temporal groupings.

(1) *User requirements*
Action research
Active listening
Activity grids
Analysis of judgments
Brainstorming
Context modeling
CRC cards
Domain analysis
Expected value analysis
Interviewing
Kelly grids
MVC analysis
Power analysis
Questionnaires
RAD
RAD workshops
Record and playback
Rich pictures
Rôle play
Scripting
Simulation
Social systems analysis
Soft systems analysis
Storyboarding
Throwaway prototyping
Videotaping

(2) *Project management and business issues*
Approval gaining
Complex adaptive systems theory
Configuration management
Cost–benefit analysis
Cost estimation
CPM charts
Critical success factors
Customer (on-site) training
Gantt charts
Impact analysis
Impact estimation table
Mentoring
Password protection
PERT charts
Physical security
Pistols at dawn

Table 6.2   (Continued)

PLanguage
Priority setting
Process modeling
Project planning
Prototyping
PSP
Risk analysis
Rôle assignment
Simulations
SMART goals
Social systems analysis
Subsystem coordination
Subsystem identification
Task decomposition
Task scripts
Team structuring
Throwaway prototyping
TQM
Traceability
Use cases
Versioning
Visioning
Walkthroughs
Workflow analysis

(2a) *Quality*

Testing

Acceptance testing
Beta testing
Dependency-based testing
Integration testing
Regression testing
Subsystem testing
Unit testing
Usability testing

Metrics

Cohesion measures
Complexity measures
Connascence
Cost estimation
Function points
Law of Demeter
Metrics collection

Table 6.2   (Continued)

Reuse metrics
Statistical analysis
Task points

Inspections

Code/document inspections
Defect detection
Fagan's inspections
Walkthroughs

Other

Assertion language
CIRT indexing
Class naming
Clusters
Exception handling
Formal methods
GQM
Literate programming
Quality templates
Rule modeling
Standards compliance
Task cards

(3) *Modeling techniques*

Technical/low-level OOA/OOD

Abstract classes
Associations/mappings
Class internal design
Class naming
Collaborations
Composition structures (or aggregations)
Containment
Contract specification
Delegation
Discriminant
Event chart
Event modeling
Genericity specification
Implementation inheritance
Interaction modeling
Mixins
Multiple inheritance
Petri nets

Table 6.2   (Continued)

Polymorphism
Power types
Repeated inheritance
Rule modeling
Scenario classes
Service identification
Specialization inheritance
Specification inheritance
State machines
Stereotypes
Task scripts
Time-threads
Traits
Use cases
Usage
Visibility

Concepts/philosophy

Abstraction
Classification
Encapsulation/information hiding
Generalization (see also Classification)
Responsibilities

Other

Assertion language
Blackboarding
BNF
Completion of abstractions
Connascence
CRC cards
Exception handling
Formal methods
Function points
Fuzzy logic
Hierarchical task analysis
Hypergenericity
Intelligent agents
MVC analysis
Object lifecycle histories
Object request brokers (ORBs)
Ownership modeling
Partitions
Pattern recognition
Process modeling

Table 6.2   (Continued)

Protocol analysis
PS–PPS
Refinement
Refinement of inheritance hierarchies
Reverse engineering
Rôle modeling
Rôleplay
Semiotic modeling
Simulation
Task cards
Task decomposition
Task scripts
Textual analysis
Transformations of the object model
Viewpoints
Visualization techniques
Wrappers
Zachman frameworks

(4) *Database*
Access analysis
Audit requirements
Clustering
Collapsing of classes
Database authorization
DBMS product selection
DBMS type selection
Indexing
Mapping to RDB
Normalization
Object replication
Object retention requirements
Path navigation
RDBMS interface specification
Reliability requirements
Security requirements
Storage of derived properties
Tuning of database
Versioning
Volume analysis

(5) *Coding*
Class internal design
Code generation
Code/document inspections

Table 6.2   (Continued)

Implementation inheritance
Implementation of distributed aspects of system
Implementation of rules
Implementation of services
Implementation of structure
Mixins
Object request brokers (ORBs)
Storage of derived properties
Traceability
Wrappers

(6) *User interface*
Color in UIs
Dialog design in UI
Screen painting and scraping
Usability testing

(7) *Reuse*
Access path optimization
CIRT indexing
Completion of abstractions
Frameworks
Generalization for reuse
Genericity specification
Idioms
Library class incorporation
Mechanisms
Pattern recognition
Redundant associations
Refinement of inheritance hierarchies
Reuse metrics
Variant analysis

(8) *DCS*
DCS architecture specification (partitioning and allocation)
DCS optimization
Early prototype to exercise DCS
Implementation of distributed aspects of system
Static analysis
Task scripts (use in DCS)

(9) *Training and education*
CD-ROM technology
Computer-based assessment
Games
Group problem solving

Table 6.2   (Continued)

Internet and web technology
Lectures
Rôle-play
Self-paced exercises
Simulation
Train the trainer
Videotaping
Workshops

They can only be grouped together very roughly (Table 6.2). They are akin to the tools of the tradesperson – a carpenter's toolbox contains many tools, some of which have superficial resemblances but may have operational affinity to tools of different outward appearance. A full description of the OPEN toolbox of techniques is a book in itself (Henderson-Sellers and Younessi, 1997).

Reference

Henderson-Sellers B. and Younessi H. (1997). *OPEN's Toolbox of Techniques.* Harlow, UK: Addison-Wesley

Chapter 7
Deliverables of OPEN

OPEN deliverables are part of the post-condition for each activity. For convenience, they are all summarized in Table 7.1 and outlined in content in the next few paragraphs.

The *project proposal* is a document that is short (typically only one page) which states the business requirement, scope, justification, sponsor, constraints, completion criteria, project costs and so on.

Based on the project proposal, requirements are elicited from the users resulting in a *users requirements statement* which is a statement representing the understanding shared by the users and developers as to how the requirements will be realized at a logical level; it represents the results of the collaborative requirements engineering process and added technical constraints. Users review this document and sign it off before further work commences. From this document, the analysts can identify, iteratively with the users, the tasks that are necessary and a TOM of these tasks. Appropriate metrics, reuse possibilities and business process definitions are all likely to be included in the resultant *users requirement specification*. This is a business-user-focused document from which the analysts then create their software-focused version in terms of a *systems analysis report*. It may be supplemented by physical and paper-based prototypes. Prototypes are needed for the *user interface* and for the *model code*.

Before the product is constructed, it is necessary to undertake serious planning and this activity will result in a number of documents as deliverables. There should be an overall *project plan*, perhaps in the form of a Gantt chart. The *quality plan* should also be a prime focus. Other important management issues require the creation and delivery of a *disaster recovery plan*, a *security plan*, a *configuration management and version control plan*, a set of *test plans* and a *training requirements report*.

Once the software development lifecycle is entered for the first of its planned iterations, the deliverables switch focus from the users and project management to technical, OO models of the system as it is first conceived and ultimately evolves towards the deliverable product. A range of deliverables are built up

Table 7.1.   Summary of OPEN deliverables grouped under the heading of the activity name with which they are most likely to be associated.

Project initiation activity
Project proposal

Requirements engineering activity
Users requirements statement

Analysis and model refinement activity
Requirements specification including physical prototype and paper-based
      counterpart
System analysis report

Project planning activity
Project plan
Quality plan
Disaster recovery plan
Security plan
Configuration/version management plan
Unit test plan, integration test plan, acceptance test plan
Participant training requirements report

Build activity

Evolutionary development activity

Class cards
CRC cards (object CRCs, cluster CRCs and rôle CRCs)
Static graphical models (semantic nets) – context diagrams, layer diagrams,
      configuration diagrams, cluster diagrams
Inheritance diagrams
Deployment diagrams
Dynamic graphical models – state transition diagrams (STDs)
Dynamic graphical models (interaction diagrams) – collaboration diagrams,
      sequence diagrams
Scenario class diagrams (use case and task script diagrams)
Creation charts
Test harness (along with code) – test cases for classes, clusters and for
      acceptance testing
Prototypes: user interface and model code
Object class specification (textual)
Source code (class code, cluster code, release code, application code)
Potentially reusable components
Frameworks

Table 7.1   (Continued)

System design report

- requirements specification
- implementation object description
- database design
- impact analysis
- back-up and recovery requirements
- audit, security and control requirements
- interfaces with system software and reusable components

Integration test plan
Acceptance test plan
System test reports
Metrics

User review activity

Agreements (written or verbal) to proceed

Consolidation activity

Documentation (full set)
Operational implications and required actions report
Implementation and conversion plan

Evaluation activity
Design report
Acceptance document
Bug report/Fault reports
Test reports
Review report
Traceability report

Implementation planning activity
System conversion plan (e.g. switch-over plan)

Domain modeling activity
List of candidate reusable classes

Use of system activity
Assessment of implementation process (conversion cutover report)
Assessment of systems acceptance test
Post-implementation review

---

during the evolutionary development activity. These include CRC cards, class cards, a range of graphical models (actually views), test cases and code.

Early in the analysis, *CRC cards* and/or *class cards* have been found to be a good way of both 'getting the discussion going' and encouraging 'object think.' The class CRC card, as used in COMN, is shown in Figure 7.1. On the front are details of name, collaborators and responsibilities and on the reverse a more detailed description and an (optional) list of logical properties, superclasses etc. The CRC card for objects also has an internal/external label; while the CRC cards for rôles and clusters have otherwise identical information apart from the different granularity of focus. These COMN-style CRC cards stick closely to those originally proposed by Beck and Cunningham (1989). The OPEN meta-model (Firesmith et al., 1997) goes further by dividing responsibilities into

- responsibilities for doing
- responsibilities for knowing
- responsibilities for enforcing.

The last of these three corresponds to rule sets. This focus, together with four types of collaboration (a-kind-of, a-part-of, associations, usage) and a hypertext-style layout are captured in OPEN's class cards (derived directly from SOMA) as shown in Figure 7.2. These are readily and successfully automated in the SOMATiK tool (Figure 7.3).

A set of graphical models is developed. Depending upon the notation used and the domain of application (MIS, real time, etc.) these may have different weights and frequency of utilization. Graphical models of the static architecture go by different names in their depiction of classes, objects, clusters, rôles and/or types. They are also used at various degrees of granularities, from context level down to the depiction of the internal 'guts' of an object's method. In OPEN's preferred notation, COMN, there are six types of semantic net which are used to describe and document the static aspects of the system. *Context diagrams* are low granular relating the proposed system to the environment and externals. *Layer diagrams* depict the layered architecture aspects. *Configuration diagrams* show the overall structure, visibility and semantically important relationships. *Cluster diagrams* are the nearest to the 'class diagram' of, for example, Booch, OMT or UML. However, they show not only classes, but also clusters (at a higher level) and objects (particularly in real-time applications). Both OPEN and Fusion urge the creation of independent *inheritance diagrams* to document all such network structures. Finally, the COMN and UML *deployment diagram* allocates software processes to processors, particularly important in distributed applications, perhaps based on ORBs.

These static diagrams are complemented by various dynamic views. These are fairly traditional in OPEN and other approaches. *State transition diagrams* are used to show the states and inter-state transitions for individual classes. *Interaction diagrams* show message passing sequences either by taking a variant of the cluster diagram (semantic net) annotated with sequence numbers (the *collab-*

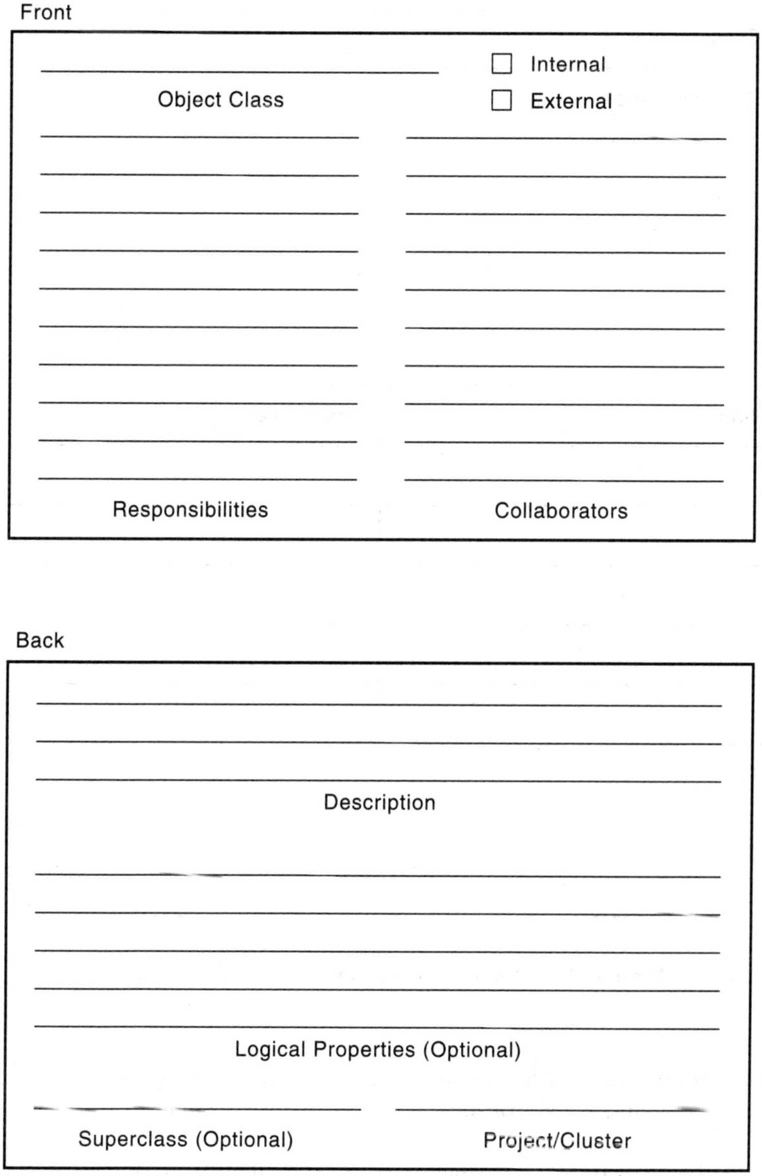

Front

```
┌─────────────────────────────────────────────────────────┐
│  _____       ☐  Internal              │
│            Object Class          ☐  External             │
│  _____    _____ │
│  _____    _____ │
│  _____    _____ │
│  _____    _____ │
│  _____    _____ │
│  _____    _____ │
│  _____    _____ │
│  _____    _____ │
│                                                           │
│       Responsibilities              Collaborators         │
└─────────────────────────────────────────────────────────┘
```

Back

```
┌─────────────────────────────────────────────────────────┐
│  _____ │
│  _____ │
│  _____ │
│                      Description                          │
│  _____ │
│  _____ │
│  _____ │
│  _____ │
│  _____ │
│               Logical Properties (Optional)               │
│                                                           │
│  _____        _____     │
│    Superclass (Optional)          Project/Cluster         │
└─────────────────────────────────────────────────────────┘
```

Figure 7.1. Example object CRC card as used in COMN (after Firesmith et al., 1997).

Class Name	Abstract/Concrete
	Domain/Application/Interface

SuperClasses:

Attributes and associations:

Operations:	Servers-messages

Rulesets:

Figure 7.2   Example class card (after Graham, 1995).

oration diagram) or in terms of the 'fence diagram' which shows for each object its interactions and collaborations in a time-focused sequence (the *sequence diagram*).

Another version of dynamism is the functionality of the system which is typically shown using a non-OO approach based on use cases. In COMN, we support not only this approach (the *use case diagram*) but also the more OO *task script diagram*, both types of *scenario class diagram*.

Creation charts, derived from the BON method, may be found useful. These are charts with essentially two columns labeled 'Class' and 'Creates instances of.' This is applied to a high level of the design and shows which classes

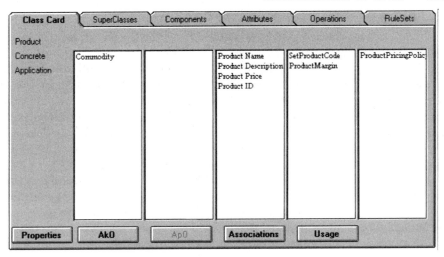

Figure 7.3.   Example class card as represented in the SOMATiK tool (after Graham, 1996).

are responsible for creating instances of which other classes. It thus supplements the collaboration diagrams with specific information on creation. It is especially useful when deferred/abstract classes are being used since, not being able to be instantiated as objects, they can never appear on the collaboration or sequence diagrams and may thus inadvertently be neglected. Conversely creation charts may identify CIRTs in the design to which *no other object* ever sends a creation message. These are called fossil classes (Waldén and Nerson, 1995) and are thus extraneous to the design and can be safely removed. Having said this, in some domains, such as artificial intelligence, these fossil classes can be essential when representing concepts that are important, if uninstantiated; for example the class of perfect men.

As part of the iterative lifecycle and, in particular, the evolutionary development activity within the build activity, testing is a major feature, that is in OPEN it is *not* a *post-hoc* activity. This means that fairly early in development, often in parallel, *test harnesses* should be designed and built. Some authorities suggest that as much as 50% of the overall system development work should be on testing so this is a critical feature of the OO software development lifecycle. Testing plans need to be documented as

- class test cases
- cluster test cases
- acceptance test cases.

Object class specifications present the completed details of the interface for an individual object class. This is basically the full design as seen from outside the class. With fully specified contracts, the use that can be made of this class by others is now finalized and irrevocable. From this specification, the coding can now be undertaken.

Source code is also a form of documentation and certainly a deliverable (some seem to think the only deliverable!). Code is needed not just for classes (assuming implementation in a class-based OOPL such as Eiffel or Java) but also for clusters. Code can also be regarded, from a deliverable viewpoint, as internal (to the development team) and also as *release code*. As the degree of sophistication and the number of iterations increase, a report on the *potentially reusable components* and on *frameworks* will become possible.

At the completion of all the iterative cycles, summary reports are required. Typically there are the *system design report*, an *integration test plan* and an *acceptance test plan*. The system design report may be fairly comprehensive including, *inter alia*, a copy of the user specification for review purposes; a full description of the implementation object model (namely the detailed design and implemented code); a *database design* where needed; an *impact analysis*, a statement on *back-up and recovery requirements*; a description of the *audit, security and control requirements* and a statement on the *interfaces with system software and reusable components*. In addition, the report should contain the test plan and the *results of the testing programme*. The results of the test plan are then reported independently against the integration test plan and the acceptance test plan (*system test reports*). Finally, all the technical and user documentation should have been prepared so that the *user manual* is ready for delivery to the customer along with the software itself.

Designs, code, other products and the process should all be measured and the *metrics reports* tabled. The rôle of metrics in OPEN is critical in monitoring, providing feedback and for process improvement. Consequently the metrics reports are endemic to the whole of the development process. They will tend to be used in the various review and consolidation activities.

The main deliverable from the user review activity within the build activity is the agreement (written or verbal) to proceed to the next iteration with proposed modifications or to the consolidation activity.

In the consolidation activity within the build activity, the main deliverables are *a full set of the technical documentation* documenting all design decisions and describing interfaces to any other systems. A *report on operational implications and required actions* is also required. Also at this stage it is necessary to delimit the mode of implementing the product and undertaking the conversion. This *implementation and conversion plan* will outline the steps to be followed in moving to the new system involving technical and end-users' rôles and responsibilities in the change process.

In the evaluation activity, the pre-release product is evaluated by a direct comparison between the current status and the planned status. A suite of reports is required: a full *design report* evaluating the technical aspects; an *acceptance document* from the users as fulfilling the requirements document; reports for *bugs/faults*; results of the testing harness runs in a *test report*; together with a *traceability report* and an overall *review report*.

In the broader scope of the overall program, the potentially reusable classes identified earlier are listed as candidate reusable classes.

Once the system is ready for implementation at the users' site, then a switch-over plan, known as a *system conversion plan* has to be created. This plan should also include a contingency plan in the event of problems with regard to the old versus the new system.

Once the system has been installed, acceptance tests are undertaken resulting in an *assessment of implementation process report* and an *assessment of systems acceptance test*. This leads to a full *post-implementation review* which must be appropriately documented.

Other documents that are needed, but may be only created once, or even acquired from a third party, are standards and guidelines documents. Coding and design guidelines are available now and will become increasingly common.

References

Beck K. and Cunningham W. (1989). A laboratory for teaching object-oriented thinking. *SIGPLAN Notices*, **24**(10), 1–6

Firesmith D., Henderson-Sellers B. and Graham I. (1997). *OPEN Modeling Language (OML) Reference Manual*. 271 pp. New York: SIGS

Graham I. M. (1995). *Migrating to Object Technology*. 552 pp. Harlow, UK: Addison-Wesley

Graham I. (1996). Requirements engineering as business process modelling, Part II. *Object Expert*, **1**(2), 54–56

Waldén K. and Nerson J.-M. (1995). *Seamless Object-Oriented Architecture*. 301 pp. Englewood Cliffs, NJ: Prentice-Hall

Appendix A
OPEN tasks in alphabetical order

This is a reference section and should be treated as such. Ordering is alphabetical, as in any dictionary or reference tome. Each task is described in a non-exciting way, laid out under identical headings of:

Task: **⟨Name⟩**   Star rating ⟨*/**/***⟩

Focus:
Typical activities for which this is needed:
Typical supportive techniques:

Explanation

As more knowledge is gained, it will first be absorbed into OPEN via these task definitions; hence, this is the portion of the book most likely to show early signs of evolution.

As well as this 'health warning,' we also give each task a 'star rating' which expresses (roughly) the industry's 'level of confidence' in the knowledge represented:

*** well tried

** reasonably well validated

* experimental or not well understood

Enjoy!

Task: **Analyze user requirements**   Star rating **

Focus: Gaining an understanding of elicited requirements.
Typical activities for which this is needed: Analysis and model refinement
Typical supportive techniques: Context modeling, CRC cards, domain analysis, rich pictures, scripting, simulation

Explanation

Identification of stakeholders' 'purposes' for the existence or the development of the system is critical; and the organization of stakeholders into groups is beneficial to the success of conflict resolution strategies.

This task aims to take the user requirements and understand their full depth. Analysis of user requirements is thus the interface between the identification of the user requirements and the first steps in creating the business model for those requirements (and the subsequent object model). One interesting way of doing this is by building a rich picture in which the complexity of the situation, as well as the wishes, concerns, agenda, aspirations and conflicts between various stakeholders is depicted as a drawing (annotated cartoons are often used) in order to highlight the issues, to open a forum for debate and discussion and to help arrive at a better understanding of the needs and wants of the stakeholders, as well as facilitating a consensus view. A rich picture is therefore a medium of communication, understanding and conflict resolution. Rich pictures are drawn and used in group situations where various stakeholders are present.

Another group technique that has proven useful is using CRC cards in which cards are created each of which represents various objects and types recognized as being, or likely to be, a part of the system. Individuals in the group then use these cards to simulate various possible iterations through the system and play out likely and/or important scenarios. Doing this has proven effective in highlighting missed opportunities, bottlenecks, overlooked functionality and a myriad of other issues potentially detracting from a good understanding of the system and the requirements.

A wide array of other techniques exist. This description will be provided in a forthcoming book in the OPEN series (Henderson-Sellers and Younessi, 1997). These include object technology-focused techniques such as use cases, task scripts, event modeling and prototyping; as well as well-established techniques from other disciplines, such as cost–benefit analysis and statistical analysis (see Chapter 6 and especially Tables 6.1 and 6.2). The aim, we must remember, is to understand the problem situation and the requirements, and to resolve any conflicts and inconsistencies that may exist. Remember: 'the end justifies the means!'

Once a composite, reconciled and stable model representing the consensus or near-consensus views of all important stakeholders is arrived at, the analyst must then check back with all parties concerned with regards to this understanding. Again techniques such as rich pictures, simulation and the use of CRC cards have proven useful. Analysis of user requirements is thus the interface between the identification of the user needs and the first step in creating the business model of those requirements.

Task: Code   Star rating ***

Focus: Translation of design into code
Typical activities for which this is needed: Evolutionary development
Typical supportive techniques: Assertion language, association, CIRT indexing, composition structures, contract specification, encapsulation/information hiding, exception handling, fuzzification, implementation of distributed aspects of the system, implementation of services, implementation of structure, mapping to RDB, mixin, object lifecycle histories, polymorphism, walkthroughs, wrappers

Explanation

The task of coding is often seen as the most important in the whole lifecycle since 'bubbles and arrows can't crash; code can' (Meyer, pub. comm., 1994/5). However, if the design is of high quality, then the translation to code should be relatively straightforward, particularly if the object model of the method and the programming language are close, as for instance in the case of when BON or OPEN is coded into Eiffel. Desfray (1994) notes that in coding 'the description of the model entities is adapted and all elements not yet described in the model are developed.' This definition stresses, quite correctly, the twin notions first of a smooth translation of the design into code yet, secondly, the need to take further, low-level implementation/coding decisions which cannot and should not be shown in the logical design. In OPEN, we include in the notion of coding those final, low-level design decisions.

Desfray (1994) notes that coding is likely to be a 'sea of detailed implementation decisions' which will submerge the modeling aspects. While this can be significant, it is perhaps most important that the code, the design and the user requirements all be kept 'in step' so that a truly seamless architecture can be achieved, with the hope of reverse engineering as described in the BON method (Waldén and Nerson, 1995).

While many of the detailed coding-level designs will be taken late in 'design,' we can consider these to be part of the coding-task. Some of these are readily represented in the normal notational sets as used in OOAD; others require the use of the coding-level extensions. These include parametrized or generic classes (OPEN Technique: Genericity), export controls (public, private and protected in C++), static/virtual/friend properties, and possibly class utilities, metaclasses, modules and/or processes (e.g. Graham, 1995a, p. 451).

Indeed the choice of language will dictate to some degree how well this SOM–IOM interface (Figure 4.4 in Chapter 4) is handled. It must be harder for a language like C++, which is very near the machine, than for a language like Smalltalk or Eiffel, which embodies the full object paradigm just as well as does the OOAD method.

Code generation is one goal of software engineering, although there are still many with significant reservations about its ultimate feasibility – mostly on the grounds that if we generate the code from the analysis (or design) diagram, then is that diagram simply not just a programming language in disguise? In its favor is the axiom that code can be generated automatically with fewer errors than when hand-coded and can also be kept synchronized with the analysis and design documentation since all artifacts across the full lifecycle are maintained within the single repository. Desfray (1994, p. 281) suggests that by using the OPEN Technique: Hypergenericity, automatic code generation can be optimized. In counterbalance, Graham expresses the concern that code generation is highly unlikely to ever suffice as a strategy for system building; but is certainly useful as a labor-saving device to create stubs and outlines – much in the mode of a structured editor.

The coding task is complete when executable code has been written and/or generated and tested.

DCS overlay

The code task absorbs much of the complexity of distributed system development. However, this complexity should not be allowed to affect the development of correct business classes. For this reason, the distribution-dependent coding work should be separated from the traditional implementation of services and structure.

Where development is for several physical nodes, different OO programming languages or compilers may need to be used. Care should be taken to ensure that development work does not cause inconsistencies across implementations. Request broker architectures (ORBs), such as CORBA and OLE (with examples such as Orbix and SOM/DSOM), are likely to require serious consideration.

Coding in a conventional language

Rumbaugh et al. (1991) and Meyer (1988) give good sets of guidelines for implementing an OO design in a conventional language. The recommendations of this section are very similar.

Classes are converted to data structures appropriate to the particular language. In C these are structs, records for Pascal, packages or records in Ada, modules in Modula 2, arrays or common blocks in Fortran, and PIC definitions in the data division of a COBOL program. In BASIC, one has only arrays.

Operations, methods or messages correspond to function or subroutine calls. Instances correspond to storage allocated to global or stack variables.

Encapsulation must be enforced by good discipline. Access functions should always be used to update or retrieve data. Application functions are thus insulated from changes to the data structures. The access functions should not access data structures from more than a single class. Global variables should be avoided and scoping used as parsimoniously as possible.

Multiple inheritance needs to be removed. There are a number of ways in which this can be done but two of the obvious ones are indicated by Figure A.1. On the left of the figure the suggestion is that the multiple subclass has the

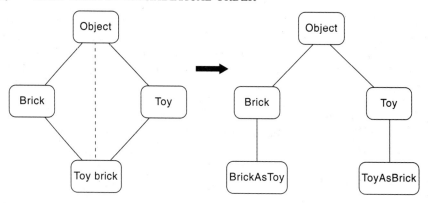

Figure A.1   Removing multiple inheritance (after Graham, 1995a).

unique features it needs from Brick and Toy copied in and inherits their common behavior from Object directly. The other suggestion is to create two subclasses with the appropriate features copied in where they cannot be inherited.

Single inheritance structures should be flattened. Each concrete class corresponds to a structure. Inherited operations are either reimplemented in each of them or, better, called as subroutines or functions.

Concurrency and polymorphism must be implemented directly using whatever features of the language are available. In the case of polymorphism, method invocations can either be resolved at compile time by identifying the class to which each instance belongs or at run time by testing each instance. The latter is normally done using select/case statements or nested if/then/else clauses.

When implementation using a relational database management system is contemplated, there are some additional guidelines and correspondences.

Implementation in a conventional language used to be an important problem but more and more organizations are now switching to OO languages. Implementation using relational databases, however, remains a key issue.

Task: Construct the object model (also known as object modeling or building the object model)   Star rating ***

Focus: Creation of static structure
Typical activities for which this is needed: Build
Typical supportive techniques: Abstract classes, association, blackboarding, BNF, collaborations, composition structures, connascence, contract specification, dataflow modeling, delegation, ER modeling, event charts, event modeling, formal methods, fuzzification, generalization, genericity specification, hypergenericity, implementation inheritance, information engineering, object lifecycle histories, ownership modeling, partitions, pattern recognition, Petri nets, power types,

polymorphism, responsibilities, rôle modeling, service identification, state machines, stereotypes, task cards, transformations of the object model, usage, use cases, visibility

Explanation

For any real-world problem, there is essentially a SOM that is to be built, first as a representation of the business problem and increasingly to represent the proposed solution: from the TOM to the BOM to the SOM to the IOM (see Chapter 4). The seamless transition across requirements engineering, analysis, design and implementation in OPEN essentially identifies OPEN as an elaborational approach – as are the majority of OOAD approaches in use today. In an elaborational approach, it is anticipated that the concepts of requirements and analysis will smoothly migrate to being similar entities in the design and code. Thus an 'object' in the detailed design/code will be easily traceable back to the same (but usually smaller) entity in the requirements (OPEN Task: Maintain trace between requirements and design). In contrast, in the translational approach, as exemplified by the Shlaer/Mellor approach and the BridgePoint tool, the analysis is translated into code, that is there are two distinct phases only.

Building this SOM can use a wide range of techniques (as listed above) dependent on whether the focus is on TOM, BOM or SOM. At each stage, candidate CIRTs are identified and the relationships between them expressed in terms of CIRT responsibilities leading to the use of associations, aggregations, containments, dependencies, collaborations and, later, inheritance structures. It is unnecessary that these relationships be fully defined or be accurate in the cardinality. It is better to draw informal connections (unlabeled and with deferred cardinality) than none at all between CIRTs (this is possible using the TBD relationship icon in COMN but not possible in UML) – mandatory constraints and cardinalities should not be enforced too soon as these are likely to change as the object model is continually refined. We find that often these rough sketches will aid in a rapid elimination of redundant or duplicate CIRTs. Once the initial relationships are identified they should be depicted in the appropriate OO diagrams and fully documented.

In the elaborational approach, the overall 'system' model becomes increasingly larger and more complex as it is built. However, at any and every stage it is important to note that the *only* reason for splitting up the model is that of complexity management. The human brain is only capable of assimilating information over a relatively small number of concepts at the same time. Trying to understand the intricacies of modern software, much of which is totally beyond comprehension by any individual, however skilled, is a pointless exercise. Divide and conquer – by extracting only certain relevant features (application of the notion of abstraction) it does become feasible.

While this is more realistically a representational issue, most methodologies, including OPEN, offer a suite of complexity management tools within the guidelines of the method itself. These are aimed at creating a self-consistent suite of diagrams which, together, document the totality of the one model. In earlier methods, the way these various model 'views' linked together was somewhat suspect. It is important that these orthogonal views, often at different abstraction levels (more or less detailed), *all* represent the same 'truth' in the model being created. For example, changing a message send in the dynamic model should change it similarly in its service representation within the CIRT interface; changing the name of a CIRT should be reflected in the use cases and vice versa. This is important particularly when CASE tool support is sought. The tool needs to have a global view despite the fact that any one diagrammatic representation – and there are several such diagram types in notations such as COMN (Firesmith et al., 1997) and UML (Rational, 1997) – only shows a subset of the total information available for the model.

Task: Create and/or identify reusable components ('for reuse')
Star rating *

Focus: Creating artifacts as a company asset for later reuse
Typical activities for which this is needed: Domain modeling, build
Typical supportive techniques: Metrics collection, completion of abstractions, contract specification, generalization, genericity specification, use cases, refinement of inheritance hierarchies, rôle modeling, service identification, fuzzification, collaborations, domain analysis, CIRT indexing, class naming, encapsulation/information hiding, abstract classes, delegation, domain analysis

Explanation

Effective reuse involves not only using classes from a library but adding new classes to the library for reuse in later projects. The objective of this task is to improve the quality of the project classes so they can be used outside of the project, and consequently to maximize the reusability of classes. This task can initially represent a significant investment of time and effort on top of the normal system development process. This task may begin at the end of the basic system development where further work is necessary to guarantee reusability for future projects – although, if the goal of reusability is borne in mind throughout the process the task actually should be actioned throughout the whole development lifecycle. This is unlikely in the first few OO projects, but as more OT skills are acquired so generalization will become integrated into the overall development process.

While one good approach is to plan to add quality and reusability to designs and classes following successful implementation in the current project, other organizations might prefer to defer incurring this cost until a future project so that classes created in project n are not generalized until it is seen that they are to be useful for project $n + 1$ (or even $n + m$). Such a strategy might, at the same time, reflect less of a commitment to reuse. However, the pragmatic view is also taken that, at least in the early years of using object technology, inexperience might lead to the generalization of classes which really should have been left as project-specific and not migrated beyond the project library to the organizational library. Empirical evaluation of these two strategies is currently lacking. This view of possible management strategies for reuse is supported by the discussion of Menzies et al. (1992) who propose that generalization *must* be undertaken before the first release of the product. Henderson-Sellers and Pant (1993) propose two further alternative reuse models:

(1) a two-library model of potentially reusable components (LPRC) and a library of generalized components (LGC), now renamed the library of adopted reusable components (LARC)

(2) an alternative cost-center model based on an emerging technology group.

As part of quality control on reusable artifacts, measurements are needed in order to effect maximal control. These measurements need to be able to assess costs of:

(1) changing the internal implementation of classes

(2) adding new classes

(3) modifying inheritance hierarchies

(4) changing a class interface

(5) changing aggregation structures

(Graham, 1991, p. 306).

From a management point of view, software developers are required to fill the rôles associated with quality assurance and class library manager.

The additional work during generalization may be simply a 'honing' or refinement of existing classes or it may require the introduction of additional classes (possibly of a deferred or abstract nature, namely ones which cannot be instantiated) at intermediate levels in the inheritance hierarchy. Furthermore, overly complex classes may require splitting into a larger number of smaller classes. The underlying guideline here is to consider whether a class developed in the current project really represents a single concept of the domain (an abstract data type) or whether it encompasses two (or more) concepts. This refinement work is needed to ensure classes are really reusable and augments any project-specific refinement of the inheritance hierarchy. Such refinements may, of course, lead to iteration and a reconsideration of the class model describing the system.

Domain analysis is a useful technique here. Creating reusable components often requires lateral thinking coupled with careful documentation, stating assumptions, limitations, expected ways for the artifact to be used (e.g. inheritance, aggregation). Goldberg and Rubin (1995, p. 105) also note that reuse producers (as here) and reuse consumers ('with reuse') should work in an interleaved fashion. Two-way feedback should be strongly encouraged.

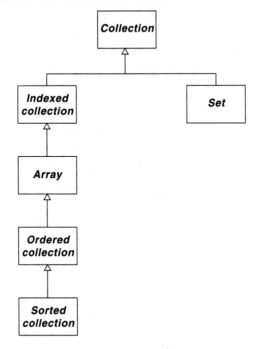

Figure A.2   Simple inheritance hierarchy in which each subclass is instantiable.

It should also be remembered that increasing refinement of inheritance hierarchies is likely not only to lead to deeper hierarchies and more multiple inheritance but also to the introduction of abstract (or deferred) classes. It is generally recommended that abstract classes should not inherit from concrete classes (de Paula and Nelson, 1991; Taivalsaari, 1996); although exceptions to this rule do exist. Another heuristic (Grosberg, 1993) is to construct an inheritance hierarchy using the rule that no concrete classes should have subclasses. With this strategy, for example, the hierarchy of Figure A.2 would be revised to that shown in Figure A.3. In both these diagrams, expressed in UML V1.0, the rectangular icon represents a class, an abstract class is a stereotyped class (as shown by the word abstract in guillemets below the class name) and inheritance is shown as a white arrow.

Subtask: Construct frameworks   Star rating *

Focus: Building a high-level, generic framework as a company asset
Typical supportive techniques: Completion of abstractions, frameworks, genericity specification, pattern recognition, refinement of inheritance hierarchies

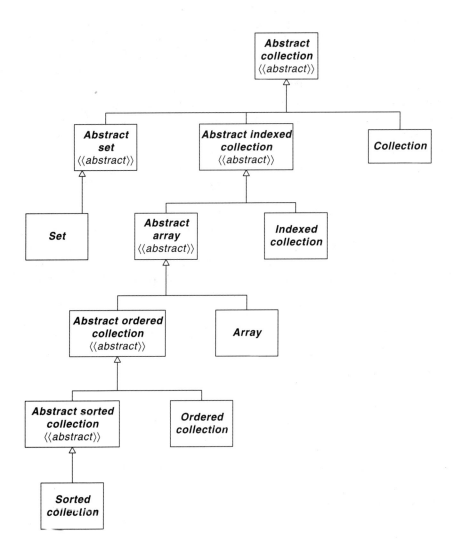

Figure A.3.   Revised hierarchy (from Figure A.2) in which classes are either instantiable or inheritable from, but never both.

Explanation

A framework is a set of cooperating classes that make up a reusable design for a specific class of software. It also expresses, at the architectural level, a fundamental structural organization for software systems by providing a set of predefined subsystems with specified responsibilities and including a set of rules and guidelines for organizing the relationships between them (Buschmann, 1995). Typically that means that the CIRT-level elements in the framework will be abstract classes. An application using a framework will then instantiate all the abstract classes by adding concrete subclasses – which in effect creates the application. It is widely reusable through synthesis and is often available as a packaged product (Reenskaug et al., 1996, p. 153; Sparks et al., 1996). The framework thus predefines a set of design parameters so that the application developer can concentrate on the specifics of the application itself. Since the framework captures the design decisions common across a whole application domain, it can be considered to be *design reuse* (Johnson and Foote, 1988; Gamma et al., 1995).

Using a rôle modeling approach, a framework has a similar definition: as 'a reusable component containing a rôle model describing a general solution, a correlated set of base classes implementing its rôles, and possibly descriptions of applicable constraints' (Reenskaug et al., 1996, p. 153). Wills (1997) goes further by viewing a framework as, essentially, a rôle pattern. He defines it to be

- a goal
- a set of typed rôles
- a set of [abstract] operations
- a set of trigger rules.

This then leads to a more powerful concept than that of subtyping in this context, moving more to the 10-year-old notion of real pluggable components.

Swaminathan and Storey (1997) classify frameworks as:

(1) *infrastructural frameworks*, particularly focusing on the ORB and concurrency management

(2) *user interface frameworks*

(3) *component class libraries*

(4) *domain-specific frameworks*, often built on top of infrastructural frameworks and for a specific business domain.

This last category of framework needs to

- be specific in its focus
- use well-understood classification relevant to the business domain
- constrain the developers' design choices without limiting their creativity

- provide a 'canonical' set of interfaces
- be prebuilt to a significant degree (more than, say, 80%)
- be open to extension.

Reenskaug et al. (1996) describe the steps to be taken in creating a framework which are, quite reasonably, similar to those for creating a pattern.

(1) Identify consumers and consumer needs.
(2) Perform a cost–benefit analysis (CBA).
(3) Perform reverse engineering of existing systems to understand all issues and some possible solutions.
(4) Specify the new framework in general terms.
(5) Document the framework as a pattern, describing how to use it to solve problems.
(6) Describe the design and implementation of the framework to aid its usefulness.
(7) Inform the user community about the existence of this new framework.

Investment in frameworks can be substantial such that a quality goal should be dominant (Sparks et al., 1996).

Subtask: Optimize for reuse   Star rating *

Focus: Reuse
Typical supportive techniques: Access path optimization, completion of abstractions, generalization for reuse, redundant associations

Explanation

Optimizing the implementation of a CIRT for reuse is another important task. Particularly important are the algorithms used, the use of extra variables to store calculated data so that they need not be recomputed, optimizing access paths, designing associations and possibly adding redundant associations for efficiency. Guidelines for these activities are discussed in Rumbaugh et al. (1991). These activities should not, in general, impact on the interface of the class, but be internal optimizations for the particular implementation of the abstraction, particularly if reuse is the focus. This task is therefore likely to be part of OOP in the evolutionary development activity. However, it may be that the CIRT model resulting from the Task: Construct the object model is not efficient in its architecture and that internal optimizations are not sufficient. In this case, the object model will need to be revisited during another iteration, this time with an optimization/design focus. Such design-oriented work should occur in later iterations once the business model has been captured.

Task: Deliver product to customer   Star rating ***

Focus: Customer
Typical activities for which this is needed: Use of system
Typical supportive techniques: Acceptance testing, customer (on-site) training

Explanation

A major task following successful in-house testing is the delivery of the product to the customer. The task is not that of pure delivery but also needs to take into account the customer need for education and training on the new product, customer site testing (often with larger databases than it has been possible to trial) and, finally, customer acceptance. Delivering an OO product to customers exhibits no real difference from non-OO product delivery.

Task: Design and implement physical database
Star rating ***

Focus: Database
Typical activities for which this is needed: Evolutionary development
Typical supportive techniques: Association, clustering, collapsing of classes, composition structures, normalization, ownership modeling, path navigation, relational DBMS interface specification, storage of derived properties, tuning of database, versioning, wrappers

Explanation

Design of the physical database involves mapping the logical data schema to the physical DBMS taking into account the issues raised in the database-specific user requirements report. In undertaking the design, consideration needs to be given to the DBMS product specifics such as recovery, security, concurrency control, versioning, distribution and query optimization. (These are discussed under the appropriate OPEN technique in the companion volume by Henderson-Sellers and Younessi, 1997 or in Case et al., 1995.)

This task is particularly pertinent to the evolutionary development activity and may need to be iterated if the first design does not meet the performance requirements. The task has three subtasks:

- distribution/replication design
- operational and performance design
- performance evaluation.

Subtask: Distribution/replication design   Star rating **

Focus: Database
Typical supportive techniques: Access analysis, collapsing of classes, object replication, reliability requirements

Explanation

Decisions on how to fragment the database and where to store each fragment must be made. The distribution of the data is based on the access paths and costs (Desai, 1990, p. 669) and on reliability requirements. The fragmentation design is determined using the database specification component of the object storage requirements document created as a delivery to the Task: Identify user requirements (DB).

Objects may be partitioned horizontally by assigning groups of objects from the same class or associated classes to different fragments in an objectbase or by making groups of tuples of a relation into fragments in an RDB. On the other hand, objects may be partitioned vertically by assigning properties or attributes in objects or relations to separate fragments. Horizontal fragmentation may improve efficiency if a class has many objects of which only a few are referenced regularly at a given site. Vertical fragmentation may improve efficiency if a class has properties with different access patterns.

Subtask: Operational and performance design   Star rating ***

Focus: Database
Typical supportive techniques: Clustering, indexing, object replication, storage of derived properties

Explanation

Operational considerations include recovery, concurrency control, security control and versioning. An implementation plan should be developed for each of these items to ensure the desired functionality as outlined in the database-specific user requirements report.

Performance is impacted by the operational considerations, distribution design and issues such as indexing, clustering, object replication, storage of derived properties, and classes that can be collapsed.

Subtask: Performance evaluation   Star rating **

Focus: Database
Typical supportive techniques: Tuning of database

Explanation

An analysis of performance is required for each identified event in order to assess
whether the user-stated performance requirements have indeed been met. This
analysis needs, at least, to be performed on the top $x\%$ of critical transactions
to ensure that the system service level requirements are met – for example, the
response time for 90% of all transactions of a specific type should be less than
two seconds.

Task: **Design user interface**   Star rating *

Focus: Creation of the HCI component
Typical activities for which this is needed: Evolutionary development
Typical supportive techniques: Color in UIs, dialog design in UI, hierarchical
task analysis, interviewing, MVC analysis, responsibilities, screen painting and
scraping, throwaway prototyping, usability testing, use cases, videotaping

Explanation

Design for human–computer interaction (HCI) is like other design problems and
the same principles apply. Designed artifacts should be fit for their purpose.
They should be natural in behavior and conform to users' expectations. There
should be no unpleasant surprises except where these are introduced deliberately
as alarms. Use of the artifact should give feedback on progress of the task
being undertaken. They should fit the mental and manual abilities of users. A
very common example of bad interface design outside the context of computers
concerns door handles. Doors in an office building with handles invite them to
be pulled and with doorplates to be pushed. We have all strained at doors with
handles expecting them to pull open only to find later that either they have been
locked but no notice to that effect is in place or, more likely, they are supposed to
be pushed to be opened and will not pull towards the user despite their interface.
     In a new telephone/fax machine purchased by one of the authors, after the
phone message has been listened to and the user wishes to delete it, the sequence
is as follows.

- Press the 'erase' button (so far, so good). The one-line LED display en-
  quires 'clear all messages. Y/N'. Question: Is clear the same as erase? Let
  us assume it is.

- Decide to press Y for yes (ah, but there is no 'Y' key). Knowing something
  about computers, choose 1 for yes (and presumably 0 for No).

- Success, but I had to make two assumptions/guesses in this very modern
  interface. I assumed that clear and erase are synonyms and that 1 is a
  good surrogate for yes.

In a similar vein, a particular e-mail package fooled another of the authors because of its two buttons labeled Send and Reply. In English if I reply to a letter that is equivalent to sending it. However, in this particular package, when answering incoming mail and pressing the obvious Reply button, none of the replied-to recipients ever received the mail. It was apparently sent correctly in that no error message was produced. Not until later did it transpire that the correct action in replying to a message was to press the Reply button *first* and not when ready to reply, type the text of the reply message and then, and only then, press the Send button.

With other packages, on trying to write a document being word processed to a disk that turned out to be full, the file is essentially thrown away with a happy message that there was no room and that the file has been burned (possibly even with a Java applet in the corner burning the wastepaper basket with the irretrievable (and presumably precious) document 'inside'). In fact straight DOS will also do this when updating an existing document on disk. This is of course equivalent to a secretary returning to the boss with the information that 'the filing cabinet was full so I burned the manuscript.' Finally, one of the authors has seen two systems with the helpful advice 'Press Enter to Exit.'

Criticizing other people's designs is far easier than designing something well yourself. The design needs to take into account the type of user, the type of computer equipment and the expectations of the users. There is also HCI research in progress regarding the use of icons in different countries (Sukaviriya and Moran, 1990; Higgins, 1997) – for instance the image of a US-style trash-can has little meaning to a user in SE Asia. There are many different ways of interacting with a computer system. These include menus, forms, command languages, natural languages and graphical user interfaces. As with input and output devices, the best style of interaction depends mainly on the task being undertaken. There is no generic best style.

Menus have the advantage that they can be learned quickly. They generally require fewer keystrokes than other styles and can use dialog management tools. Menus help to give structure to the dialog and make it far easier for the designer to manage errors. However, there are several disadvantages too. The menu tree may be deep and difficult to remember and navigate. This may slow frequent users down significantly. Menus consume screen space, are inflexible and impose a need for a rapid display rate. The most significant factor with menu interfaces is the need for the task analysis to be complete.

Forms-based interfaces are mainly suitable for data entry and tend to make it easier. Users of such interfaces require modest training but they are not very good for casual users. They too consume screen 'real estate' and tend to be inflexible. On the plus side, form generators can be readily used to cut down development times compared with coding everything in a 3GL.

Modal dialog boxes, where the dialog is constrained strictly to the questions and values in the current box, represent a sort of combination of the forms- and menus-based approaches.

Command languages have the advantage of ultimate flexibility and are usually tailorable with macros or a programming language. However, they are notoriously hard to learn for many end-users, hard to remember and easy to make errors with.

Graphical user interfaces combine the advantages of several of the above styles. They are easier to remember than command languages because they provide visual aids to memory and can be quite flexible. They encourage exploration while at the same time making it possible to encourage consistency and enforce a standard interface across different software products. Novice errors can be constrained by warnings or modal dialog boxes. However, graphical user interfaces (GUIs) are very costly indeed to write and may need extra and more expensive hardware, though this must be judged in the light of hardware prices continuing to fall.

Demming and Duffy (1996) suggest that using design patterns can be highly beneficial in creating quality GUIs. They discuss in particular the efficacy of three patterns from the Gamma et al. (1995) book:

- visitor, which allows objects to be presented in different formats
- bridge, which separates abstract GUI objects from their implementation
- composite, which allows creation of recursively defined aggregations of objects.

It is also crucial that the interface designer, like the software engineer, does not stop at merely analyzing and automating existing practices. Computers can, and should, change the tasks they were designed to assist with and this is often their largest contribution. Word processing, for example, has largely changed the nature of document preparation work in offices, and groupware and hypermedia systems and the global internet are continuing the trend.

HCI design involves the following issues.

- Functionality: How does the interface help users carry out tasks and how does it impede them? Does the interface itself make something possible or impossible?
- Usability, covering:
    - learnability
    - memorability
    - productivity
    - propensity to errors
    - support for tasks (task analysis)
    - safety
    - range of users
    - suitability for different locations and conditions.

- Aesthetics.
- Acceptability.
- Structure.

- Reliability.
- Efficiency.
- Maintainability.
- Extensibility.
- Cost.

It is remarkable that the most-liked features of a given GUI are often the aesthetic ones. For example, one of the most popular innovations in windowing systems has been the introduction of a three-dimensional push button that seems to depress and is then clicked or held clicked. It apparently contributes nothing but is loved by users to the extent of being a prerequisite for all such modern systems.

Guidelines for user interface design

In the context of a user interface, both the user and the system must fulfill their responsibilities toward each other. The responsibilities of the user include knowing what tasks can be attempted, being able to perform the procedures needed to accomplish these tasks, understanding and interpreting messages (including their interpretation under different modes) and being able to use the appropriate I/O devices.

The responsibilities of the system include those of helping the user to carry out the tasks specified during design, responding correctly to commands, pre-empting destructive input, meeting performance constraints and sometimes explaining itself to the user. These responsibilities are task-oriented rather than user-oriented because the same user may have quite different responsibilities when adopting a different rôle when a contrasting set of tasks is implied. For example, the same user might approach the system as a manager enquiring on performance or as a data-entry clerk adding new financial assumptions.

Figure A.4   Culturally-dependent icon (after Graham, 1995a).

Designers should remember that there are considerable variations among users. The fact that icons are images which are culturally dependent is demonstrated by the icon in Figure A.4. For those who have still not guessed the meaning of this icon, it represents the choke of an automobile. Recognizing it depends either entirely on memory (used as a symbol) or on the knowledge that some carburettors contain a 'butterfly' (i.e. an icon); a device consisting of a flat metal plate that pivots about an axial pin to allow more or less air into the combustion process. Once you know this, the meaning is obvious. If you do not have this fundamental engineering knowledge, you have to memorize the meaning. Icons thus evoke direct association (if you have that knowledge); symbols derive their meaning from tradition and extensive use. Symbols can thus be more difficult to learn because their associations with reality are, in the final analysis, arbitrary (Constantine and Henderson-Sellers, 1995). Furthermore, users vary widely in their visual ability and will react accordingly. In addition to this natural variation in ability there may also be very great variation due to handicaps such as color blindness, fingers missing, fatigue, illiteracy, memory disorders, deafness and so on.

The power law of practice says that practice has a log-linear effect on skill or that practice makes perfect. The more opportunity the users have to explore the interface the better they will become at using it. This implies that both regular use and an exploratory style will help. It also tells us that systems that will be used by infrequent users need more attention to the user interface.

Users come to the system with different backgrounds and knowledge levels. Psychology tells us that during skill acquisition, knowledge is first stored as declarative knowledge, often in the form of rules and objects to which those rules apply, and can be directly recalled as such. Practice helps people store associations between items and form chunks based on these associations; this is associative knowledge. More practice compiles the rules into procedural knowledge by which stage it is often inaccessible to consciousness; as with the knowledge of how to ride a bicycle or read a sentence. On this basis designers should design for the knowledge level of the users they anticipate using the systems and preferably provide both novice and expert modes.

Some commonly used heuristics for user interface modeling which add to the above principles are listed here.

- Use strong, natural metaphors and analogies.
- Keep it simple.
- Model the domain objects directly.
- Use semantic structures (classification, composition, usage, mapping).
- Minimize semantic primitives.
- Capture rules.

Remember that documentation, training and the user's knowledge are all part of the user interface.

Task: Develop and implement resource allocation plan
Star rating **

Focus: Project management (plan, estimate, control)
Typical activities for which this is needed: Project planning, resource planning

Typical supportive techniques: Cost estimation, Gantt charts, PERT charts, priority setting, project planning, risk analysis, traceability, workflow analysis

Explanation

Project management focuses on planning for the allocation of time, money, people, range, tools and techniques and quality. In addition, control and measurement, following the project initiation, is part of this overall task. Here, each of these areas is investigated (see the following subtasks) in order to provide an overarching project management strategic plan and then instantiate it into a tactical project-level resource allocation plan (see also Henderson-Sellers and Dué, 1997).

The project schedule identifies temporal constraints, possibly temporal orderings (particularly of deliverables), units of work (tasks) and milestones by which to measure progress. Goldberg and Rubin (1995, p. 152) suggest as possible milestones:

- feasibility prototype completed
- market-viability report based on the feasibility prototype available
- first technical prototype completed
- prototype usability study completed
- engineered product released for test
- alpha (internal) release of product available
- updated product, based on alpha feedback, released for test
- beta (external) release of product shipped to customers for test
- updated product, based on beta feedback, released for test
- master copy of product released for manufacturing test
- first customer release of product shipped.

A good project manager realizes what the knowns and unknowns of the project environment are; what needs to be done to eliminate the uncertainties and unknowns; what needs to be done to ensure milestones are technically and politically feasible; and is able to replan as the project unfolds and needs correction mid-course (Goldberg and Rubin, 1995). A winning OO project management strategy delivers results incrementally, building management trust and retaining customer involvement, if possible on a three to six monthly time basis. Timeboxes (Section 4.1) can also be usefully deployed here.

Subtask: Choose hardware   Star rating ***

Focus: Identification of appropriate hardware
Typical supportive techniques: Cost–benefit analysis

Explanation

In many instances, the hardware will be no constraint on the objectives of the current project. In others, it will be necessary to have a faster CPU to undertake calculations faster, to run a more sophisticated GUI, and so on. OO environments such as VisualAge were originally memory hungry and required computers with around 32 MB of RAM. When this software was introduced these computers were relatively rare. Nowadays, however, the hardware is not a constraint on adoption of such a programming environment; although many OO tools and software are pushing hardware and software to the limits. To overcome this state-of-the-art equipment may be needed to create a sensible and efficient environment for the project under discussion.

In other instances, there may be choices between a small platform such as Windows (probably on a Pentium machine) or Mac/Powerbook with their different flavors of GUIs. Other systems demand an AS/400 size midi or a mainframe. While workstations are increasingly powerful, they are still not adequate for main database interactions for a major bank, for example. Also the whole topology of networked workstations is a critically different technical and management controllable environment than a central mainframe with relatively dumb terminals (thin clients).

Selection of hardware may thus simply be from what is currently available or may require a commissioning process. For large systems, this might require going to tender and evaluating the options proposed. Benchmarks need to be considered, particularly those that realistically represent the mean and maximum transaction rates likely to be experienced.

Subtask: Choose project team   Star rating ***

Focus: Team building
Typical supportive techniques: Rôle assignment, team structuring

Explanation

Selecting both a team structure and members of that team can be critical to the success of the project. A team consists of many individuals, each playing one or more rôles – McGibbon (1995) suggests ideally 7–15 members. Project success will be determined both by leadership and by interteam member communication skills.

Team structure can vary – from hierarchical (layered) to fully cooperative (flat). Teams may also have different foci – from application production to reuse. Rôles within the team may also vary, depending upon organizational culture, type of project and available resources. All of the participants should be chosen carefully in order to optimize the possibility of success. Various behavioral characteristics (mover, collector, informer, clarifier, philosopher, evaluator, guide, communicator, encourager, mediator and fixer: McGibbon, 1995, pp. 133–4) should be noted and rôles assigned to take best advantage of contrasting skills. For initial projects, the best team members should be selected from the best and most highly motivated people available. They should be given every opportunity to succeed with access to just-in-time training, time to investigate and understand the new paradigm, protection from unrelated interruptions, and sufficient and timely resources.

Subtask: Choose toolset   Star rating **

Focus: Selection of languages, compilers, debuggers, libraries, browsers, CASE tools, methodology, process, and so on
Typical supportive techniques: Cost–benefit analysis, usability testing

Explanation

One of the difficult tasks, often for the project manager, is the choice of the tools to be used on the project. Sometimes there are organizational standards; yet often a specific project will need specially selected tools. An organization needs to retain a balance between an internal standard and the inflexibility that it brings. It is often a mistake to use, say, C++ for *all* projects simply because you are 'a C++ shop.' Choose the appropriate tools for each new project; watch as technology changes and matures, do not get locked into a single language vendor, methodology marketer or inflexible (and definitely not open systems) CASE tool. (Note that we are not categorizing all CASE tools as inflexible, all methodologies as being only marketing hype and so on – some are, but many are not.)

In choosing tools, defer the language choice. Most languages can be used effectively. However, if there are no supporting tools for browsing, debugging, documentation, then other choices should be considered. In addition, more important determinants to success than language are

- organizational culture
- project management style
- effective lifecycle development method
- knowledge of the object paradigm

in no particular order. Goldberg and Rubin (1995, p. 347) recommend the following criteria for tool choice. The tool should:

- provide explicit support for each step of the method
- manage all of the information that the method requires you to collect or to specify

- be able to handle the quantity of information you require (that is, it should scale to the size of your problem)

- include a mechanism by which you can check that the information that you have collected is consistent

- take on as much of the burden of layout and pretty-printing as possible for drawing the various diagrams

- handle the number of simultaneous users on single or multiple projects that you require for your organization

- (optionally, and dependent on the kind of system being built) be able to generate an initial executable implementation and hardcopy documentation. If any generated implementation is to be modified by the users, then the tool should provide a reverse engineering mechanism to make sure that implementation changes are consistent with the OOAD models.

Tools may also be ranked by urgency of need (Table A.1).

It should also be noted that Booch's (1991, p. 158) warning that 'one of the things that [automated] tools can do is help bad designers create ghastly designs much more quickly than they ever would in the past.'

Browsers typically support navigation through a library based on the class hierarchy and can often be quite rudimentary in nature (McGibbon, 1995, p. 114). A browser is thus an automated tool to manually search through vast amounts of information, often the class definitions (or maybe just the names)

Table A.1   Software tools by category (after Williams, 1995).

First-level tools
  CASE tool
  Word processor
  Development environment
  Project tracking tools

Second-level tools
  Source-code control/configuration management software
  Additional documentation tools
    spreadsheet
    drawing tool

Third-level tools
  Interface builders
  Third-party libraries
  Group work tools
  Testing tools

inside your class repository/library. Another missing feature is the assembly (for prototypical testing) of clusters of classes from within the library being browsed.

Libraries currently represent coded classes, coded in some specific OOPL. As those distributed applications based on CORBA increase, the interoperability provided via CORBA and IDL should make it more possible for the language of coding to become less relevant. As early as 1994 demonstrations were made at conferences of objects written in Smalltalk, say, running on a DOS platform communicating with objects written in C++, say, running on a UNIX platform.

What is probably of more importance is the semantic model underlying the library architecture. How inheritance is used to connect classes, and which are parents and which are children, is *very* different between libraries (Yap and Henderson-Sellers, 1997). This mitigates against reusability.

When choosing a library, consider not only these semantic issues, but also vendor stability and market penetration and their degree of openness and interoperability. Too many libraries force a single vendor linkage which is the antithesis of modern, open, distributed computing. Advice on what to look for before purchasing a software library is given in Table A.2.

An *appropriate method* should also be chosen. While OPEN targets certain commercial audiences, there are some it currently does not, but there is a choice. Some aspects of OPEN will fit well with your organizational goals (we hope the majority). However, be sure that our philosophy and approach are in accord with yours. Some of the questions you need to ask when choosing a method are summarized in Table A.3. If you want good arguments why you should choose a single, homogeneous published method, such as OPEN, read Henderson-Sellers et al. (1994).

Underlying the method should be a *process lifecycle model*. This will describe the typical project management environment. Choices are a rapid prototyping environment or a more formal, structured or OO lifecycle such as the spiral, the fountain, the pinball, the baseball or the contract-driven model. The choice of which lifecycle model is most appropriate may depend upon the method chosen (some advocate a particular process lifecycle model; others essentially ignore the need for it) or may be determined by the corporate culture or the developers' skills and expertise.

CASE tools are often not chosen independently of methods since the degree to which a method is supported by a specific CASE tool (drawing or full CASE) varies greatly. So is the difference between capabilities for code generation and semantic checking. Some CASE tools support only one method (e.g. ROSE, OOATool) while others contain a common metamodel which permits them, at least in principle, to model a wide variety of methods and notations (for example, ObjectMaker, Paradigm Plus, Simply Objects, Graphical Designer, MetaEdit, System Architect).

Of course, the cost of these tools must also be considered as well as their track record. Most vendors will supply an evaluation period before purchase and details of an existing customer who could give a developer's insight into the tool's use. Other factors important in any assessment of a tool include:

- its completeness in supporting a methodology (remember many support little more than the notation and semantic checking)
- the support facilities of the vendor
- the update agreements
- ease of use
- the availability of training
- the tailorability of the tool to the organization.

Table A.2. Advice on what to look for in a commercially supplied library (derived from information in McGregor and Sykes, 1992).

The library should
- give a complete general model (logic to classes and their interrelationships)
- be designed around a few key abstractions
- model standard knowledge in the domain
- use inheritance
- be designed as networks of classes without free-standing data or procedural items (avoid hybrid styles)
- be designed with a low level of coupling between classes
- provide a consistent and easily understood approach to error handling
- provide 'inspector' functions to check preconditions
- make it impossible for users to violate abstractions represented
- conform to a minimal set of standards
- have maximum efficiency
- provide a consistent naming scheme
- provide generic classes
- provide full documentation as specified below
- provide commercial-strength support (from vendor)

Documentation required for library classes (after Korson and McGregor, 1992)

Documentation on the state of completeness of each class implementation
Documentation reflecting the structure of the library
Documentation containing an overview of the library, including contents and structure
Different documentation for different levels of user
Documentation accessible by a minimum of three methods:
- alphabetic by class name
- hierarchical via inheritance structure
- keyword facility

Table A.3   Summary of method selection criteria.

Concepts addressed by the method	The method should support basic concepts that you believe are significant in solving your problem.
Is the choice a method or not?	Choose a method with concepts, techniques, and well-defined process steps, not merely a set of recommendations for a process model or notation.
Notational appropriateness	The notation should be immediately understandable, and there should be a minimal subset for beginners. It should be drawable by hand.
Process model coverage	Choose a method that addresses well-identified activities of the process model.
Types of applications	Choose a method geared towards the kinds of applications your organization builds.
Customizability	If you expect to refine any method you choose, then select one that identifies appropriate aspects for customization. Alternatively, if you expect to compose several methods, make sure the inputs and outputs (or points of overlap) are complementary.
Evolutionary versus revolutionary	Choose a method that is consistent with your organization's ability to bring in new technology.
Learnability	Make sure your people can learn the proposed method.
Traceability	Choose a method that maintains a clear and consistent mapping among artifacts.
Scalability	Choose a method (and related tools) that address the size of the problem you must solve. A method needs to scale up and scale down to the needs of the project.
Collateral material	Choose a method that produces the collateral documents required by your organization.
Tool environment	Choose tools that are well integrated, with an open access to the information collected using the different tools.
Marketplace momentum	Choose a method and tools that you are confident will have a sustaining life in the marketplace, ones for which there is ample training and consultants available.

It was estimated that the total US OO CASE tools market in 1991 was just over \$90 million (9.3% total OO market) with projections to grow to \$500 million in 1997 (17% of total market). The newsletter *OO Strategies* (1992) argued that they expected 'this market to grow very briskly in 1992.' However, a survey of its readers, undertaken in early 1992 by *Object Magazine*, reported in the April 1992 issue that 0% of their respondents were using OO CASE tools. Partly this response may be a result of the lack of availability of CASE tools in the survey period of 1990–1991; partly it may be that developers are not to be seduced by solely notations and drawing support, but rather are awaiting CASE tools which support a total integrated environment of methodology and project management support as well as notation.

For OOPLs, the major choice is between a statistically typed language like Eiffel or C++ and a dynamically typed one such as Smalltalk; an effectively procedurally based (at least internally) language such as Eiffel and Java versus a logic based one such as CLOS; a hybrid language such as C++ or Objective C and a pure OOPL such as Smalltalk or Eiffel; mainstream commercial languages such as Smalltalk, C++, Eiffel, Objective C, Java or more experimental languages such as Self, Kea, Cecil or Emerald or newer OO versions of non-OO languages such as OO COBOL and Ada95. Most languages are now available from multiple vendors, have full debugging/CASE-type environments (Visualworks, VisualAge for Smalltalk; EiffelBench for Eiffel) and have full technical support and a wide range of industry types using them. While many pundits regard Eiffel as the best language (which academically it undoubtedly is!) the larger market share to date has gone to C++ (much of it non-OO usage) and increasingly Smalltalk. Then 1996 saw the ever rising star of Java!

Languages do currently offer slightly different object models and differing degrees of support for OO features. In some, particularly the pure OOPLs, the coder has less to do in order to utilize these features (for example, assertions in Eiffel, polymorphism in Smalltalk), in some encapsulation violation is supported (for example, friends in C++), in many the inheritance mechanism default encourages feature redefinition in such a way that the is-a-kind-of generalization hierarchy is easily destroyed. Default dynamic binding is found in Smalltalk and Eiffel (although in Eiffel the compilers automatically replace it with static binding if dynamic binding is not needed) whereas in C++ static binding is the default – which could lead to later changes (from static to dynamic binding) to necessitate the opening up of code modules in the library, thus thwarting true reusability. Goldberg and Rubin (1995) sum up the pros and cons of these, and other, language features (Table A.4).

Table A.4.   Benefits and drawbacks of language mechanisms (after Goldberg and Rubin, 1995).

Concept/ mechanism	Benefits	Drawbacks	Languages
Object Abstraction Class or templates	Capture similarity among like objects	Overhead for applications that have many one-of-a-kind objects	C++, CLOS, Eiffel Objective C, Smalltalk
Encapsulation Multiple levels	Flexibility in controlling visibility	Reduces potential for reuse	C++, CLOS
Circumvention	Potential performance boost by avoiding message passing as a way of accessing data	Violates an object's encapsulation and introduces tight coupling between objects	C++, CLOS, Objective C
Polymorphism Unbounded polymorphism	Flexibility in prototyping and maintenance to replace an object with another object that supports the required interface	Inhibits static type checking	CLOS, Objective C, Smalltalk
Bounded polymorphism	Provides additional information for type checking and optimization	Reduces the flexibility of object references	C++, Eiffel
Inheritance Of interface specification without implementation	Promotes behavior reuse and object substitution	In isolation no drawbacks,but if there is no implementation inheritance, then forces redundant coding	C++, Eiffel
Of implementation	Promotes code reuse	Inheritance hierarchies may not reflect object type specializations	C++, CLOS, Eiffel, Objective C, Smalltalk
Multiple	Useful when a class is viewed as a combination of two or more different superclasses	Can lead to exceedingly complex inheritance patterns, difficult to understand and maintain	C++, CLOS, Eiffel
Typing No declaration	Less work for the developer	Omits important information that could improve implementation understandability	CLOS, Smalltalk

Table A.4   (Continued)

Formal declaration	Makes implementation easier to understand and provides necessary information for static type checking	More work for the developer	C++, Eiffel
Static type checking	Detects type errors before execution	May impede prototyping by rejecting implementations that could run	C++, Eiffel, Objective C
Dynamic type checking	Allows flexible construction and testing of implementations	Detects type errors only at run time	CLOS, Objective C, Smalltalk
Binding			
Static	Avoids runtime lookup, or use of large amounts of memory to store compiled code for alternative execution pathways	Requires unique names for all system operations, and may require multiple code changes when requirements change	(C and Pascal)
Dynamic	Creates a very flexible code that is resilient to the addition and removal of types	Incurs the overhead of binding at execution time, or the creation of extra code for alternative execution pathways	CLOS, Smalltalk
Both	Can choose the appropriate form of binding for the situation	Requires the developer to know the difference and to specify the information needed to support both	C++, Eiffel, Objective C
Object lifetime			
Classes are objects available at runtime	Additional abstraction capability and runtime flexibility to modify and add classes	Overhead for maintaining the class information in the runtime environment	CLOS, Objective C, Smalltalk
Manual runtime storage reclamation	Allows the developer to control reclamation in special situations	Is error prone and forces the developer to deal with a low-level systems issue	C++, Objective C
Automatic runtime storage reclamation	Frees the developer from determining when space is to be reclaimed	Imposes an overhead on the runtime system to do the reclamation	CLOS, Eiffel, Smalltalk

Subtask: Decompose programme into projects   Star rating *

Focus: Management, business decision making
Typical supportive techniques: Subsystem identification

Explanation

The normal approach to software development is to focus only on a single project. In OPEN, however, we acknowledge the wider context in that any single system development has to be set in the context of an ongoing suite of deliverable software systems. This suite is the overall 'programme.' Any company developing software would recognize this need and equate this level with domain analysis/architecture and strategic planning as opposed to the more tactical notions of developing a single project.

   In some instances, a programme will emerge by the consequential development of a suite of individual projects. For larger, more organized organizations, the overall mission will be to develop the programme, that is a full suite of software tools and systems. Now, the problem of the (probably technical) management is to break down the programmes which reflect the organizational mission and goals into projects, each of which can then be handed over to a project team and its associated project manager or project management team. The project is likely to have a deliverable deadline of the order of a year or so; a programme might continue for a decade – although increasingly it is *much* too difficult to create an environment that will survive unscathed (technologically speaking) for such a long period of time.

Subtask: Develop education and training plan   Star rating **

Focus: Identification of appropriate training (in-house and external consultants)
Typical supportive techniques: CD-ROM technology, computer-based assessment, cost–benefit analysis, games, group problem solving, internet and web technology, lectures, rôle play, self-paced exercises, simulation, train the trainers, videotaping, workshops

Explanation

Education and training are often confused – although many education/training programmes have elements of both. Education develops problem-solving skills; training inculcates a zombie-like ability to do specific skills. For example, knowing the control commands for accessing a windowing-based programme requires training (and memory); knowing how a windowing operating system operates requires education.

   Traditionally education is the realm of universities and schools; training is what is done on the job for a particular purpose. In reality, training and education must go hand in hand throughout a person's lifetime. Required life skills

Table A.5. Months to reach each of the four proficiency levels for various OO skills areas (based on data given in Goldberg and Rubin, 1995).

Skill	Conceptual	Basic	Functional	Advanced
OOAD	0–1	1–3	6–8	18–24
Framework design	0–1	4–5	12–24	24–48
Implementation	1–2	1–3	4–6	18–24
Project management	0–1	1–2	12–18	24–36

change rapidly and an ongoing education, whether personal or organizational, is demanded for success in business and in life.

Developing an education and training plan requires an evaluation of the current skills base in your organization or project team. Goldberg and Rubin (1995, p. 405 et seq.) identify four proficiency levels.

- Conceptual (level C): the individual has a preliminary grasp of the concepts but not a working knowledge. To reach this level, reading journals and books usually suffices.

- Basic (level B): the individual has a working knowledge and can work on small assignments but not yet mission-critical projects. Initial training and simple assignments are required to reach this level.

- Functional (level F): the individual has a good working knowledge and needs minimal guidance on projects. This is the necessary level for a successful project team. This level is attained through a combination of training and direct experience over several projects.

- Advanced (level A): the individual has expert skills and is an authority to whom people turn when they have problems. This level is attained by sustained experience over multiple projects.

Goldberg and Rubin suggest that the time required to achieve these four proficiency levels varies for the particular OO skill being sought (Table A.5). They also recommend the creation of different training plans for different rôles, based on the level of proficiency required in each of the OO skills areas (Table A.6).

Training formats vary. On-the-job experience figures highly in Table A.6. Seminars and other training courses are valuable but need to be followed up by opportunities to try out these new ideas (the combination of education in the seminars – often mistakenly called 'training courses' – and on-the-job training). Mentoring at this stage, by external consultants or by the internal object coach, is usually highly beneficial. The most successful mentoring programmes are those where the mentor watches and advises and *does not* take an active lead on the projects. Most people learn by a combination of study and then experience in

Table A.6.   Training plans for several rôles within the project team (after Goldberg and Rubin, 1995).

Subject and sequence	Level	Training format
Non-technical managers		
OO concepts	C	Executive seminars; self-study
First-line project managers		
OO concepts	F	Executive seminars; self-study
Project management	A	Conference tutorials; classroom; on-the-job experience
OOAD	B	Self-study (optional)
Implementation	B	Self-study (optional)
Reuse managers		
OO concepts	F	Executive seminars; self-study
Project management	F	Conference tutorials; classroom; on-the-job experience
OOAD	B	Classroom
Frameworks	B	Classroom
Technical managers and object coaches		
OO concepts	A	Classroom; on-the-job experience
Project management	F	Conference tutorials; classroom; on-the-job experience
Implementation	F	Classroom; on-the-job experience
OOAD	F	Classroom; on-the-job experience
Frameworks	F	Classroom; on-the-job experience
Analysts and designers		
OO concepts	A	Classroom; on-the-job experience
OOAD	A	Classroom; on-the-job experience
Implementation	B	Classroom
Frameworks	B	Classroom; self-study
Framework designers		
OO concepts	A	Classroom; on-the-job experience
OOAD	A	Classroom; on-the-job experience

Table A.6   (Continued)

Implementation	F	Classroom
Frameworks	A	Classroom; self-study; on-the-job experience

Product programmers and prototypers

OO concepts	F	Classroom; on-the-job experience
Implementation	F	Classroom; on-the-job experience
OOAD	B	Classroom

Reuse evaluators

OO concepts	F	Classroom; on-the-job experience
Implementation	F	Classroom; on-the-job experience
OOAD	B	Classroom
Frameworks	B	Classroom

practice (with someone more experienced on hand to help out). However, it must be noted that traditional classroom-based education and training is still most popular – Goldberg and Rubin (1995, p. 417) observe that the number of projects using classroom-based training approximately equalled those using mentoring or self-study (combined).

While formal education in terms of college and university degrees offers useful long-term benefits, organizational education and training are, unhappily, seldom so strategically focused. Much more prevalent, and a lot more targeted towards teaching system functionality, are short-period training courses which may be provided as intense one to five day offerings composed usually of lectures and practice sessions. The alternative is two to three hourly offerings over a period of several weeks. It is customary that during the practice sessions, hands-on interaction on an appropriate problem is provided. Written course notes are usually the main source of information in these traditional training courses.

In-organization mentor-based training uses the train-the-trainer principles. This is when the developer trains one or a few individuals in every or various aspects of the system and then the organization uses this individual or these individuals to train the rest of the staff. It must be mentioned that in-organization mentor-based training must be used with extreme care in that the choice of instructor is critical in the success of this approach.

Multi-media technology may be used to enhance or replace the role of the lecturer, or provide practice opportunity. CD-ROM, written course notes and videotape material may be used as sources of information. CD-ROM or computer based assessment (CBA) technology may be used for assessment and evaluation purposes. Computer networks may be used to simulate a multi-person work environment and interactivity, which adds to the real-world applicability of the training course. The obvious advantage of this approach is that CBA may be administered on a self-paced basis, or at least reduce reliance on expert instructors. This characteristic makes this technology particularly useful for those situations where the software is installed by numerous customers, or the developers are geographically dispersed.

The potential of the internet, particularly the World Wide Web, as a training-provision vehicle must not be ignored. This medium allows virtually all of the technologies mentioned above to be made available virtually instantly and world wide.

Finally, a lot of organizations forget the importance of what we call indirect training. Into this category fall things such as publication of product newsletters, user-group meetings, provision of books and other instructional articles, help desks, and so on. It is of the utmost importance that, irrespective of the technology or context of the training course provided, they must be informative, targeted and relevant, precise and error free, and, most importantly, interesting. Games, rôle plays, simulations, and group problem solving have all proven useful.

Setting up a training plan depends upon available resources, and existing and desired skills levels of team members. Each organization should construct its own training plan based on these three factors. Some case-study examples are given in Goldberg and Rubin (1995, Chapter 19). Some of the most important training and education considerations that the project manager will have to cope with include:

- taking three or more years for an organization to migrate fully to an OT environment

- taking 30–40 days of just-in-time training spread over 6–12 months to migrate individual project participants to an OT environment

- perhaps as few as 20 or 30% of traditionally trained analysts and technicians will become proficient with the object paradigm.

Subtask: Develop iteration plan   Star rating **

Focus. Project management of technical build
Typical supportive techniques: Gantt charts, priority setting, process modeling

Explanation

In this subtask, a project plan is developed which describes in detail the required resources, objectives and timeframe for the forthcoming (next) iteration.

In developing an iteration plan, there are a number of considerations (Lorenz, 1993).

(1) *Update and prioritize system requirements* (by capturing new insights and documenting the rationale behind decisions taken).

(2) *Document external dependencies and deliverables* (and minimize dependencies on external sources outside your control).

(3) *Determine specific goals for each iteration* (involving users and usability testing).

(4) *Establish a schedule* (maintaining links to the requirements).

Approaches useful for the development of a schedule include listing all project tasks, determining intertask dependencies, estimating the duration of a task and defining the earliest and latest completion dates for a task. To support this subtask, a PERT, CPM or Gantt chart could be usefully developed for the iterations.

Subtask: Develop timebox plan   Star rating **

Focus: Delivery by stated deadlines
Typical supportive techniques: Impact analysis, project planning, RAD workshops

Explanation

The timebox plan outlines the activities and resources required to build an agreed part of the system by a fixed date. Timebox planning also involves estimating and resource and infrastructure procurement. The plan takes account of the overall project plan and should be sent to those responsible for the overall plan. The timebox planning activity will normally last for between one and four weeks as well. Each timebox may last for between one and six months and a three-month period is to be considered normal. Evaluation and reuse analysis should never take more than two weeks. These limits are subject to an overall maximum of six months elapsed time from the end of the workshops to implementation.

One or more parallel timeboxes are planned. Each timebox will ideally last around three months elapsed time though this will depend on the tools used. There is also a higher-level planning context which plans, or at least predicts, sequences of timeboxes and considers the interrelationships with the domain model.

Deliverables and observable milestones should be agreed when the project plan is produced and reviewed regularly.

Timebox planning involves:

- reviewing the requirements discovered in the RAD workshops and reviewing the analysis report (O)

- reviewing the domain model and existing systems and identifying existing components for possible reuse (R)

- ensuring a participant training programme is planned (R)
- applying source-code control tools to the existing system if a proposed solution is a change to an existing system (M)
- revising development plans (R)
- identifying the impact of proposed change on hardware, including response times (M)
- setting the timebox objectives and publishing them (M)
- setting the number of planned prototype iterations (R)
- establishing the development team, confirming the lead user, project manager, developers and the sponsor (M)
- establishing the evaluation team – sponsor, project manager, user representatives, facilitator, demonstrator/reader, corporate auditor, operations representative, librarian, legal expert, and so on (M).

Timebox planning produces a timebox plan, including a Gantt chart, and an estimate in task points with resource requirements and delivery dates.

Each of the timeboxes results in deliverables in the form of one or more of the following:

- a system and its documentation
- a specification/report, including defect analysis and other metrics
- a set of candidate classes for reuse.

Each timebox may last between one and six months subject to an overall limit that the time from the end of the RAD workshop activity (q.v.) to implementation is under six months. The ideal timebox lasts three to four months.

A short participant training requirements report should be produced to ensure that the costs, rôles, systems training and business training needs of systems and business participants are clearly understood and planned. Emphasis is placed here on requirements and testing. This report identifies the broad skills required to undertake the project, then the skill set of the individuals allocated to it, to identify the mismatch. It is necessary to ensure that:

- staff members are named
- training requirements are identified and scheduled
- business and technical needs are covered
- equipment can be obtained on time
- inspections are included in the plan.

Subtask: Identify project rôles and responsibilities   Star rating ***

Focus: Team building
Typical supportive techniques: Rôle assignment, team structuring

Explanation

Within a project team there are needs for a variety of skills. While the actual team members will vary from project to project, the likely skills base will include developers with special skills in

- abstract thinking
- component reuse
- mentoring
- component construction (coding skills)
- objectbase administrator
- requirements engineering
- methodology
- prototyper
- toolsmith
- domain analyst
- testing
- metrics and QA.

Even within the reuse team, there may be specialist rôles (McGibbon, 1997):

- reuse manager
- reuse administrator
- reuse maintainer
- reuse evaluator
- reuse librarian
- reuse engineer.

Project team members will also have non-OO skills which provide psychological complementarity in a team and ensure it functions holistically and successfully. These include members with such skills as:

- mover
- collector
- informer
- clarifier
- philosopher
- evaluator
- guide
- communicator

- encourager
- mediator
- fixer.

Subtask: Manage subsystems   Star rating **

Focus: Identifying and controlling subsystems
Typical supportive techniques: Subsystem coordination, subsystem identification

Explanation

Subsystems (or clusters in COMN and BON) need a management plan. The project manager is responsible for identification of the most appropriate subsystems – an architecture decision (see OPEN Technique: Subsystem identification) which requires skills not necessarily possessed by a typical project manager. Subsystems are needed particularly in large systems as a tool by which to manage technical complexity. It is also necessary to coordinate the development of subsystems. Often, one team is responsible for each subsystem; however, someone needs to be responsible for ensuring compatibility between subsystems. This could be a linchpin person (Thomsett, 1990) or a member of the cross-project team (see OPEN Technique: Subsystem coordination and subtask Choose project team).

The OPEN contract lifecycle model makes the assumption that subsystems can be developed in parallel. Concurrent development shortens time to market drastically but creates new problems in terms of coordinating multiple, concurrent activities. When the development is distributed too, the complexity may be double that of centralized sequential developments. However, this is the ultimate model for downsizing the development organization and its processes. Figure 4.8 shows the four possibilities. OPEN will support any of the models shown in this figure. However, if a concurrent approach is adopted there is additional complexity to manage. The problem is to ensure coordination across projects (and timeboxes when used): that integration of timebox products is adequately planned for and that timebox synchronization is accomplished. The model we adopt is shown in Figure 4.9.

The diagram shows how the consolidation activity within each timebox integrates the results of other efforts to produce a product which is then subjected to evaluation. In some cases the timeboxes communicate directly and informally, in others only after evaluation. If the products of the two final timeboxes interact there would have to be a combined evaluation.

To make everything work and maintain consistent levels of quality, everyone involved must speak the same development language and that language must be sufficiently expressive, or semantically rich. OPEN is offered as the basis of just such a *lingua franca.*

Subtask: Set up metrics collection programme   Star rating **

Focus: Identification of best way to collect metrics data
Typical supportive techniques: Reuse metrics, task points

Explanation

Management of any production process is simplified if some measures of progress towards a quality product are collected and analyzed. In manufacturing, tolerance limits are prescribed and individual components assessed against these 'standards.' Excessive product rejections suggest that the process producing them is at fault. Costs are tracked during the process and compared with estimates made initially.

It is necessary to know with what precision software development data are obtainable. Clear goals and objectives of the metrics programme need to be elucidated early on in the planning process. Are the data to be used to assess, to predict or to control (Goldberg and Rubin, 1995)? Careful planning is required before any collection commences. Those involved and who feel they are being measured need to be intimately involved with both collection and analysis; in other words, the aims of the metrics collection programme need to be widely advertised throughout the organization.

Software development shares with manufacturing industry the need to measure costs, productivity and quality. The main difference lies in the 'one-off' nature of software. Nevertheless, quality can be evaluated against prespecified criteria, progress towards the goal evaluated on a temporal basis and final costs compared with estimated costs (the differences often called variances by accountants). Specific goals could include the ability to

(1) do cost estimation from the requirements analysis

(2) estimate maintenance costs from the code

(3) evaluate the reusability of designs, frameworks and code

(4) allocate resources most wisely.

Such aims require collection of data on the process, effort expended (often measured in time resources times people resources) and objective measures of the code itself.

In introducing a measurement programme, an initial question is often: What is to be measured? A more appropriate question is: What is the goal which we wish to attain? For example, is the goal to increase programmer productivity; to decrease the number of defects reported per unit of time (of course, this can be easily abused – by just not *reporting* any defects); to improve the efficiency of the overall development process; or to attain ISO 9000 accreditation? Until that goal is defined, recommendations on the optimum measurement programme cannot be made. This is the goal–question–metric (GQM) paradigm (Basili and Rombach, 1988) in action.

In another framework approach, Rowe and Whitty (1993) describe the application of metrics to industry (AMI) programme which focuses on an interlinking of the actions of assess, analyze, metricate and improve. Here the framework encompasses a 12-step method which embodies both the GQM paradigm and the five-level CMM. The four activities are themselves distinct but interlinked. The AMI method proposes that you:

- *Assess* the project environment in order to define the goals (for GQM)
- *Analyze* these goals in terms of achievable sub-goals
- *Metricate* in terms of a measurement plan
- *Improve* by using the measured data to feed back to the process.

Metrics can be used as a mechanism for evaluating staff performance. Such a use is fraught with problems since it can be counter-productive. Staff resistance can be high because of the appraisal element or staff may work to optimize one specific metric (e.g. size) if that metric is, unwisely, being used as the sole adjudicator of their productivity/'worth.' In discussing the etiquette of applying software metrics programmes, Grady (1993) divides his set of 'rules' (Table A.7) into three types: those relating to functional management, those to project management and those to the project team. At each level it must be made clear that metrics are to be used for mutual improvement, not to chastise individuals.

Another use which is often overlooked is the objective assessment of various competing methodologies, techniques, organizational structures or work patterns (or indeed whether the object paradigm is being used at all!). Although, as Ince (1990) notes, there is little practical experience with this mode of application of metrics, Fenton et al. (1994) underline that the difficulties and realities of research in these areas need to be stressed (Henderson-Sellers, 1995).

In a study of the introduction of a metrics programme to Contel (Pfleeger, 1993), the appropriateness of the metrics was linked to the SEI maturity level (Table A.8). Several common themes that contributed to the project's success in Contel can be readily identified. These should be equally important in an OO environment:

- begin by focusing on the process
- keep the metrics close to the developers
- focus initially on those who need help – they will then 'spread the good word'
- automate data collection as far as possible
- keep things simple to understand
- capture whatever information is possible but without burdening developers
- do not force the developers to implement a metrics programme against their will
- some metrics is better than using no metrics

Table A.7   Rules of etiquette for applying software metrics (after Grady, 1993).

Functional management
- (1)   Do not allow anyone in your organization to use metrics to measure individuals.
- (2)   Set clear goals and get your staff to help define metrics for success.
- (3)   Understand the data that your people take pride in reporting; never use it against them; never even hint that you might.
- (4)   Do not emphasize one metric to the exclusion of others.
- (5)   Support your people when their reports are backed by data useful to the organization.

Project management
- (6)   Never try to measure individuals.
- (7)   Gain agreement with your team on the metrics that you will track and define them in a project plan.
- (8)   Provide regular feedback to the team about the data it helped collect.
- (9)   Know the strategic focus of your organization and emphasize metrics that support the strategy in your reports.

Project team
- (10)   Do your best to report accurate, timely data.
- (11)   Help your managers to focus project data on improving your processes.
- (12)   Never use metrics to brag about how good you are or you will encourage others to use other data to show the opposite.

Table A.8   Capability Maturity Model – the five levels (after Pfleeger, 1991).

	Level	Characteristics	Metrics to use
(5)	Optimizing	Improvement fed back to process	Process + feedback for changing process
(4)	Managed	Measured process (quantitative)	Process + feedback for control
(3)	Defined	Process defined, institutionalized	Product
(2)	Repeatable	Process dependent on individuals	Project
(1)	Initial	Ad hoc	Baseline

- tailor the metrics used to the individuals responsible
- criticize the process and the product, but *not* the people.

Goldberg and Rubin (1995, p. 462) highlight the need for data collection to be an integral part of all software development job rôles. Insofar as it is possible, automated collection of metrics information assists in creating a successful programme. The success of any metrics programme requires total commitment and understanding of what can and cannot be achieved and in what timeframe. Success can be considered to have been achieved when

- measurement programme results are actively used in decision making
- they are communicated and accepted outside of the IT department
- the programme lasts longer than two years.

On the other hand, failure is more likely if

- management did not clearly define the purpose and later saw measures as irrelevant
- systems professionals resisted the introduction of a metrics programme, perceiving it as a negative commentary on their performance
- already burdened project staff were taxed by extensive data collection requirements and cumbersome procedures
- programme reports failed to generate management action
- management withdrew support for the programme perceiving it mired in problems and 'no-win' situations.

There are three potential causes for low satisfaction:

(1) measurement is often regarded as an immature (and hence untrustworthy) discipline
(2) measurement programmes are often incorrectly implemented
(3) the data collected are often used for other (ignoble) purposes, as highlighted above.

In a recently published study of the Sydney Area Health Service (Lynch, 1995), the necessary objective nature of the data to be collected is stressed, as is the need to negotiate the details of the programme before its instigation. Metrics must be linked to business needs and must be useful (i.e. both timely and sensitive) as well as economical to gather.

An OO metrics programme can certainly accomplish a number of goals: greater understanding leading to identification of a repeatable and hence manageable process for software development. Greater quantification of the process also enhances the organizational process maturity level, as described by a process maturity model. Early, immature prototypes for such models already exist as in the SEI CMM (Humphrey, 1989) but they need massive improvement if they are not to be merely costly and bureaucratic overheads (Jones, 1994). They should be used merely as a map by which to judge location and must *not* be viewed as a hurdle to be overcome and then forgotten.

At a more technical level, metrics can provide information on which to base standards for assessing maintainability; to evolve best practice for responding to user change requests and, in the future, to determining 'how OO' a particular design or program is. The whole use of metrics is compatible with moving software development towards scientific understanding and engineering practice, that is to make software engineering a more mature discipline. Finally, for the people concerned, their involvement in improving the process and the product should lead not only to higher-quality systems but also to a sense of ownership and pride.

But instigating a metrics programme does not bring immediate 'magical' answers to all software development. It cannot and should not be used to assess the performance of the developers themselves; nor can it create non-existent skills in the developers (although it can enhance their awareness of the extent of their skills). A metrics programme will not provide a single number for complexity or for quality. Neither will it, overnight and by itself, create a one-off version of a rigid development process which can thereafter be mechanistically (slavishly) followed. Productivity gains are likely but they are a consequence of other factors not a necessary result *per se*. Finally, almost all managers want a cost estimation tool (e.g. Haynes and Henderson-Sellers, 1996). Instigating a metrics programme will lead to the ability to create one for your organization; it cannot provide a 'magic formula' applicable in all situations.

A metrics programme provides knowledge and understanding; it does not provide quick fixes.

Subtask: Specify individual goals   Star rating *

Focus: Plan for personal achievement
Typical activities for which this is needed: Project planning
Typical supportive techniques: PSP, SMART goals

Explanation

Management is about getting the best out of people: out of the members of your team. While software engineering professionals typically get pleasure out of working hard and working well, they also seek some recognition of their skills. Blanchard and Johnson (1983) suggest that managers need to set out clearly what is expected of an individual. One technique they suggest is that of SMART goal setting. SMART is an acronym for

- **S**pecific: Is it clearly understandable?
- **M**easurable: What would a good (and a bad) job look like?
- **A**ttainable: Is it realistic for the individual?
- **R**elevant: Will it make any impact?
- **T**rackable: How will anyone know?

Setting SMART goals requires three stages (McGibbon, 1995, p. 146):

(1) identifying the objective and areas of responsibility

(2) specification of priorities

(3) detailing of at least three ways in which success can be measured.

Another approach to individual goal setting is provided in the personal software process (PSP) of Humphrey (1995). PSP uses a series of interrelated exercises, grouped into four levels (PSP0 to PSP3). These exercises are designed to help the software engineer arrive at a defined and measured personal software process. This is done through collecting statistics on a number of metrics relating to planning and management of these 'personal (individually performed and completed) software projects.' This develops a framework for a well-defined and statistically managed software engineering approach that is defined, disciplined, measured and predictable. Once the personal process reaches such a level of definition, it will significantly improve the way in which the software engineer plans, controls and improves his or her work in the future. The PSP is therefore based on the principles of plan, do, measure and improve, all in the context of statistical quality control.

Given such a basis, the defined and measured personal process of a software engineer, created through the application of PSP, will allow a degree of predictability in terms of how hard and how well (i.e. how productively) the individual works or can work. This can be a useful guideline for specifying individual goals – goals that are meaningful and attainable, and their achievement measurable.

Subtask: Specify quality goals   Star rating *

Focus: Plan for high quality
Typical activities for which this is needed: Project planning, programme planning
Typical supportive techniques: Contract specification, quality templates

Explanation

A major focus of OPEN is quality – quality of product, quality of user interface, in terms of usability and quality of process. While metrics programmes need to be in place to make the necessary measurements (Subtask: Set up metrics collection programme), before this can be done, there need to be some decisions made about how to use these metrics data. Collection of data just gives us numbers. These numbers need to be usable to answer questions such as: Did we achieve an appropriate quality? In order to answer that question of course, we first need to state what we mean by 'appropriate quality.' This subtask focuses on that decision-making process (see OPEN Technique: GQM).

Quality goals need to be stated in terms of code quality (for example, internal complexity for maintainability estimates and external quality in terms of usability, flexibility and so on – see for example Fenton, 1994; Henderson-Sellers, 1996). This gives rise to product metrics. Quality also needs to be assessed in terms of process, probably based on the TQM approach (see OPEN Technique: TQM).

We mentioned earlier (Chapter 2) that a high-quality software process has to be understandable, enactable, repeatable and improvable. We also said that to achieve these attributes, a software process has to be formal, granular, precise and measurement based. These characteristics in a software process contribute directly to, and can *en masse* be assessed in terms of, the capability and maturity of the software process in question. In other words the level of capability and maturity may be deemed as a good measure of the quality of a software process and, indirectly, an indication of the quality of the product artifact that may be produced as a result of the process.

In order to measure the capability and maturity of a process however, we need a yardstick. An effective way of producing such a yardstick is to observe the behavior and structural characteristics, together with the output of a wide array of processes, and categorize them into progressive graduations or levels of capability and maturity. A candidate process may thus be compared in terms of its behavioral and structural characteristics with those belonging to such an ordinal framework and can, therefore, be placed at some level of such a scale.

Measurement for measurement's sake is of very limited use. The essential utility of the measurement of capability and maturity is for the purpose of process improvement as embodied in convergent engineering (Taylor, 1995) and OPEN. In this sense all frameworks of this nature have at their core the essential principles of TQM. TQM puts 'process improvement' on a firm basis of statistical control through:

- identification and separation of common and special causes

- measurement and control of special causes.

In short, TQM attempts to measure and statistically isolate special variations and its causes within a process. It then uses the resources available to work towards the elimination of these special variations by removing their causes through the improvement of the process of production. At the same time TQM ensures that time and money are not wasted in trying to eliminate common causes.

A wide array of process capability assessment frameworks with varying degrees of sophistication, popularity, and applicability exist, some of which are

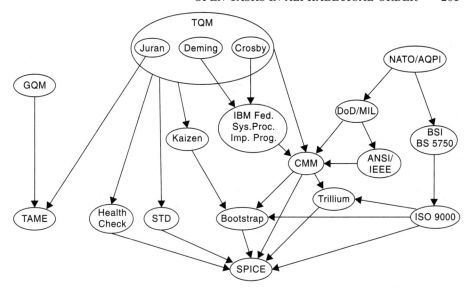

Figure A.5.   An influence diagram of concepts, architecture and principles involved in process assessment approaches.

enumerated below:

(1) CMM developed by the SEI (Paulk et al., 1993).

(2) SPICE, under development by the ISO to be promulgated as the ISO standard for software process assessment and improvement (Dorling, 1993).

(3) ISO 9000, promulgated by ISO as a general process and service quality certification framework (ISO, 1991 – see also below).

(4) Bootstrap, developed by the European ESPRIT project (Koch, 1993).

The concepts, architecture and principles involved in many of these process improvement approaches currently being elaborated have been influenced by those preceding them. In turn they carry influences from earlier formulations and concepts.

Figure A.5 is an attempt at capturing and illustrating at least some of the more obvious, fundamental and explicit of these influences. The diagram is by no means exhaustive in terms of coverage of either various schemes or their mutual influences.

Software process assessment and improvement frameworks, if applied and utilized correctly and with the right intent (genuine improvement not the mere obtaining of a certificate or rating), have a great potential in increasing the level of quality of the organization.

Threshold values

One application of internal metrics, used frequently by software engineers during development and which may be justifiable and pragmatically useful, even in the absence of any link to an external characteristic, is in terms of a threshold value which would occur whenever the value of a specific internal metric exceeded some predetermined threshold. While it is clearly not the case that there is a discontinuity in the range of values whereby a value less than or equal to the threshold is acceptable and a value greater than the threshold indicates a problem that *must* be solved, values not in the acceptable range should be used merely to draw attention to that particular part of the code. It should also be stressed that exceedance of a threshold value does not, for certain, imply a problem; rather it should be interpreted as a higher than average probability of finding a problem, that is providing a focus of attention only. In many instances, rapid inspection reveals no cause for concern. Another alternative would be to predetermine three ranges for each metric: safe, flag, alarm. Thus, without presuming either a causality or even a high enough correlation to propose any type of model, these flags and/or alarms draw a developer's attention towards a particular program module or chunk requiring further evaluation. Finally, it should be noted that such indicator levels should not be absolute (as many metricians might read into McCabe's (1976) threshold value of 10 for control-flow complexity) but rather relatively dependent on the particular development environment, especially the complexity of the problem itself – an area of metrics almost totally ignored, as noted earlier.

ISO 9000 standards (contributed by B. Unhelkar)

OPEN deliverables satisfactorily fullfill the requirements of many clauses of AS3563.1 which is the Australian Software Quality Assurance Standard based on ISO 9001. Clause 4.2 Quality System of AS3563.1 requires the developer to 'demonstrate ... an organized approach to control' the factors which affect quality within an organization. Production of well-documented OPEN deliverables and checkpointing them using deliverable sheets satisfies a large part of this requirement – especially sub-clause 4.2.2 Development Standards and Procedures. While clause 4.3 Contract Review, Planning and Requirements Control is reflected in the business-focused activities (the business planning stage of Figure 2.1), OPEN particularly facilitates the satisfaction of the design control and reviews requirements of clause 4.4 Design, Programming and User Documentation Control of AS3563.1. OPEN also has specific deliverables for inspection and testing (clause 4.10). In an industrial application of OPEN (from which this mapping to ISO 9001 was derived), the development team were surprised to find that no other methodology examined (for example, Booch, Coad and Yourdon, Wirfs-Brock et al. 1990) gave sufficient importance to testing – some did not even mention it. The OPEN requirement for test cases and test reports and specific activities, tasks and techniques to achieve them helps this clause to expand into the detailed test documentation as seen above.

Metrics in OO systems are a subject of debate in the industry at this stage. However, OPEN conforms well to clause 4.20 Statistical Techniques of AS3563.1 in its specification of the measurement requirements and its associated collection of several metrics-focused tasks and techniques. Finally, OPEN, being a full lifecycle methodology, has helped the industry user to comply with the requirement of clause 4.21 Control of Development Environment, by assisting in the identification and change control of all the factors that could affect the quality of the software being developed. The iteration planning task also helped with the configuration management.

While most contemporary methodologies concentrate on the actual development process, OPEN gives due importance to quality assurance and testing by means of Task: Evaluate quality and Task: Test and the various testing and metrics-focused deliverables such as the test report and the review report (see Table 7.1). Thus, overall, by following OPEN, industries have found that they are readily complying with many requirements of the recognized quality assurance standards.

Interface (GUI) quality standards

The various style guides from Apple, IBM, Microsoft, NeXT, OSF and Sun all adopt a broadly OO approach to user interface design. Therefore, given a sufficiently correct and expressive object model, these guides may be used to select standard components to represent the objects in the model. This is especially easy when there is an interface object library available. Apple provides MacApp and the User Interface Toolbox. Microsoft Windows can be approached with the Microsoft Foundation Classes or the Borland Object Windows Library (OWL). NeXT provides possibly the best combination of ease of use and power in an integrated environment. OSF and Sun provide 'widget' libraries both based on X-open's Xt Intrinsics. All these support the 'look and feel' recommended by the appropriate style guide. However, each one uses a different terminology for common features. A simple example is the term 'mouse-down' (Apple and Microsoft) which appears as 'ButtonPress' in X-Windows variants. Some concepts, such as 'mouse-over,' are not supported uniformly across all styles. Also the class libraries have very different classification structures and this can be confusing for developers moving from platform to platform. Furthermore, the structures might well be incompatible with those of an earlier OO analysis, leading to the need for careful implementation remodeling.

IBM's CUA'91 provides a standard look and feel for the presentation manager applications and, in fact, for DOS, AIX and Windows applications too. The intention was to make all CUA-compliant applications look and behave similarly on all platforms. CUA'91 also contains guidelines on how to go about designing a user interface and amounts to the rudiments of a structured method for graphical user interface design. Microsoft has also published similar, detailed guidelines on user interface design when the context is MS Windows. Apple, Sun and the Open Systems Foundation have all published style guides defining a standard for the Mac, Open Look and Motif workstations respectively, with

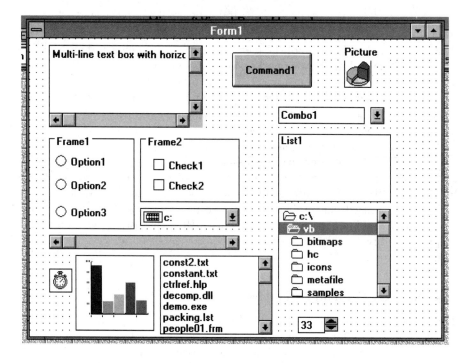

Figure A.6   Some typical CUA-style objects (after Graham, 1995a).

the Apple document being generally regarded as the paradigm for all the others mentioned so far. Most of these standards give a lot of detail including: positioning standards for controls (for example, the cancel button should be 3 mm below the OK button or to its right), standard control types and layouts (such as those shown in Figure A.6), and standards for menus and naming conventions. Visual Basic includes an on-screen, tutorial style guide.

There are certain things that all the style guides have in common, despite terminological variations. All permit the display of one or more windows that can be divided into panes or child windows and used to provide views of different parts of an object, file or document. One may have either modal or modeless dialog boxes to give additional information or contextual clues. The windows contain objects to be acted upon and there is a menu bar detailing the actions permissible. The style guides agree on issues such as the use of single words for menu items. Most require a status bar at the bottom of the screen and 'gray out' unreachable menu options. They all support push buttons, radio buttons, check boxes, text fields, scroll bars, gauges and some kind of hierarchical menu display. Only some have spin buttons, list boxes, combo boxes, hierarchical scrolling lists, scrolling menus and so on, but there is usually an equivalent way to implement such features. Lee (1993) gives a high-level list of the features of these style guides.

One word of caution about these interface standards is in order. These are early days; documents do contain some standards – on issues like control positioning, color and so on – but they mostly contain only guidelines on design. It is a capital mistake not to be willing to vary your design away from the standard when you can justify the deviation as an improvement that is at least roughly compatible with the guidance.

Subtask: Use dependencies in the BOM to generate a first-cut project plan (Gantt chart)   Star rating **

Focus: Project planning
Typical activities for which this is needed: Project planning
Typical supportive techniques: Gantt chart, process modeling, project planning, subsystem identification

Explanation

It is reasonably easy to generate a first-cut project plan from the agreed BOM. The inheritance, composition, association mapping and usage links between classes define the dependencies in terms of the order that classes must be built in. Servers must precede clients and the complexity metrics can be used to give an estimate of relative build duration (absolute when we have properly calibrated the estimation model). Class builds can then be back-sequenced from the most dependent client. With a tool like SOMATiK that stores all these dependencies and the product metrics, these data can be exported to a project management package such as MS Project for subsequent amendment by a skilled project manager.

Task: Develop BOM   Star rating **

Focus: Modeling the business
Typical activities for which this is needed: Requirements engineering, analysis and model refinement
Typical supportive techniques: Agents, rôle play, scripting, task decomposition, task scripts, use cases

Explanation

The TOM focuses on business processes and is at the high level. It can be best described by tasks, task scripts, task cards and so on. Although tasks can be regarded as objects, they are reified processes and need to be translated (smoothly as it happens) into business objects. Business objects can be considered to be at the same level of abstraction as system objects but in the business rather than the technical domain. Business objects thus have a technical flavor while retaining a nomenclature immediately recognizable as belonging to the business domain. Once agreed with management and users, the business object model is the starting point for technical development and from this can be derived cost estimates and a first cut at the project planning, perhaps using Gantt charts.

Task: Develop software development context plans and strategies   Star rating **

Focus: Organizational standards and strategies
Typical activities for which this is needed: Resource planning
Typical supportive techniques: Database authorization, password protection, physical security, process modeling, wrappers

Explanation

Large-scale software planning must depend upon business decision making. In this task, OPEN focuses on those organizational-level (as opposed to project-level) decisions which define the organizational culture and the software development paradigm. Planning at this level must also take into account the existing culture.

Constantine and Lockwood (1994) describe four stereotypical organizational cultures: closed, random, open and synchronous. They argue that unless such organizational self-assessment is undertaken, project management – and also change management (from traditional to OO) – will likely be unsuccessful.

Subtask: Develop capacity plan   Star rating ***

Focus: Hardware/software size
Typical supportive techniques: Cost-benefit analysis, DCS optimization, internet and web technology, statistical analysis, volume analysis

Explanation

Capacity planning focuses on calculating the required sizes for CPUs, disks and so on. For OO systems, it is no different than for non-OO ones. There are basically two techniques: simulation or queuing-theory approaches. A standard text may be consulted.

Subtask: Develop contingency plan   Star rating ***

Focus: Failsafe plan with respect to unforeseen catastrophes
Typical supportive techniques: Cost-benefit analysis

Explanation

A contingency plan is a plan to avoid failure should some catastrophe occur. Contingencies vary depending upon the organization and the criticality of its operations. For banks and other financial institutions, hot sites may be needed so that should physical or software failure cause the system to shut down, the business is not disrupted for more than a few hours – several days' failure can mean the total failure of the business. Contingencies might also include, in the context of OT, the development of some plan should the selected compiler or CASE tool be unavailable or should it fail in some unforeseen way. What is the back-up strategy? What is the contingency should delivery be delayed? A company without a contingency plan is either non-commercial or lacking in common sense.

Subtask: Develop security plan   Star rating ***

Focus: Access violation protection
Typical supportive techniques: Database authorization, password protection, physical security

Explanation

Security should be considered for a variety of vulnerable areas. User security and authorities should be considered to protect the system against unauthorized access to information through system screens and reports.

Secondly, communications security should be considered to protect the system against unauthorized monitoring of or interference with information as it is communicated between physical nodes. Ideally, this should be an issue for the choice of DCS or for the implementation of the communication logic, rather than an issue for design of the application.

Furthermore, software component security should be considered to prevent unauthorized client processes requesting services of system resources through the standard message-passing mechanism. This last area is mostly affected by object orientation.

Object-level access control should be considered. In this way, an object may be designed and built so that it will only provide its services to authorized client objects. This provides a way of implementing software component security. If the DCS provides adequate security then little is required of the designer. However, if the DCS does not adequately support security, it should be considered in the modeling process (for example, Task: Identify CIRTs) and built into objects in Task: Code.

Information must be obtained from users pertaining to security requirements. This information should include data on the organizational rôle responsible for creating objects, those rôles with the authorization to create, read, update and delete objects. Further information should include the methods taken to prevent invalid access to and tampering with objects and how and where objects should be stored off-site as part of the contingency plan.

Subtask: Establish change management strategy   Star rating ***

Focus: Delineate appropriate strategy for change management
Typical supportive techniques: Risk analysis, team structuring

Explanation

Transitioning to OT is not just a simple matter of replacing a structured method and a set of tools by an OO one. OO is a way of thinking, a mindset, and not merely the adoption of a language (especially if that language is C++!). Some of the organization issues which must be addressed seriously by those transitioning to OT are as follows.

- Creating the 'new culture': this includes a focus on quality, reuse, high modularity in both design and coding, more emphasis on requirements engineering and analysis, a cleaner and more frequent dialog between developer and user.

- Evaluating what rôle reuse has to play in the organization: initially, focus should *not* be on reuse as a rationale for adopting OT. However, it should be part of the new culture insofar as it should become second nature and should certainly not be an 'add-on.'

- How to assess and award productivity bonuses: in a software development environment where reuse of analysis, design and code is practised, the best developers are those who *do not* write code. Traditional productivity metrics emphasize personal productivity in terms of output of lines of code per unit time. In good OO projects, that can be a negative value. One manager at the OOPSLA 94 metrics workshop was puzzled in how he reported to his management that the size of his software as it neared completion was shrinking yet proposing that the members of his team were being highly productive and deserved recognition. The number of completed task points may serve as a good preliminary metric for this purpose since it ought to be correlated with business benefits.

- Whether to move to OT wholesale or incrementally and, in the selected scenario what is, or should be, the rôle of retraining. A total commitment is dangerous in the sense that any failure is a company-wide failure. On the other hand, an incremental move brings with it the danger that the move will not be considered seriously by either developers or managers. Indeed, it is more likely that developers will not put in any effort to learn the new paradigm and will continue to code in a non-OO framework despite using an OO language, such as C++ or Java, in which to do it. It is better to invest heavily in retraining at *all* levels and commit to the move. Having done so, it then becomes feasible to move the organization part by part or project by project – so long as the overall elapsed time is not overly long. In this way, small glitches can be isolated and treated without disrupting the whole of the organization's day-to-day business.

Change management is so important and wide in its remit that whole books have been written about the possible pitfalls that may degrade the experience (Webster, 1995).

Subtask: Establish data take-on strategy   Star rating *

Focus: Delineating of policy for incorporation of non-OO data
Typical supportive techniques: ORBs, wrappers

Explanation

There is nothing different here about OO systems. There is the usual choice between big-bang and phased approaches – and the usual cost and ennui.

Subtask: Integrate with existing, non-OO systems   Star rating **

Focus: Legacy systems, migration
Typical supportive techniques: ORBs, wrappers

Explanation

There are a number of scenarios in which an OO application should interoperate with existing non-OO systems (Appendix D).

Object wrappers can be used to migrate to OO programming and still protect investments in conventional code. The wrapper concept has become part of the folklore of object orientation but, as far as we know, the term was first coined by Wally Dietrich of IBM (Dietrich et al., 1989) though it is also often attributed to Brad Cox and Tom Love, the developers of Objective-C, but in a slightly different context. There are also claims that the usage was in vogue within IBM as early as 1987.

The existence of large investments in programs written in conventional languages such as Assembler, COBOL, PL/1, Fortran and even APL has to be recognized. It must also be understood that the biggest cost associated with these 'legacy' systems, as Dietrich calls them, is maintenance. Maintenance is costly because, in a conventional system, any change to the data structure requires checking every single function to see if it is affected. This does not occur with OO systems due to the encapsulation of the data structures by the functions that use them. However much we would like to replace these old systems completely, the economics of the matter forbids it on any large scale;

there are just not enough development resources. What we must do is build on the existing investment and move gradually to the brave new world of object orientation.

It is possible to create object wrappers around this bulk of existing code, which can then be replaced or allowed to wither away. Building object wrappers can help protect the investment in older systems during the move to OO programming. An object wrapper enables a new, OO part of a system to interact with a conventional chunk by message passing. The wrapper itself is likely to be written in the same language as the original system, COBOL for example. This may represent a very substantial investment, but once it is in place virtually all maintenance activity may cease; at least this is the theory.

Migration and interoperation with non-OO systems are discussed in full detail in Appendix D.

One may conclude that, until much more experience has been accumulated, the best approach to migration of legacy systems with significant data management complexity is to build wrappers that support OO front-ends and to build the required new functions within the front-ends. The tandem strategy can be used only when there is little overlap and separate databases will have to be maintained. The exceptions to this are when the existing system already has a coherent data-centered structure that facilitates translation or when the benefits of the migration are large enough to justify the cost of building a very complex wrapper along the lines of the take-over strategy. If there is an existing DBMS this can be wrapped as a whole and maintained for a long time as the wrapped functions are gradually migrated. Then, at some point, one can move all the data at once to an OO database if desired and eliminate the database wrapper. This is a special variant of the translation strategy where the database is one huge 'coherent chunk.' It is probably the ideal option for many organizations already obtaining satisfactory performance from their relational databases. A good wrapper for Oracle or Sybase, probably written in C++, is a very sound investment in terms of migration strategy.

Subtask: Tailor the lifecycle process   Star rating *

Focus: Identification of an industry-specific process based on OPEN guidelines
Typical supportive techniques: Process modeling

Explanation

It is clear that no one methodology can satisfy all projects. If it could, then it would be so unwieldy when applied to small projects as to be unusable. OPEN offers the middle ground with a methodology that contains many options from which to choose. When that choice has been made, the resulting method, tailored to your organization and your project, is readily learnable and becomes your organizational standard. However, the method is completely compatible with the published (and larger, more comprehensive) OPEN methodology, as described in this text.

The OPEN lifecycle model, the contract model (Section 2.6), offers an overall number of activities and some likely connection paths. In this task, you choose which of those paths are appropriate; which tasks should be used to support those activities. Which techniques should be used can be left as less prescriptive since the way you accomplish the result (the outcome of the task) has less impact on project management – so long as the choice is one from several, all being equally efficient and effective techniques, the choice being merely that of personal taste, past experience, and so on. In this way, the methodology description can be likened to a salad bar (Reenskaug et al., 1996, p. 6): the chef prepares a number of dishes for your delectation, but it is up to you the customer (read developer) to choose what delights your palate and avoid those items you find unpalatable. This type of self-selected or tailored methodology approach is also advocated in MOSES and OOram, particularly.

Task: Evaluate quality   Star rating **

Focus: Quality of all deliverables
Typical activities for which this is needed: Evaluation, user review
Typical supportive techniques: Assertion language, BNF, class naming, code/document inspections, cohesion measures, complexity measures, connascence, contract specification, defect detection, encapsulation/information hiding, formal methods, function points, fuzzification, GQM, metrics collection, responsibilities, reuse metrics, simulation, standards compliance, TQM, task points, usability testing, use cases, videotaping, walkthroughs

Explanation

A prime focus in OPEN is quality since it is imperative that any classes generalized for future addition to the company's library of classes be of guaranteed quality. This involves not only code testing but also an assessment of the compatibility of the class with other library classes (in other words, the class library structure). Its potential usefulness in the company's specific business domain is assessed. In other business domains an assessment is made of whether profits can be reaped by resale. Finally, and perhaps most importantly, there is the assessment of the standard of its documentation. Continuous monitoring of classes during development, using quality mechanisms such as assertions, assists here.

Quality is more than end-phase testing. Testing identifies 'OK' or 'needing rework' (Zultner, 1989; as quoted in Adams, 1992). Quality is built in *throughout* the development process, not as a one-off quality assessment test of the final product. Thus this task spans the whole lifecycle. Adams (1992) advocates short cycle times in a 'constant quality management' framework (Figure 5.7). Metrics provide the tool to accomplish this quality goal.

Table A.9. Design guidelines (after Henderson-Sellers and Edwards (1994) – derived from information in McGregor and Sykes (1992)).

---

(1)   The only members of the public interface of a class should be methods of the class.

(2)   A class should not expose its implementation details, even through public accessor operations.

(3)   An operator should be a member of the public class interface if and only if it is to be available to users of instances of the class.

(4)   Each operator that belongs to a class either accesses or modifies some of the data of a class.

(5)   A class should be dependent on as few other classes as possible.

(6)   The interaction between two classes should involve only explicit information passing.

(7)   Each subclass should be developed as a specialization of the superclass with the public interface of the superclass becoming a subset of the public interface of the subclass.

(8)   The root class of each inheritance structure should be an abstract model of the target concept.

(9)   A set of reusable classes should make maximum use of inheritance to model relationships of the problem domain.

(10)   Limit the number of methods that must understand the data representation of the class.

Evaluating quality is difficult and seldom quantitative. Heuristics do, however, exist for 'good design' (see the guidelines in Table A.9) and are closely linked to and quantified by OO metrics – a rapidly developing area of OO research and technology transfer (e.g. Lorenz and Kidd, 1994; Henderson-Sellers, 1996). Software metrics or software measures attempt to quantify either the software product or the software process. Product metrics are typically code-oriented, measuring parameters such as module size or the complexity of the intramodule logical structure. Process metrics typically attempt to relate estimates of the product metrics, made relatively early in the lifecycle, to overall effort required in order to produce costing estimates.

Assessment reports are useful for evaluating the degree to which any desired objective is being met. The relevant information is defined using quality templates and one informal assessment procedure is shown using assessment scorecards in Figure A.7. Goldberg and Rubin (1995, p. 78 et seq.) have found this informal approach to be most useful. Here the focus is on stating the objective and then comparing the results with this stated objective. Each column of the scorecard describes a particular dimension such as related processes, product or resource objectives. For example, on a product process model scorecard the dimensions may be testing, coding, interproject reuse, configuration manage-

Activities	Dimensions			
	Dimension 1	Dimension 2	Dimension 3	Dimension 4
Activity 1	●/√		● /√	
Activity 2		●/X	● /?	●/√
Activity 3	●/√		● /X	●/?
Activity 4		●/√	● /X	●/√
Activity 5	●/?	●/?	● /√	
Comparison	●	○	◒	◒
Theory/Practice	Theory	Practice	Practice	Theory
Overall Assessment	◒	○	◉	●

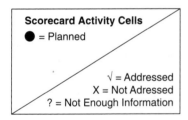

Scorecard Activity Cells
● = Planned
√ = Addressed
X = Not Adressed
? = Not Enough Information

Comparison with Early Adopters
◉ Well Ahead of the Game
◒ Ahead of the Pack
○ Par with the Industry
◐ Trailing the Majority
● Far Behind the Pack

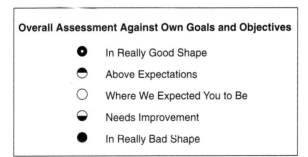

Overall Assessment Against Own Goals and Objectives
◉ In Really Good Shape
◒ Above Expectations
○ Where We Expected You to Be
◐ Needs Improvement
● In Really Bad Shape

Figure A.7   Assessment scorecard (after Goldberg and Rubin, 1995).

ment, and so on. The first column of the scorecard lists the activities performed. Each row of the card thus describes the extent to which the activity supports each dimension, each cell being divided in two. The legend of Figure A.7 notes that the top half of the cell is either empty or has a bullet which indicates that the activity was planned to address the dimension. The lower half contains information as to what degree the activity did in fact do this. The last three rows of the scorecard use:

- comparisons against other companies in an overall ranking compared with the 'pack'
- an assessment of theory versus best practice
- an overall aggregate assessment based on all the information presented.

Each project is recommended to have between 4 and 10 of these assessment scorecards which are found (Goldberg and Rubin, 1995, p. 80) to be easily understandable and can also be used to indicate temporal progress.

Another important measure of quality is the number of defects. Defect measures may be in terms of numbers of defects and their temporal trend (industrial statistical quality control may be useful here); the absolute number of occurrences of defects; the number of defects fixed.

Defects numbers should be tracked, using the templates described using appropriate OPEN techniques. Inspections, walkthroughs and reviews are all useful in uncovering the existence of defects. Testing is also of prime importance here. Defects should be reported, in some organizationally standardized format – and acted upon.

Subtask: Analyze metrics data   Star rating ***

Focus: Quality evaluation
Typical supportive techniques: Statistical analysis

Explanation

Following metrics data collection, appropriate statistical techniques are required to analyze and understand the implications of the raw data. Since this is pretty much standard inferential statistics, not too much time will be spent discussing it while recognizing that you might wish to stop reading here and pick up your favorite statistics text to refresh your mind on the topic!

Box whisker plots are a useful way of representing robust statistics (medians and quartiles rather than means), needed to describe the non-Gaussian, ordinal-scale data sets typically associated with typical structural complexity metrics (Kitchenham and Linkman, 1990). They provide an immediate visual representation of the main features of the distribution and can be supplemented by detailed distribution information in tabular format.

Care must be taken *not* to use means and standard deviations unless the data is for a metric taken on the interval, ratio or absolute scale. Much of software metrics data is on the ordinal scale.

Subtask: Evaluate usability   Star rating *

Focus: Quality evaluation from a user's perspective
Typical supportive techniques: Usability testing

Explanation

This is not a specifically OO issue but is discussed in outline in Graham (1995a).

Evaluation of the user interface is very important. HCI reviews and expert walkthroughs are usually enormously useful. Other valuable evaluation techniques include questionnaires, observational studies and test script reports. Nielsen and Mack (1994) suggest the use of the following.

- Performance tests – in which a user is given a prototype GUI and asked to perform some task depicted in a single use case. Errors made are videotaped and timed for later analysis.
- Cooperative evaluation – a performance test but conducted by a team (usually of three) involving both users and designers.
- Usability measurement questionnaire – a standard statistical survey based on predetermined questions on usability.
- Expert review – usually in terms of an internal or external consultant.

Useful GUI metrics include the time it takes to learn an operation or to use a whole system, the time it takes to carry out a particular task, the average user's error rate, satisfaction indices and the skill retention over time. These metrics imply that a budget for experimentation and data collection be created. Also, it should be noted that the existing system should be measured with respect to these metrics during requirements capture if the metrics are to be of use in assessing benefits.

For mass-market products it is often worth investing in full-scale usability workshops wherein trial users are recorded, observed and measured carrying out common operations. This is usually too expensive for custom developments but would be worthwhile for systems going into very wide use or where paybacks are very high and sensitive to usability. Observational studies of any kind imply the need for usability metrics to be agreed. One can measure learnability by comparing task execution times before and after extended use. Other metrics have already been discussed. Usability testing is easier if it is supported by specific software support tools although this is most beneficial for a mature product where comparisons with earlier versions are possible. Usability testing also uses task analysis as a key technique.

Usability tests should examine users' rôles, skill levels, frequency of use and the possible social, cultural and organizational variations. OPEN emphasizes the centrality of user rôles; that is neither the users nor their rôles but the combination of a user adopting a rôle: an actor. This notion combines the skill level and organizational rôle in a single, finer-grained concept. Usability studies may further distinguish computer and application skill levels and most approaches to HCI use a simple knowledge-level model such as:

(1) beginner (no knowledge)

(2) learner (knowledge incomplete, encoded as rules)

(3) competent (knowledge complete, compiled and not accessible to consciousness)

(4) expert (knowledge subject to critique and refinement).

Usability testing requires careful experimental design and statistical analysis. It is therefore expensive. At the simplest level it must identify the categories of the most frequent users, such as: frequent, competent with computers, domain learners, English-speaking or well-educated. The tests should take account of transfer effects between different environments and this may, for example, lead to the need for a user interface that looks the same on different platforms. An additional difficulty with testing GUIs arises from their graphical nature. Whereas a command-line interface can be tested by producing a test harness that compares textual output across trials, often GUI tests have to compare bitmaps of output. This is complicated by the need to ignore irrelevant variations, such as the final position of the mouse pointer, which makes careful design of the tests very important. For all this, studies of two projects at IBM have showed that big savings can result from thorough usability engineering; as large as $2 saved by productivity gains for every dollar spent.

Subtask: Review documentation   Star rating ***

Focus: Quality review of final documentation in comparison with stated goals and objectives
Typical supportive techniques: Code/document inspections

Explanation

The purpose of reviewing documentation is to ensure that the current design is being adequately documented in the various deliverables. Documentation review should be carried out at regular intervals (i.e. weekly, monthly) or at predetermined 'breakpoints' in the development process – for example, at the end of each activity. In particular, the evaluation activity should have documentation assessment as a prime focus.

All documents must be reviewed in the contexts of

(1) Existence – a check can be made for mandatory and recommended documents. These could be mandatory because of the lifecycle being used or mandated by the organization.

(2) Accuracy and consistency checks of the models used. For example, all CIRTs shown in inheritance diagrams must have a class specification and should appear in one of the layered class diagrams. CASE tools, as they become increasingly available, can be useful here.

This task is essentially a check on the deliverables before final presentation.

Task: Identify CIRTS   Star rating **

Focus: Identify classes, instances and types (CIRTs)
Typical activities for which this is needed: Evolutionary development, requirements engineering
Typical supportive techniques: Agents, class naming, ER modeling, event modeling, fuzzification, interviewing, Kelly grids, partitions, responsibilities, rôle play, scripting, simulation, textual analysis, use cases

Explanation

A core task in an OO systems development is the identification of likely or candidate CIRTs. Early in the process of deriving a model, the task will essentially be one of discovery, whereas later in the process it will be more one of refinement and invention. Refinement will never result in a 'perfect' model but will, after a few iterations, lead to a stable model. Newly discovered CIRTs should be documented in the CIRT model and in the class specification and will be refined as the development proceeds.

Subtask: Determine initial class list   Star rating **

Focus: Initial CIRTs
Typical supportive techniques: Abstraction, agents, CRC cards, responsibilities

Explanation

Identification of CIRTs is at the same time both easy and hard. Meyer argues that 'objects are just there for the picking!' (Meyer, 1988, p. 51). However, while this may be true in a well-understood and defined domain such as data structures, well-defined business objects are significantly harder to find.

Firesmith (1992) suggests using the following list:

- nouns
- DFDs
- recursion
- ADTs and abstract state machines
- states
- attributes operations and exceptions
- requirements
- CRC cards
- OO diagrams
- object abstraction
- personal experience
- OO domain analysis
- previously developed software
- repositories.

Noting that identification of CIRTs is a difficult step, he offers a wide selection of techniques and a variety of conceptual abstraction levels. In a later publication (Firesmith, 1993) he groups these into recommended, traditional and miscellaneous approaches (Table A.10) together with additional elaboration.

Possible candidate classes thus include:

- real-world objects of the model, such as tanks, pipes, chairs
- abstract concepts of the model, such as a race, a demand curve, a maintenance schedule, an asset
- abstract or real processes, such as a waste-water process, cruise-control process
- rôles, such as manager, student, employer, a threat
- events in a system, such as commands in a user interface
- events to be remembered, for example ATM transactions, overflow events in a tank
- physical devices, such as sensors and printers.

Classes should typically represent a large collection of actual objects. If there is only a single object (single instance) within one specific class it is unlikely (though not impossible) that this class will remain in the system.

Identity is the fundamental notion of objects. If objects of a class cannot be counted, that is they do not have identity in their own right, then they are not true objects and the classes from which they are derived are probably not good ones.

Table A.10. Some recommended approaches for finding CIRTs (after Firesmith, 1993).

Recommended approaches
- Using object abstraction
  - using the types of the modeled entities
  - using the definitions
  - using object decomposition
- Using inheritance
  - using generalization
  - using subclasses
- Using OO domain analysis
- Using repositories of previously developed software
  - reusing application frameworks
  - reusing class hierarchies
  - reusing individual objects and classes
- Using specification and design languages
- Using personal experience

Traditional approaches
- Using nouns
- Using traditional data-flow diagrams (DFDs)
  - using terminators on context diagrams
  - using data stores on DFDs
  - using complex data flows on DFDs

Miscellaneous approaches
- Using abstract data types and abstract state machines
- Using states
- Using resources
  - using attributes
  - using operations
  - using exceptions
- Using requirements
- Using CRC cards
- Using entities on entity–relationship attribute (ERA) diagrams
- Using OO diagrams
  - using nodes on semantic nets
  - using nodes on message diagrams

Each class should immediately be given a unique name that is concise yet informative. A description of the meaning of each class should also be given. Classes may also be identified from scenarios. Once again, nouns within the scenario are candidate classes. Other sources of classes are class libraries or already specified components. Also data models or database schemes provide indications of classes useful in the domain.

Graham (1995a, p. 304) observes that, *inter alia*:

- a good reusable object represents something universal and real
- an object is a social animal and its services may be used by other classes; if not, then ask: What is its function? – or delete it from the model
- although an object should not be so complex as to defy comprehension, it should encapsulate some reasonably complex behavior in order to justify its existence
- avoid 'accidental' objects, that is those objects that are characterized by nothing but a list of adjectival phrases.

Subtask: Identify persistent classes   Star rating **

Focus: Persistence/data storage
Typical supportive techniques: Object retention requirements, path navigation, RDBMS interface reliability requirements, security requirements, specification, versioning, volume analysis

Explanation

Specification of persistence should generally be undertaken during OOP, although it may be possible to indicate it during OOAD. Persistent CIRTs are the results of a particular program execution, for example the results of a simulation run, or information that outlasts the program execution such as configuration information. This information may be read from a file, or stored as a persistent CIRT depending upon the nature of the storage environment (for example relational database, objectbase or operating system files). Unless persistence is a major part of the application, for example a database system, specifying CIRTs that are to be saved to secondary storage can be left until quite late in the development process.

Specialized CIRTs may be needed for interfacing to relational and object databases and for addressing the concerns of concurrency, distribution, versioning, security and real-time.

Subtask: Identify rôles   Star rating *

Focus: Modeling
Typical supportive techniques: Rôle modeling

Explanation

It is only just recognized how often rôles occur in an object model. Consider a typical example in an introductory OO text: 'Consider an employee who is (of course) a person.' Thus, they say, this is a simple example of inheritance since an employee is a type of person and thus CIRT employee inherits from person. This is wrong.

The person is only taking on a rôle temporarily and may indeed take on more than one rôle contemporaneously. Thus an individual is a person (permanently), a teacher (Tuesday nights), a researcher (Fridays), an administrator (Wednesday) and an international speaker (occasionally). In fact in the last rôle, we might also be a teacher and a traveler and probably a foreigner (or alien).

How significant rôles are in the object paradigm, in contrast to classes and objects and, more recently in OOAD, types, is still open to question. OPEN and OOram support rôle identification much more strongly than in other approaches.

Subtask: Refine class list   Star rating **

Focus: Iterative refinement of CIRT list
Typical supportive techniques: Abstraction, responsibilities

Explanation

Identification of CIRTs will likely produce a long list of 'candidate objects.' In this task, we re-evaluate that initially identified list of CIRTs and iterate around a small number of times to try to refine the list of CIRTs.

During refinement the aims are (Wirfs-Brock et al., 1990; Graham, 1995a, p. 301):

- elimination of duplicates
- classification of objects as either within or outside the system
- elimination of 'accidental' objects and demotion of them to attributes; for example, the noun phrase 'expensive, prickly red roses wrapped in grease-proof paper' is not a new class of objects, but rather a rose object with many attributes
- insertion of relationship objects (if any)
- detection of nouns used as stand-ins for verbs.

Task: Identify context   Star rating *

Focus: Identify the needs of the business (end-)user
Typical activities for which this is needed: Requirements engineering

Explanation

It is important that the context of the problem be identified. This is the OO equivalent of the standard context model and is, in many ways, little different. The aim of this task is therefore to set the boundaries, to identify what is feasible and what should be deferred as 'too hard' or irrelevant.

Task: Identify source(s) of requirements   Star rating **

Focus: Identify the needs of the business (end-)user
Typical activities for which this is needed: Requirements engineering

Explanation

Identification of sources of requirements is logically the first step in eliciting system requirements. Initially, the analyst must be able to identify the specific requirements made on the system by various stakeholders. He or she must also become acquainted with the problem and the problem domain. Information must be collected spanning not only the hard and quantitative aspects (specific tasks and boundaries), but also qualitative aspects (level of service expected, conflicts, politics, powerplays, aspirations, and so on of the stakeholders in the problem situation). This is then followed by the process of deciding on the level of relevance and significance of such knowledge to the problem situation.

There is, however, some confusion about where requirements come from. Loucopoulos and Karakostas (1995) state that some requirements elicitation approaches restrict the sources of requirements to human stakeholders only, while others also consider other potential sources. This is a statement that requires clarification. It must be noted that a distinction can be made between, first, sources of requirements, and, secondly, sources of requirement knowledge. While the latter may be a myriad of sources, the former must only include human stakeholders. After all, a 'form' does not and cannot 'require' the new system to behave in a certain way!

Sources of requirements

Business, being a human activity, implies that, in viewing the requirement space, various stakeholders might view the problem differently and regard, propose and expect different solutions to what they view to be the problem. It is therefore crucial to consider (at least) all stakeholders and stakeholder categories that could potentially have an interest in the system. Experience with systems methodologies (Mumford, 1985; Checkland and Scholes, 1990) has shown that an important classification of the roles that various stakeholders play within each system may be presented as below.

(1) Client(s): those for whom the system has been established. These can be beneficiaries, or victims.

(2) Actor(s): the participants who actually run or operate the system.

(3) Owner(s): the authority or entity, represented by a person or a group of people, that has the power to abolish it.

For example, in a typical MIS system (say a health insurance system), clients could include:

- members of the public and policyholders (for example patients lodging a health insurance claim, or a member of the public making an enquiry regarding membership conditions)

- end-users that interact with the system (for example health insurance claims-processing clerks)

- the accounting division of the health insurance company

- the Government (for example Ministry of Health or the Bureau of Statistics).

Actors could include:

- end-users that interact with the system (for example health insurance claims-processing clerks)

- systems administration staff

- systems maintenance staff.

Owners could include:

- the insurance company (board of directors)

- the Government (for example the insurance ombudsman).

From the above list, it is evident that a particular group of stakeholders may play a rôle as members of more than one category (for example end-users that interact with the system).

These stakeholder categories and their sub-groupings must be identified and their requirements sought with respect to each potential system implementation.

Having identified the sources of requirements, it is also essential to recognize that the acquisition of requirements information from these sources is not always a smooth and simple process. Some of the most important reasons for this are because stakeholders may:

(1) have difficulty describing their knowledge of the problem domain (for example when a nuclear scientist finds it difficult to explain the intricacies of a nuclear reactor control mechanism to a software requirements engineer with only a basic understanding of physics)

(2) have difficulty describing what they want (for example when a user finds it difficult to describe exactly how a user interface should behave, although quite clear in their own mind how it should operate)

(3) lack clarity about what they want (for example when the same user is not too certain whether to include or exclude a certain feature or style of presentation)

(4) be unwilling to cooperate (for example an employee who has a personal hidden agenda against the development of the system or some aspect of it).

Sources of requirements knowledge

As previously mentioned, knowledge of requirements may also come from sources other than human stakeholders. These other-than-human sources of requirements knowledge may be categorized into groupings such as:

- artifacts that are inputs into or are outputs from the system (perceived or actual), for example:
  - existing forms
  - procedures for interaction with the outside world
  - existing inflow and outflow of goods

- artifacts that relate to the process carried out or envisaged to be carried out by the system, for example
  - existing internal flows of information (internal procedures)
  - planned or perceived flows of information (plan documents and models)
  - existing transformations (internal procedures)
  - guidelines
  - existing scenarios and descriptions of the system
  - existing software systems in the domain

- artifacts that relate to the structure of the system. These may include:
  - existing prototypes
  - existing or planned databases and repositories
  - organizational arrangements and relationships (for example organizational charts)

- artifacts that belong to the environment of the system. Such as:
  - standards
  - legislation and conventions
  - associated organizations and regulatory bodies
  - sponsors
  - existing software systems belonging to other similar or associated domains.

Specific techniques of identification and categorization of these sources of requirements and requirements knowledge are explained elsewhere (Henderson-Sellson and Younessi, 1997).

Task: Identify user requirements   Star rating *

Focus: Identify the needs of the business (end-)user
Typical activities for which this is needed: Requirements engineering
Typical supportive techniques: Brainstorming, hierarchical task analysis, interviewing, questionnaires, RAD, RAD workshops, rôle play, scripting, simulation, use cases, videotaping

Explanation

The purpose of this task is to develop and refine a formal and stable user requirements specification. The *systems requirements documents* are prepared in the language of the user, as normal, and include timing details, hardware usage, cost constraints as well as problem specification and functional user requirements.

User requirements may be quite general. For example, the desire may be as broad as 'automate the accounting system at a cost of less than $200 000 using existing PCs and workstations.' In other words, it is a statement of a problem and some notion of constraints that apply, usually derived from external world budgetary consideration. For example, client–server architectures are currently gaining popularity. In such a distributed system, where several machines are networked together, such that the processing is distributed across several CPUs (several machines or one multi-processor machine), determining the appropriate configuration may be a business planning constraint. In this case, evaluation of the impact of such a choice may be important. At this stage, a software solution may or may not be indicated. Alteratives are evaluated by a feasibility study.

In summary, user requirements engineering therefore involves initial interviews with business users, followed by the development of scenarios which should be validated either by a prototyping effort or by walking through the scenarios with the users.

Subtask: Define problem and establish mission and objectives
Star rating **

Focus: Identification of the problem to be solved
Typical activities for which this is needed: Project initiation
Typical supportive techniques: Expected value analysis, interviewing, RAD workshops, scripting, simulation, throwaway prototyping

Explanation

Before embarking on the creation of a piece of software to 'do something neat,' it is clearly requisite (but so often ignored) that the business problem should be identified and clearly delineated. This is encapsulated in the organization's mission statement and its business objectives. These may already exist or require elicitation through interviews or RAD sessions with senior managers and other key personnel in the organization.

It is too easy to see the problem as 'automate the accounting system' or 'give the customer a faster turnround.' The first statement does nothing to define the problem (which is more likely to be something along the lines of create an efficient means to manage the accounts) and the second leaves us wondering who the customer is. Do we mean *all* customers or just the majority (say 90%)? What does faster mean? – Should it be measured for all customers? Should it be a relative or percentage change or ...? Feature creep often results in projects becoming stultified, never being delivered due to the new add-on feature being always 'almost ready.' This is a direct result of the original problem not being clearly defined and not being set in the context of the business ethos of the company.

The problem-solving literature is highly relevant here. What is the problem requiring a solution? What is the system to which this all applies? Where are the system borderlines? BON advises that the system borderline allows us to focus not only on the problem area to be modeled at the highest level, but also on the communication mode between the system model (of interest) and the external world (of no interest other than as a boundary condition). Good use of scenarios, use cases and task scripts can help by drawing a box around the system that is of relevance (the business system in the first instance). The inside of the box needs our further consideration; the outside does not.

Waldén and Nerson (1995) quote Marmolin (1993) on some guiding principles for user considerations.

- Identify the way in which the system will be used: enterprise goals, rôles, information flow and so on.

- Identify user groups and what degree of usage they will exhibit.

- Define the UI on the 'worst-case principle.'

- Use metaphors to help in delineating the system.

- Adopt a minimality principle by which only the required users' needs are solved – no more, no less (this prevents feature creep).

- Identify potential semantic errors by trying to understand the differences that must result when moving from a personal mental model to a different mental model and hence to the requirements, analysis, design and implemented system (see also Goldberg and Rubin, 1995, p. 337).

- Use transparent modeless dialogs so that the interface does not have to be learned and posits no barriers to the user.

External inputs and desired outcomes need to be clearly stated. For database applications, if timing considerations offer an important problem, then these need to be identified.

All of these analyses of the business domain and the problem that has been encountered will permit the objectives to be set. These should be realistic in terms of required usage, budget, technology (hardware and software) and resources (human and time). Awareness of the current 'state-of-the-art,' particularly in hardware and software, assists in setting realistic and achievable objectives. Prioritization of the objectives can be accomplished using techniques such as expected value analysis.

Subtask: Establish user requirements for distributed system   Star rating *

Focus: Distributed computing
Typical supportive techniques: Early prototype to exercise DCS

Explanation

User requirements can affect the decision of whether a distributed system is required. It also affects the relative priorities given to performance, fault tolerance and scalability via Task: DCS architecture specification (partitioning and allocation). Therefore location, concurrency and distributed systems specific constraint issues should be included in Task: Identify user requirements.

Location

Understanding the location of users and information sources assists in the allocation of processes and data to different physical nodes in the network. Furthermore, requirements may differ for users in different locations (Jain and Purao, 1991).

Concurrency in the problem domain

Requirements engineering should also look for concurrency in the problem domain. To identify that concurrency exists would often be enough in the requirements engineering stage. Concurrency is identified in scenarios using a distinction between concurrency within scenarios and concurrency between scenarios (Jacobson et al., 1992).

Constraints

Constraints are another form of requirement, that may be collected in the Task: Identify user requirements. Examples of constraints that are relevant to distributed systems (or the need for distributed systems) are performance, reliability, scalability, portability, human engineering and security. Of these, performance, reliability and scalability are often the most discussed in relation to distributed systems. Each of these should be considered and may lead to a decision to utilize a DCS approach.

Subtask: Establish user database requirements   Star rating ***

Focus: DB needs
Typical supportive techniques: Access analysis, audit requirements, object retention requirements, reliability requirements, security requirements, volume analysis

Explanation

Quantitative information on the volume of the objects stored, the ways in which the objects are accessed, the frequency of the accesses and so on is required from the users when designing a database for an OO system for the same reasons as when designing a traditional system, since one must ensure that the final physical design of the database maximizes all the criteria of the database system being developed, that is, time and storage requirements as well as the functional requirements. Performance issues are important.

Task: Maintain trace between requirements and design
Star rating *

Focus: Auditability

Explanation

One of the benefits of an OO development is the feasibility of auditability and traceability across the full lifecycle by use of the virtual seamlessness of an OO lifecycle. However, in order to gain full benefit from this traceability, it is an important task to have mandated a trace maintenance capability within the project. This means annotating design decisions in such a way that each code decision can be traced back first to design and then to the customer's problem. It is all too easy to lose this trace by ignoring the documentation. Even in an automated tool, such traces are vital and may not be automatically provided.

Task: Manage library of reusable components   Star rating **

Focus: Reuse
Typical activities for which this is needed: Other projects
Typical supportive techniques: Library class incorporation, refinement of inheritance hierarchies, reuse metrics

Explanation

The main management task for reusable libraries or repositories is to ensure that, once library components have been created, they can be easily accessed by potential future users. In particular, we need to consider

- classification of CIRTs; indexing and cataloging
- the need for browsing and retrieval tools and techniques

Classification of CIRTS; indexing and cataloging

Despite much research and experiment (e.g. Freeman and Henderson-Sellers, 1991; Waldén and Nerson, 1995; Thorne, 1997), there is still no accepted classification scheme for OO components. One favorite classification scheme is derived from the faceted classification scheme first discussed in detail by Prieto-Diaz and Freeman (1987) in a non-OO context. Some of the factors which need to be indexed include the particular functionality, perhaps constrained by a specific industry domain, possibly (if at the class level) written in a selected OOPL.

In selecting items for cataloging and storage, it is important that redundancy is avoided. Populating a library with essentially many versions of the same abstraction is counter-productive. As in good design of product or UI, it is also important to devise a scheme by which consistency is maintained. In other words, all components are documented in a clear and consistent manner. These goals are exemplified in the Eiffel class library documentation (Meyer, 1994).

The need for browsing and retrieval tools and techniques

It is critical that high-quality browsing and retrieval tools be available for managing OO component repositories. As these grow rapidly, it is of paramount importance that the developers can identify a component that fits their current need – and to do so within a short time span (possibly as short as 10 minutes). Otherwise, they are likely to recode/reinvent the abstraction rather than search in a library for an item they are not even sure exists therein.

In retrieving components, it is important that the tools utilized permit access to multiple users. Perhaps more importantly, it is the responsibility of the library manager to make all developers aware of the potential of the repository by advising them of what is available. On many occasions, this actually requires an advertising campaign, perhaps in the form of Cox's Software-IC catalogs. If developers are not aware of the existence of components, they are unlikely to seek them out in the repository.

Chargeback

The politics and chargeback of a library can be accomplished in several ways. The most likely is that of the two-library model (Henderson-Sellers and Pant, 1993). In Figure 4.10 we have library 1 of potentially reusable components (LPRC) and library 2 of adopted reusable components (LARC). Components are identified as 'potentially reusable' in the current project but are not generalized for future use (at a cost of possibly several hundred percent of the development cost) until their use is perceived in a later project. Only after refinement and testing by their use in (preferably) at least three projects can they be considered to be of high enough quality to be moved into the LARC.

Other chargeback options include the following.

(1) At the end of each project, investing effort (and hence money) into creating reusable, domain-level components from the best of the classes created for the current project. This was an early proposal which in reality does not work since there is neither time to undertake this, nor are there any obvious 'customers' who will pay for it.

(2) Bound into the project, the generalization for future reuse is accomplished incrementally: the G-C1 model (Menzies et al., 1992). Although some success in practice, it is not generally advisable for the same reasons as (1) (no obvious and equitable chargeback mechanism).

(3) Setting up an independent cost center. This is similar to (1) except that the 'customer' is the organization itself at a future date. Similar in operation to a standard 'emerging technology' group within an organization, this cost center is envisaged to run at a loss for the first couple of years (absorbing the overhead of creating reusable components from project-specific ones) and only later feeding these back (with an associated charge) to future projects within the IT development group. Because of the large initial investment, this is only a viable option for large companies and has been shown to work in some large telecommunications companies.

It should also be stressed that there is unlikely to be a single repository (or two if the two-library model is adopted). Libraries will be associated with different management levels within an organization and, at each level, will require different quality characteristics. Each individual developer will be likely to have their own 'library' of components. These may have (at least initially) few quality checks. As these are released to team developers, most developers prefer to 'spruce up' their code. Similarly, before an individual project team will release their components to the higher and broader divisional level, they will make sure that the components have been thoroughly tested. If not, they can anticipate many irate calls from a large number of users (whom they are unable to manage, limit or control in any way) to fix errors. Defects fixed late are well known to cost *significantly* more than errors caught and corrected early.

Task: **Map logical database schema**   Star rating **

Focus: Database
Typical activities for which this is needed: Evolutionary development
Typical supportive techniques: Normalization

Explanation

Mapping of the object class model to the database schema can be carried out only once the database model has been selected. The mapping to an objectbase is straightforward; only when a relational, hierarchical or network database is being used does this stage require any effort.

When a relational database is in use, the behavioral aspects of the object interaction diagram are not supported directly by the database management system. Some developers may prefer to convert the object model to an ER model, on the basis of familiarity. Undertaking such a mapping, while throwing away behavioral information, should nevertheless be fairly straightforward. Rules have already been presented (e.g. Rumbaugh et al., 1991; Jacobson et al., 1992, pp. 272–6; Crowe, 1993) for mapping the properties and relationships depicted in an object (structure) diagram into third normal form relations.

The output associated with this task is a logical database schema. If an objectbase is being used, the schema consists of a definition for each class of its properties and operations and its inheritance, aggregation and association relationships with other classes. For a relational database, the database schema consists of a list of relations and their attributes.

Task: **Map rôles on to classes**   Star rating *

Focus: Implementing rôles in code
Typical activities for which this is needed: Evolutionary development (OOP)

Explanation

Since rôles represent dynamic classification and since no current commercial OOPL supports rôles directly, there is the task of mapping the rôles identified in the analysis and design onto the classes which will eventually represent them in code. Since there is not necessarily a one-to-one relationship between rôles and classes/types in the language, other mappings may be needed (although a pattern for implementing rôles is to be found in Renouf and Henderson-Sellers, 1995 and much discussion on this topic in Reenskaug et al., 1996).

Task: **Model and re engineer business process(es)**
Star rating *

Focus: Evaluate and possibly restructure business processes
Typical activities for which this is needed: Programme planning, resource planning
Typical supportive techniques: Context modeling, cost–benefit analysis, visioning

Explanation

Business process engineering is all about profit optimization. If the new system is designed using systematic process engineering principles, is customer focused and targeted towards the real aims of the business, then it has a good chance of contributing to a lowering of costs and to customer satisfaction and hence to increased sales. Once these two aims are achieved, higher profits follow. The essential elements of doing business (re-)engineering are as follows.

Identify and state the purpose for the business engineering project

This purpose must be central, real, clear and profit oriented. By central, we mean that it must be critical to the business operation. As an example of the importance of this, we may note a major insurance conglomerate that went through a business re-engineering exercise which resulted in a significant and measurable improvement of certain of its processes; yet in six months the company was almost bankrupt. The reason was that the areas re-engineered were not central to the business. By real, we mean that the concern must not only be central but also believed by influential stakeholders to be so. Its achievement must be part of the vision of the organization. To be clear, the purpose must be stated in terms of measurable entities; only then can we be assured of the achievement of our purpose. Profit-oriented means that the purpose when achieved will significantly improve sales, lower costs or both. To do this, customer orientation is essential.

Use the purpose identified to clearly define and model the problem situation

Although related, defining the problem is not the same as stating the purpose for business process engineering. Here, an investigation into possible contributing factors is conducted and individual opportunities for redesign are identified. Sometimes it is useful to create a model of the present situation. This is done for a number of purposes including understanding, communication and analysis of the way things currently are. It must be stated that creation of such a model must not be allowed to stifle creativity, ingenuity or a revolutionary approach to business process design. This can happen easily if the engineer's views become biased towards the existing way of doing things.

In modeling problem situations, object technology, particularly context modeling (the topic of the first subtask), will prove beneficial.

Commence analysis using the identified opportunities and context models created

Note that this analysis is possible only if a defined and clear model of the process exists. Ishikawa diagrams, root cause and statistical analysis are amongst the main tools here. The purpose for this analysis is to identify and separate the common cause from the special cause. Once the common and special causes are identified, then a decision may be made whether to go for 'gradual process improvement' – that is the removal of special causes – or whether a whole new process is needed. If the latter is the case, then we have a design task on our hands: the task of designing a new business process.

Design a new business process

Here, the principles of process engineering, such as maximization of cohesion, minimization of coupling, parallelism, piping, boundary value analysis, flow analysis and process control, may be applied to the design of a new business process. This new process is aimed to be fundamentally different in its internal characteristics (that is the structures, transformations and interactions composing it), yet still fulfill the same purpose as the previous process. The new process must be demonstrably better or a new process must be developed that implements a new purpose, inspired by a new vision.

Model the new process

One central issue here is how do we capture and communicate this design? The answer is through creating a model of it. This is where object technology (business context modeling, see below) becomes an enabler.

Implement the model

Here the business engineer will decide on the performance of various tasks or roles. To do so a number of considerations such as the vision of the organization, best practices, current technology, funds and human resources available become prominent. Another critical task here is to decide what level of automation and technology to use. In terms of information support technologies, the re-engineered organization is in an enviable position as there is, through the application of object technology, a largely seamless path to the design and implementation of software systems.

Subtask: Build context (i.e. business process) model   Star rating *

Focus: Business
Typical supportive techniques: Context modeling

Explanation

Consider some business process or enterprise area within the grid. It could be an entire company, a division or department of that company or just a sole trader. It is most likely to be a process-oriented business area and may be represented by one cell in the grid or a few cells representing strongly linked processes. The cells of the grid carry the mission statement for this 'business area.' Our first

Figure A.8   External context model of placing orders (after Graham, 1995b).

task is to refine it into a series of measurable, prioritized objectives as discussed later. The business area is regarded for this purpose as an independent business. This business must communicate with the outside world to exist at all and, if it does so, it must use some convention of signs and signals thereto. These signals are called *semiotic acts* and are *carried* by some material substratum and involve a number of semiotic levels from data flows up to implicit social relationships. (Semiotics is the comparative study of sign systems and has been important in such diverse fields as mathematical logic, natural language processing, anthropology and literary criticism. It holds that signs can be analyzed at three levels at least: those of syntax, semantics and pragmatics.) For example, the substrate may consist of filled-in forms in a paper-based office environment and the social context might be that one assumes that no practical jokes are to be played. If the substratum is verbal (or written natural language) communication then we can speak instead of *speech acts* or *conversations*. These are the speech acts of Austin (1962) and Searle (1969). Semiotic acts can be represented by messages, which are directed from the initiator (source) of the communication to its recipient (target). A typical such message is represented in Figure A.8 where a typical customer places an order with the business. This message includes the definition of the reply: {order accepted|out of stock| etc.}. By *abus de langage* we shall identify semiotic acts with their representation as messages from now on although strictly they are different; the same semiotic act may be represented by many different messages. This defines equivalence classes of messages and we can think of our actual message as a representative of its class.

Note particularly that every message should support at least one objective and, contrarily, every objective must be achieved through the medium of one or more conversations (messages). This is an important check for the modeler to perform.

Of course, in business process re-engineering, we are anxious to capture not just the messages that cross the business boundary, such as order placement, but model the communications among our customers, suppliers, competitors, and so on. This provides the opportunity to offer new services to these players, perhaps taking over their internal operations – for a fee of course.

Figure A.9 shows how this might be applied in the simple case of delivering medical supplies, based on what actually happened at Baxter Healthcare (Short and Venkatramen, 1992). Originally, Baxter took an order from the hospital's

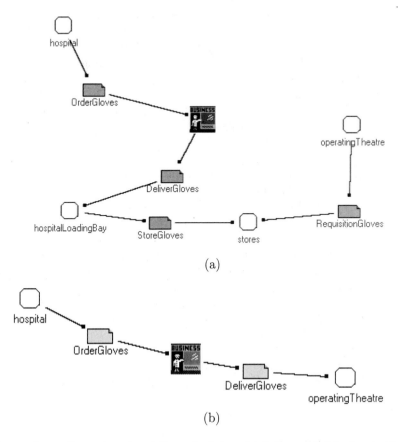

Figure A.9. Re-engineering delivery logistics: (a) before and (b) after implementation (after Graham, 1995b).

procurement department and delivered it to its loading bay. Then the hospital was responsible for storing the goods and delivering them to the appropriate operating theater (Figure A.9(a)). After re-engineering, goods such as surgical gloves are delivered direct by the supplier to the operating theater where they are required (Figure A.9(b)). Of course, the message labeled `OrderGloves` has been modified. This gives an advantage over other suppliers in terms of service, reduces the hospital's inventory and logistics costs and means that a higher price can be charged by the supplier while remaining competitive. It also makes the hospital more dependent on the supplier.

A semiotic or speech act is characterized at the semantic and pragmatic levels by a (possibly implicit) contract that both parties understand. The pragmatics of this contract represent a social relationship just as a message represents a semiotic act. Many contracts may express the same relationship so we choose one to represent its equivalence class.

A message implies that data flow, so that this approach generalizes data-flow modeling. However, it also enriches it considerably. For one thing, data flow in both directions along message links. This is why we have chosen to terminate message links at the recipient end with a filled rectangle rather than an arrowhead. The line segment is directed from the *initiator* of the communication not from the origin of the data.

A *business process* is a set of related messages. The relationship between the messages is encoded in a task ruleset.

It is inconceivable in most businesses that the message initiator does not wish to change the state of the world in some way as a result of the communication. This desired state of the world is the *goal* of the message and every message has a goal even if it is often unstated.

A goal is achieved by the performance of a *task*. The tasks we perform can often be reduced to a few stereotypes: typical tasks that act as pattern-matching templates against which real tasks can be evaluated and from which real tasks (or use cases) can be generated. This overcomes a possible objection that there could be an explosion in the number of tasks. Our experience indicates that there is no such explosion of tasks. It turns out that tasks can be modeled as objects within a *bona fide* object model in the task domain.

Tasks can be described in several ways but it is most useful to describe a task using a task script. A task script represents a *stereotypical* task (see e.g. Graham, 1995a; Henderson-Sellers and Younessi, 1997). This provides a notion of generalized exception handlers that does not seem to be available with use cases; where an exception (extends) path is specific to the use case.

Subtask: Build task object model   Star rating **

Focus: Business
Typical supportive techniques: Task scripts, hierarchical task analysis, task decomposition, task cards, textual analysis

Explanation

The external context model is a model of the messages that pass between the business (as defined earlier) and the external objects that represent its customers, suppliers and so on. It also includes messages that pass between external objects that are, as it were, out of context. This permits business process modeling and thus process innovation. The internal context model extends the external context by introducing an object representing the 'business support system' within the business that is to be built (usually a computer system). Also, within the business, we define actors in exactly the manner of Objectory: users adopting a rôle. The internal-context model is a model of messages that pass between the support system, actors and external objects. Note that a message sent by an external object to the business in the external context

Figure A.10   Internal context model showing an actor (after Graham, 1996a).

could, in the internal context, go directly to the support system (implying perhaps an electronic interface) or go to an actor. External objects and actors are *bona fide* objects with a contractual relationship to other objects in the model.

Messages are triggered by *events*. In the case of messages initiated by actors or objects internal to the support system, we usually know the causes of these events, because they are the direct result of task execution. When the initiator is an external object we nearly always lack this knowledge and the triggering event appears as a given object.

In Figure A.10 a salesman receives the customer's order and enters it into a business support system. The order is triggered by some unknown condition within the customer. Of course, this business support system is likely to be the computer system that we are trying to construct, but it could just as well be a card index or similar. Let us examine the RecordOrder message in more detail. Figure A.11 shows the detailed description of this message.

This high-level task can be decomposed into component tasks that, in SOMATiK (Bezant, 1995), are entered using a structure known as a task card. The decomposition may then be displayed in graphical form automatically as shown in Figure A.12.

The task card shown in Figure A.13 emphasizes that tasks are to be regarded as objects (either classes or instances). Tasks may be classified and (de)composed. They may send messages to exception handling tasks and may be associated with other tasks; for example, this task 'reminds one' of that task. Tasks have complexity and take time. This is usually only recorded for atomic tasks (defined below) since it can often be inferred for the composite tasks; the time taken is assumed to be the sum of the times for the components at the next level and so on. This of course can be overridden. Complexities are also additive unless otherwise stated. An atomic task is illustrated in Figure A.14.

External objects differ from actors in two senses: actors work within our business and we know more about the tasks they are carrying out. External objects may conceal tasks that we have no knowledge of, which will affect us because they lead to events that trigger messages or *triggering events*. Messages always have triggering events, though for actors and the system we usually know the task that has led to the event. External objects, such as customers, are usually represented in the BOM by objects with few or no operations but typically

```
┌──────────────────────────────────────────────────────────────────┐
│ ▭                        Message Properties                        │
├──────────────────────────────────────────────────────────────────┤
│ Label│RecordOrder│      │      OK      │     │ Glossary │   │ Cancel │ │
│                                                                    │
│ Source              Target         Trigger              Goal        │
│ │salesman│          │__SYSTEM│     │Receipt of order from c│ │Orders up to date│ │
│                                                                    │
│ Definition  │RecordOrder                        │   Task │enterOrder│ │
│ Description                                                         │
│ │See task card                                                  ▲│ │
│ │                                                               ▼│ │
│                                                                    │
│ Information                                                        │
│ │Customer details                                               ▲│ │
│ │Product details                                                 │ │
│ │Price details                                                  ▼│ │
│ Expected Result                                                   │
│ │Order accepted by system                                       ▲│ │
│ │                                                               ▼│ │
└──────────────────────────────────────────────────────────────────┘
```

Figure A.11.   The structure of the semiotic act: RecordOrder (after Graham, 1996a).

several attributes. It is important not to confuse these internal representations, which cannot do anything except store static data, with their real-world counterparts that do exhibit, often complex, behavior. Such internal representations of external objects are nearly always persistent objects.

Rulesets in tasks allow the sequencing and coordination of tasks to be described in the high-level SOMA rule language. This effectively describes the way tasks combine to form complete business processes.

Task modeling begins with a model of the business processes expressed in terms of messages between actors, external objects and systems. Each message has a goal which is associated with a unique task that, if performed, will help achieve the goal. This task can be decomposed into atomic tasks, each of which is given a task *script*.

The idea of task scripts has its theoretical roots in the AI script theory of

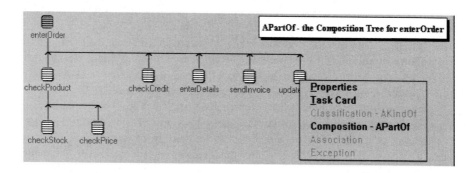

Figure A.12   Task decomposition (after Graham, 1996a).

Task Card
SuperTasks
Components
Associates
Exceptions
RuleSets
enterOrder
transactionCapture
checkCreditRating
checkProduct
enterDetails
sendInvoice
updateStock
outOfStock
Properties
AkO
ApO
Associations
Exceptions

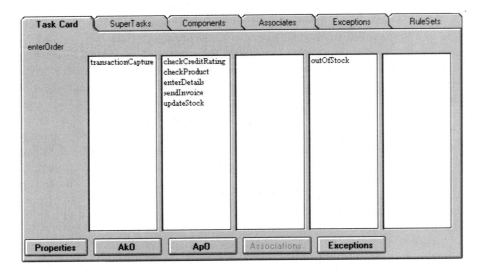

Figure A.13 A task card (after Graham, 1996a).

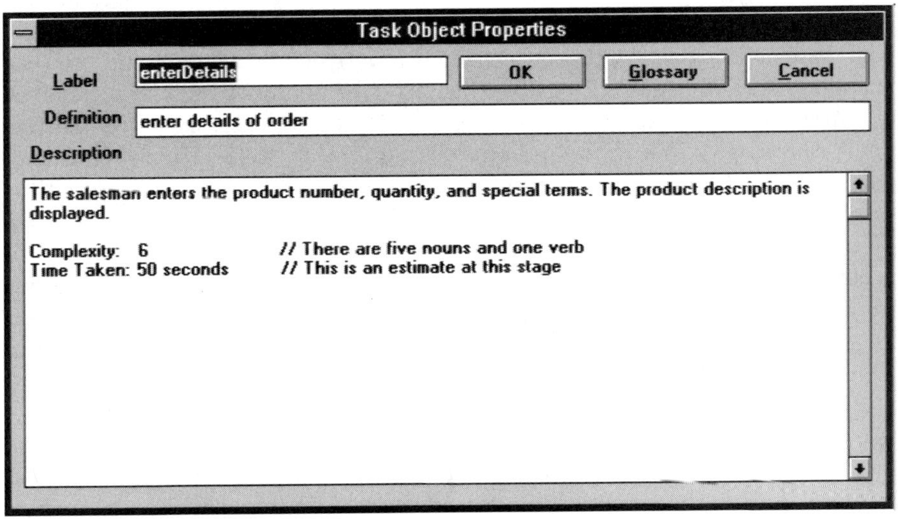

Task Object Properties
Label
enterDetails
OK
Glossary
Cancel
Definition
enter details of order
Description
The salesman enters the product number, quantity, and special terms. The product description is displayed.
Complexity: 6 // There are five nouns and one verb
Time Taken: 50 seconds // This is an estimate at this stage

Figure A.14 An atomic task (after Graham, 1996a).

Schank and Abelson (1977) and in the hierarchical task analysis popular in HCI work. Also, task scripts can be regarded as generic use cases. Use cases may be one sentence or an essay whereas task scripts should consist of a single sentence. This means that measurement of process models based on task scripts is much easier than with use cases. After building a TOM we use textual analysis to find objects and responsibilities and begin the construction of a BOM. Unfortunately this process is not seamless, violating one of the key benefits claimed for OO methods.

While conventional methods offer different modeling techniques for almost every lifecycle phase, OO methods introduce no such seams between analysis and logical design. There may be a 'seam' between logical and physical design when language-dependent features are introduced, but using a language such as Eiffel effectively eliminates this seam too. Thus OO development is claimed to be seamless (Waldén and Nerson, 1995). However, leaping from the requirements model to the system model, there remains more than a seam: a veritable abyss which, once leapt over, cannot be easily retraversed.

OPEN, in this context derived from SOMA, is supported by Bezant's SO-MATiK software tool.[†] Using SOMATiK there is a neat solution to this problem of the World/System seam which we will attempt to explain using a simple example.

An example

In our approach to OO requirements capture the first thing we do is establish the project mission and then drill down to a number of specific, measurable, prioritized objectives. Next, we build a business process context model showing: *external objects* (the stakeholders in our business area), internal *actors* and support systems. Messages representing semiotic acts between these items are then introduced. Figure A.15 shows how this might be applied to a system designed to capture foreign exchange trades. In this figure, the external object c/party sends a message to an actor (dealer) inviting him to strike a foreign-exchange bargain. The dealer then must negotiate the terms and enter the deal into the system. This is represented by the message `enter_deal`.

A goal for each such message and its associated task must be found. This is called the root task because it is at the root of a composition tree. The tree for `enter deal` is shown in Figure A.16. Analyzing and decomposing the tasks for each goal in this way is completed when atomic tasks, the leaf nodes of this tree, have been identified. Next task scripts for the atomic tasks are written.

Figure A.17 shows the script for the task `Enter Details`. It is easy to see from this script that a number of classes are mentioned; for example instruments, counterparties and deals. Also there are some obvious attributes, such as buy/sell. Finally the operation `enter` is mentioned. After a preliminary analysis of this and all the other scripts and a walk through the system design, we realize that the Task: Enter deal at the root of the tree corresponds to a responsibility of the class deals: `captureDeal` in this case.

---

† Bezant Ltd: `100073.1340@Compuserve.com`; Tel: 00-44-(0)1491-826005.

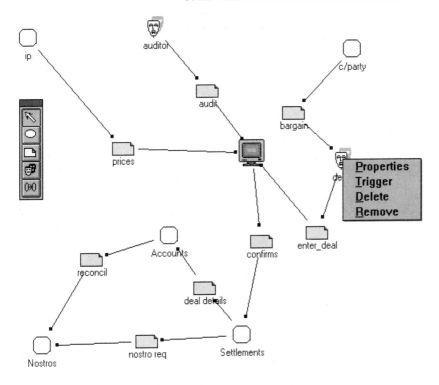

Figure A.15. Business process context model for Forex deal capture (after Graham, 1996b).

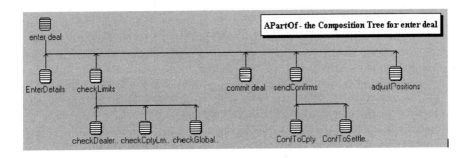

Figure A.16   Task tree for enter deal (after Graham, 1996b).

> The dealer enters the following data:
> counterparty, instrument, amount, rate, buy
> or sell, special settlement conditions

Figure A.17   Task script for EnterDetails.

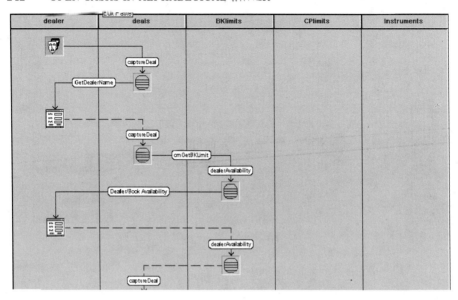

Figure A.18.   A small fragment of the active event trace of deal capture produced by SOMATiK.

The initiating operation field of the root task object **enter deal** contains the text: 'deals → captureDeal.' This makes a permanent link between the process plan represented by the root task and the software that will help the user execute this plan. As a consequence of this link we can animate the specification.

Selecting the trigger option on the menu shown in Figure A.15 will display a list of events that are relevant to the dealer actor. Selecting the event deal done will trigger the task **enter deal**. This, in turn, triggers its initiating operation: captureDeal. Any operation scripts and windows that the developer has created are executed and displayed for interaction now, and any calculations specified performed. While this is happening SOMATiK records a trace of the entire interaction in script form, which can be saved, replayed and displayed graphically in the form shown in Figure A.18.

Should the execution crash, some flames appear in this diagram directly underneath the operation that failed. The analyst can click on the operation, emend it and rerun the trace. The code is written in a high-level scripting language that can be learnt in a day or less. SOMATiK thus produces a prototype. However, this prototype must be thrown away because there are no facilities to develop sophisticated user interfaces. Code can, however, be generated at this point (currently in C++, Smalltalk or Newi).

Subtask: Convert task object model to business object model
Star rating **

Focus: Modeling

Explanation

Once the analysis of the context models, business processes and messages is completed, we end up with a set of task cards representing decomposed tasks. It is assumed that the decomposition continues to 'atomic' level where an atomic task is one that cannot be further decomposed without introducing terms foreign to the domain. Each atomic task is represented by a sentence – in a standard subject/verb/object form where possible. We call this the TOM, the sentences in which are now analyzed (preferably, we find, by users) to discover the true business objects. The technique used is basically textual analysis where nouns indicate objects and verbs operations. The classes so discovered are represented on class cards in the form shown in Figure 7.3. This process creates the BOM. Note that the class and task cards have exactly the same structure; they are both 'objects.' Class cards contain the entire model and, as with task cards, structure diagrams can be generated from them. These class cards are printed out on paper in a different format (see example in Figure A.19) for use in CRC-style walkthroughs to validate the model and produce event traces.

Subtask: Do user training   Star rating **

Focus: Education
Typical supportive techniques: CD-ROM technology, computer-based assessment, games, group problem solving, internet and web technology, lectures, rôle play, self-paced exercises, simulations, train the trainer, videotaping, workshops

Explanation

It is obvious that competent and effective utilization of a product goes a long way in ensuring the satisfaction of the user's needs. Customer training is therefore a most important element of the software lifecycle. Unfortunately, however, this is one step that is often missed, or considered to be outside the software process system boundary. This practice must cease if successful product utilization and happy customers are desired.

Customer training has three equally important facets; two have a process and the third a product focus.

1. Educating the customer (stakeholders) in the process, and in what is possible

The customer might know best about their requirements as they pertain to the business solution they are seeking. When it comes to how to satisfy these

```
Class Name        Product                                          Concrete
Description: A product has a code, a name, a description, and a price    Application



SuperClasses:
Commodity


Component Classes:




Attributes and associations:
Product Name
Product Description
Product Price
Product ID(Product, 1, 1)






Operations:                                        Servers
SetProductCode                              (Product - Create Product)
Establishes the product code and other details in the system database

ProductMargin




Rulesets:
ProductPricingPolicy



```

Figure A.19   An example printed class card (after Graham, 1996a).

requirements, however – that is how to build the product – 'the customer often does not know best.' Yet they invariably suggest, and often even dictate, a particular course of development action. Faced with this reality the first customer education task of the developer is to sufficiently educate the customer so as to ensure that project goals are attainable given current capabilities.

2. Educating the customer (stakeholders) in how to help you

Despite what most developers may have felt from time to time, customers do want a successful project outcome! And they are willing to help you achieve such success. It is after all to their own benefit. However, they often do not know how best to do this. It is again the responsibility of the developer to educate the customer in so doing. This educating exercise may take the form of the provision of short courses, workshops, or discussion sessions. It could be as simple as providing them with relevant literature from appropriately selected magazines, journals or research paper articles or books, or the introduction or provision of a consultant.

3. Educating the customer in how to best use the business solution provided

Amongst the three, this is the only facet of customer education that is somewhat frequently practiced by developers. This is the kind of customer education we call 'user training.' User training has a very precise aim. Its aim is to ensure that those users who interact with the system know how to do their jobs precisely, effectively and efficiently. As such, training programmes must be clear and understandable, targeted, precisely defined, and repeatably deliverable; but there is more. Most training programme developers make the mistake of only teaching functionality. Functionality is important but it has to be taught within context. The customer has to be introduced to what the system will do for him or her; not in terms of the system functions, but in terms of his or her organizational responsibility. As such, training must be provided in terms of: 'what the system will do for you,' and not in terms of: 'what the system can do.' To achieve this, it is important to do the following.

(1) Identify and put into groups those users whose interaction with the system is identical or very similar (for example data entry, claims processing, system administration and so on.)

(2) Identify those aspects of the system that impacts all users similarly and that all users need to know about. If sufficient material of this nature exists, create an 'introduction to . . .' course that is available to everyone who might come in contact with the system. If it is not sufficient to make up an independent course, then include these as the starting part of the first round of training courses.

(3) Then for each group identified in (1), develop a training course that describes how their jobs can be done more effectively using the system (their view of the system) and why. That is, what aspects and functionalities in the system ensure this. To contextualize your training, provide examples and exercises from the immediate area of responsibility of the group being trained. Make sure these examples are real, understandable and of high impact. Also let them get a glimpse of the workings of the product lying just outside their own immediate system view (up stream, down stream, side stream). This will help them understand how their utilization of the system might impact the effectiveness of their colleagues elsewhere.

(4) Pay particular attention to the training of those with systems administration responsibilities. The quality of system administrator training has an inverse relationship with the number of maintenance calls to be received!

In terms of techniques, a wide array of customer education techniques and technologies are available. These include:

- formal education
- short-term traditional training courses
- in-organization mentor-based training
- interactive multimedia
- the net
- other indirect training

Formal education, university or technical college education

Usually a prerequisite of entry into the organization, this type of training may also be provided as part of a long-term staff development strategy and not for the purpose of acquiring specific skills to use a particular system. This type of education finds importance in relation to the process facets of customer education (see above). The need for such education is usually determined by the user organization's management and not by the developer, although suggestions of system developers have often been considered. This is particularly the case in customer/developer relationships that span a number of years or relate to large and long projects such as defense contracts.

Short-term traditional training courses

Much more prevalent, and a lot more targeted towards teaching system functionality, are short-period training courses which may be provided as intense one to five day offerings composed usually of lectures and practice sessions. The alternative is two to three hourly offerings over a period of several weeks. It is customary that during the practice sessions, hands-on interactive experience with the product is provided. Written course notes are usually the main source of information in the traditional training courses.

In-organization mentor-based training

This approach uses the train-the-trainer principles. This is when the developer trains one or a handful of individuals in every or various aspects of the system and then the organization uses this individual or individuals to train the rest. It must be mentioned that in-organization mentor-based training must be used with extreme care in that the choice of instructor is critical in the success of this approach.

Interactive multimedia

Multimedia technology may be used to enhance or replace the role of the lecturer, or provide practice opportunity. CD-ROM, written course notes and videotape material may be used as sources of information. CD-ROM or CBA technology may be used for assessment and evaluation purposes. Computer networks may be used to simulate a multiperson work environment and interactivity, which adds to the real-world applicability of the training course.

The obvious advantages of this approach is that CBA may be administered on a self-paced basis, or at least reduce reliance on expert instructors. This characteristic makes this technology particularly useful for those situations where the software is installed by numerous customers, or the customers are geographically dispersed.

The net

The potential of the internet, particularly the World Wide Web, as a training-provision vehicle must not be ignored. This medium allows virtually all of the technologies mentioned above to be made available virtually instantly and worldwide. Considering the fact that your customers are very likely to have access to the internet, this becomes a really powerful training vehicle.

Other (indirect) training

A lot of organizations forget the importance of what we call indirect training. Into this category fall things such as publication of product newsletters, user-group meetings, provision of books and other instructional articles, help desks, and so on.

Finally it is of the utmost importance that, irrespective of the technology or context of the training courses provided, they must be informative, targeted and relevant, precise and error free, and most importantly interesting. Games, rôle plays, simulations, and group problem solving have all proven useful.

Subtask: Prepare ITT   Star rating *

Focus: Document preparation prior to letting a contract

Typical supportive techniques: Cost estimation, DCS architecture specification, interviewing, project planning, soft systems analysis, task points, TQM

Explanation

ITT preparation is the same as for conventional systems except that objects and OO products may be specified.

Task: Obtain business approval   Star rating ***

Focus: Seek and obtain management approval to proceed
Typical activities for which this is needed: Project initiation, project planning
Typical supportive techniques: Approval gaining, cost-benefit analysis, cost estimation, critical success factors, prototyping, risk analysis, throwaway prototyping

Explanation

Building software is undertaken to support the activities of the business and for no other purpose. Consequently, there needs to be senior management (business) support for the technical department of IT. Building a piece of software that fulfills no useful function to the business is a waste of money. So are projects that proceed and are later canceled.

It is recommended that at various stages during the software engineering lifecycle an evaluation is made of the utility of the software being developed in the context of the business domain. While being politically hard, it may sometimes be tactical to cancel a project before completion rather than let it fail later and at significantly greater expense and loss of kudos.

Task: Optimize reuse ('with reuse')   Star rating **

Focus: Capitalize on existing reuse assets
Typical activities for which this is needed: Other projects, build, project planning, program planning
Typical supportive techniques: CIRT indexing, contract specification, library class incorporation, pattern recognition

Explanation

The objective of this task is to maximize the reuse of library components that already exist. OO development emphasizes the importance of reuse in the development process and, as we have already discussed, the successful outcome of this methodology is a software base of reusable components. The fountain model of

Henderson-Sellers and Edwards (1994) (Figure 2.2) or of Reenskaug et al. (1996) (Figure 5.18) graphically represents this.

Surprisingly, as pointed out by Goldberg and Rubin (1995, p. 345), most methodologies do not provide support for optimizing the reuse of software assets (one exception being MOSES). They note it is insufficient to make statements such as: 'Now you are ready to pick a design – see if one already exists to handle the event.' Techniques and guidelines are needed; for instance ensuring there is a common vocabulary of object names and messages. OBA recommends as a step the explicit searching for architecture design models and then utilizing the existing rôles and responsibilities by folding them into the current model. In OPEN these OBA directives are fulfilled by the techniques listed above.

Task: **Optimize the design**   Star rating *

Focus: Optimization of code and architecture
Typical activities for which this is needed: Other projects, evaluation, consolidation
Typical supportive techniques: Abstract classes, assertion language, association, class naming, collapsing of classes, composition structures, contract specification, DCS optimization, encapsulation/information hiding, fuzzification, implementation inheritance, indexing, object replication, polymorphism, refinement of inheritance hierarchies

Explanation

When computing resources are scarce and/or the problem demands are high, the design may require optimizing. This occurs after the basic business model has been defined. Unlike the optimization subtask which supports generalization for reuse, this task is focused on changing class structures and interfaces. The changes are due to a redesign/optimization of the design rather than individual algorithms.

Optimization requires a detailed knowledge of physical information storage and processing. Optimized code may avoid excessive paging in the machine, may minimize loops, excessive resetting of attribute values and so on.

Optimizations take place at two levels. One is redesign of the objects model in order to optimize the time/space parameters of the system. Such redesign may involve removing classes and relationships on adding design classes to store information. For DB applications, Rumbaugh et al. (1991) suggest a number of guidelines for optimizing the object model based on the 'hit' rate of queries in the search for objects. They suggest the use of indexes to reduce the search and traversal requirements of the model. Alternatively, redundant relationships may be added to reduce traversal paths and message sends. Re-evaluation and optimization of the object model is best undertaken during late stages of specification when certain 'hot spots' can be identified. For DCS, there are a variety of techniques.

The second level is that of breaking the object model to optimize a solution. For example, violating encapsulation or the use of friend mechanisms can lead to reduced overheads albeit at the expense of flexibility and reuse. Such optimizations and redesign are largely system specific including a reworking and prototyping iteration to ensure that performance criteria are met. Quite often the designer may be able to identify critical optimization points during its specification. In these circumstances, the developer may undertake a prototyping exercise to provide a proof of concept. Such prototypes can be incorporated as short iterations at the start of the project to minimize the risk that the development will fail based on performance criteria.

It is also critical to remember that optimization can only be assessed by measuring 'before and after.' There is no point in optimizing code that has only a miniscule contribution to overall running time. Reenskaug et al. (1996, p. 126) point out that our intuition about where the program spends most of its time is highly unreliable – a point any developer (including ourselves) has learned from bitter experience.

There is also a need to optimize the GUI (Redmond-Pyle, 1996). For example, for frequent or time-critical cases, the normal OO GUI which separates multiple objects distributed across two or more windows may need revision so that these several objects are gathered together in a single window designed to support this specific use case.

Task: Test   Star rating *

Focus: Quality evaluation through continual testing
Typical activities for which this is needed: Evolutionary development
Typical supportive techniques: Beta testing, code/document inspections, contract specification, defect detection, early prototype to exercise DCS, generalization, integration testing, regression testing, responsibilities, scripting, simulation, subsystem testing, unit testing, usability testing, videotaping, walkthroughs

Explanation

Software artifacts must undergo testing (verification and validation). However, testing and quality assessment must be distributed across the whole lifecycle with short cycle times between tests. In OPEN, testing is also part of the post-condition on the tasks of each activity.

In software engineering, the term verification is summarized by the question: Is the system being built correctly?; whereas validation relates to the question: Is the correct system being built? Complete OO testing methodologies are currently under development. Testing can be either specification-based (or 'blackbox') or program-based (or 'whitebox'). In the former, the behavioral specification is tested; in the latter the implementation of each class. One might also differentiate between static testing and dynamic testing. In static testing, the software is evaluated without executing on a processor; whereas dynamic testing involves actual execution of the code.

Testing can occur at a variety of scales. Traditionally, the smallest scale results in unit testing – in OT that is generally taken to be the class *not* the method. Subsystem testing evaluates structures at the subsystem level and, at a higher level still, integration testing evaluates all the system when the pieces (the already-tested subsystems) are all put together – the OO equivalent of the 'big-bang test' in a traditional environment; except that now there is likely to be less fallout from the integration!

Smith and Robson (1992) note that, since object systems have no explicit threads of control, traditional testing techniques, which attempt to examine all routes through the system, are not directly applicable. Nevertheless, the ideas of walkthroughs are still valuable in which the author(s) explain their analysis/design/code to peers under the control of an impartial moderator who schedules and runs the meeting. Only a small number of people should be involved in such inspections.

Testing evaluates, *inter alia*

- all public messages are commented correctly
- messages received but not sent are documented as to intended use
- any reimplementation of an inherited member function does not simply duplicate the implementation in the superclass
- all subclasses conform to the expectations of the superclasses for providing deferred functionality
- subclasses do not implement inherited messages for the purpose of blocking functionality
- no superfluous redundancies exist
- all redundancies are documented as to why they are required
- all public functions are documented with an example of use

(Goldberg and Rubin, 1995, p. 127).

It also needs to be remembered that without a 'control' set of results to provide a baseline against which test results are to be compared, any testing programme is virtually useless. A list of test cases, and their expected outcomes, needs to be prepared. Indeed, test harnesses are OPEN deliverables (Table 7.1). Scenarios form a useful basis for blackbox testing of components.

The results of each of these testing techniques should be documented in the OPEN test reports.

DCS overlay

Non-determinism in distributed systems means that dynamic analysis, the traditional model for testing, does not give sufficient confidence that a system will work adequately in production. Static analysis is required, in an attempt to find problems that may not appear in dynamic testing. Other testing is required for performance and stress/load issues.

Subtask: Acceptance testing   Star rating *

Focus: Testing

Explanation

Acceptance testing focuses on the user's evaluation undertaken in conjunction with the user review subactivity of the build activity. At each increment, it is important that the user is involved in acceptance testing so that they can then use the current instantiation of the system. In some organizations, it may be necessary to undertake acceptance testing after system delivery, but in a fully OO, incremental lifecycle, as described in OPEN, this should be unnecessary or, at worst, trivial.

Subtask: Class testing   Star rating *

Focus: Testing

Explanation

The main unit of management in an OO system is the class. It is thus at the class level that 'unit' testing occurs. Class testing is not only fundamental to creating a high-quality system, it is also able to be undertaken incrementally thus ensuring reusability in the future.

Subtask: Cluster testing   Star rating *

Focus: Testing

Explanation

Clusters or subsystems are typically designed within a single team. Cluster testing thus occurs when members of the team, each responsible for a number of classes in the subsystem, put together their work and test the collaborations at this subsystem/cluster level.

Subtask: Regression testing   Star rating *

Focus: Testing

Explanation

In concept, regression testing for OO systems is little different from testing in non-OO systems. Following any modification, the product is retested against previous test cases to ensure that the behavior of the rest of the system has not been adversely affected. This, of course, requires the retention of previous test harnesses and test results.

Task: Undertake architectural design   Star rating *

Focus: Create the large-scale architecture in its context
Typical activities for which this is needed: Analysis and model refinement, project planning, domain modeling
Typical supportive techniques: Domain analysis, pattern recognition, throwaway prototyping, Zachman frameworks

Explanation

A good architecture extends the object paradigm to the large scale. Rather than just whitebox connections between subsystems, each subsystem is individually encapsulated with its own responsibilities (Mowbray, 1995a) – see Figure A.20. At the conceptual framework level, an OO architecture extends these notions of encapsulated interfaces (Mowbray, 1995b) – Figure A.21.

Subtask: Develop layer design   Star rating *

Explanation

Layers in OPEN support architectural design. The notion of a layer has been introduced (e.g. Figure 5.4) in terms of the standard two- or three-layer client–server application; for instance each layer addressing the application model, the domain, the server interface, and so on. Layer design is thus not only inextricably linked with such large-scale and architectural design decisions, it is also crucial to creating a flexible and extensible system.

Subtask: Establish distributed systems strategy   Star rating *

Focus: Determination of whether or not to use a DCS architecture
Typical supportive techniques: DCS architecture specification, static analysis

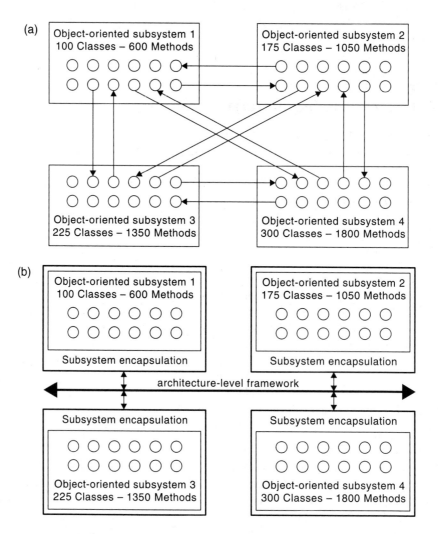

Figure A.20. Subsystem design: (a) programming-level solution and (b) architecture-level solution (after Mowbray, 1995a).

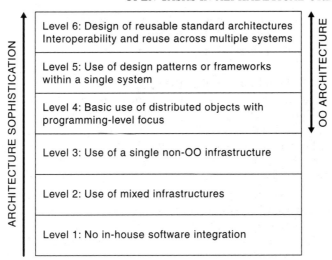

Figure A.21.   Conceptual framework for OO architecture practices (after Mowbray, 1995b).

Explanation

DCS development may include development work in different cities or even countries. In this case, the development team may need to be split to allow for geographical distribution of its members. Leadership, planning, standards, skills and support need to be planned in cognizance of this split. DCS issues, hardware and business requirements are likely to place constraints on the alternative configurations and system designs that may be considered in the feasibility study. Furthermore, the distributed hardware impact on users and team planning issues will also have direct impacts on the technical, economic and operational feasibility of the DCS alternatives. When considering economic feasibility, the future value of experience with DCS design and the cost of the extra risk should both be considered.

The object-based taxonomy for DCS (Martin et al., 1991) can be used to determine what distributed and concurrent concepts are provided by the DCS and what must be done to implement features which are not completely and transparently provided by the DCS. The main areas to be considered are the support provided by the DCS for:

- threads of control

- object properties, including issues such as persistence, restoration, replication, protection and existence

- object separation; the main issues are identification, communications, partial failures and migration.

It is envisaged that this task be performed towards the start of the design, before implementation environment concerns arise.

However, before discussing partitioning and allocation decisions in distributed systems, physical issues such as the communications semantics and concurrency control should be shown in the dynamic object models. Active objects may be identified as those objects that require their own thread of control because they monitor other objects or because they are a source of events. These are identified as such in the CIRT model. Once the dynamic and static object models have been updated with these details, Task: DCS architecture specification (partitioning and allocation) may be performed. Database distribution would also be considered at the same time (Case et al., 1995).

Partitioning and allocation are of vital importance in the development of a distributed information system. There are several approaches that may be taken to the partitioning and allocation decisions – two possible techniques are described in Task: DCS architecture specification (partitioning and allocation). They are not mutually exclusive.

Code distribution (DCS)

Once the partitioning and allocation process has been completed, it is possible to determine the code distribution of executable images. Decisions must be made on what code is included in each executable image based on partitioning and allocation decisions and migration possibilities. Here, the developer takes advantage of the features of the DCS and implements all the physical attributes of the dynamic and static object models. The OPEN Technique: DCS architecture specification provides the information on what features are provided by the DCS. This task also provides designers with information on what must be done to implement features which are not completely and transparently provided by the DCS.

Different compilers (and even programming languages) may be required for the software modules to be compiled onto their physical node. Copies of the class code that are slightly changed to allow for a different compiler should be well documented to ensure that they are maintained along with the primary copy.

The procedures for updating software once it has been installed on the physical nodes around the network should be planned.

Interoperability is encouraged by an open and distributed computing system. With the advent of ORBs, middleware, which permits interaction between components of different character and language, becomes even more practicable. The ability to call on services from distributed objects makes it easy to update reusers. The reusable asset is maintained in one place known to the object broker. Reusers are automatically updated because the broker accesses the latest version of the object. Standards such as CORBA and OLE are emerging to facilitate such interoperability within a distributed computing environment.

Code testing occurs after programming and has to recognize the existence of non-determinism as well as the need for stress testing. Security should also be considered during system construction as well as design – object-level security may be implemented through features provided by the DCS. Other levels of security may need to be designed into the application. Optimization may occur if testing discovers problems with response, stress handling or inefficient use of network resources.

Subtask: Select database/storage strategy   Star rating **

Focus: Determination of appropriate persistence mechanisms
Typical supportive techniques: Database authorization, DBMS product selection, DBMS type selection, storage of derived properties, versioning, volume analysis

Explanation

Selection of a database (i.e. storage strategy) is a management task supported by two complementary OPEN techniques: DBMS model selection and DBMS product selection. The first of these can be performed at any point up until the first iteration in which the CIRT model is mapped on to the logical database schema in the Task: Map logical database schema. The second OPEN technique is appropriate at any point until the first iteration of the Task: Design and implement physical database.

Task: Undertake feasibility study   Star rating ***

Focus: Decision making
Typical activities for which this is needed: Project initiation, programme planning
Typical supportive techniques: Cost estimation, critical success factors, simulation

Explanation

A standard feasibility study, which involves cost estimation, thus linking strongly with the CBA, is undertaken. Both hardware and software solutions are sought and evaluated in terms of both technology availability and cost. The costs are maintenance, training, and so on. For example, in considering improvements to an insurance claim system, the options may be as follows.

(1) Add new functionality to the current 3GL system (perhaps pushing to the limits of currently available hardware, for example PCs).

(2) Develop a new system on a faster platform, say SPARC-based workstations. This has a short-term cost (hardware and training) but a long-term payoff since future upgrades are foreseen which would be impossible with (1).

(3) Redesign the system from scratch with a 4GL or package.

(4) Redesign the system from scratch, using OO techniques to create a new system flexible enough to have a long life.

(5) Do nothing at present, anticipating more mature/cheaper hardware/software in n months time by which time (2) or (4) may look more economically appealing.

Task: **Undertake in-process review**   Star rating ***

Focus: Evaluate success in users' environment
Typical activities for which this is needed: Use of system
Typical supportive techniques: Code/document inspections, walkthroughs

Explanation

Some of the worst disasters in the short history of software have been traced back to the lack of in-process review. Reviews should not be undertaken solely at the project end (the danger of 'bolting the stable door after the horse has bolted') but at various predetermined times *during* the development process. In OPEN, such review stages are implicit in the post-conditions of the activities and explicit in the user review activity.

Task: **Undertake post-implementation review**   Star rating ***

Focus: Evaluate success in users' environment
Typical activities for which this is needed: Use of system
Typical supportive techniques: Videotaping

Explanation

In addition to in-process reviews (q.v.), it is traditional (no less so in OO) to undertake a final review, most often after the software has been installed into the customer site. Not only does this review the comparison of realization with expectations (specification/user requirements statement) but also involves the issues of whether the software has scaled to a non-technical user community.

Task: **Undertake usability design**   Star rating *

Focus: Design for user-friendliness and maintainability
Typical activities for which this is needed: Evolutionary development
Typical supportive techniques: Possibly completion of abstractions, simulation, videotaping

Explanation

Usability is a key element in creating high-quality software. While usability can be tested *post facto*, it is more important to adopt a user-centered focus throughout the design and *design in* the usability from the commencement of the project. One way of assisting is to involve the user throughout the project, as well as inculcating in individual designers a mindset which moves away from 'gee-whizzery' at the technical level to a more considered and client-focused approach to designing software.

While usability is well practiced in the user interface design community, these ideas have had little penetration into OO methods (but see Redmond-Pyle and Moore, 1995). Four key aspects of usability have been identified by Shackel (1990) as:

- Effectiveness: with respect to the performance of tasks by the user

- Learnability: how much training time is needed

- Flexibility: how effective is the UI when the task changes

- Attitude (user satisfaction): do users like the system and feel it is helpful in their work?

Another viewpoint on usability is given by Redmond-Pyle (1996) who suggests some common usability problems. These include:

- a long sequence of actions needed in order to accomplish a relatively common task

- functionality classified obscurely (that is in a menu where the user is unlikely to anticipate finding it)

- backtracking is difficult

- arcane terminology in menus

- inconsistencies in UI or actions between different parts of the system

- inadequate feedback on success or failure of user's actions.

Redmond-Pyle points out that a failure because of poor usability is as (or more) important to the user than missing functionality   a point ignored by most software developers. Good usability comes from a higher amount of design work, which involves the user. A highly usable system will require less costs for training, higher productivity rates when in use and reduced user error rates.

In terms of Task: Undertake usability design, the design needs to be user-centered and there are three techniques advocated for facilitating this: some sort of use case/task script modeling; object modeling and prototyping, which are all OPEN techniques (see Henderson-Sellers and Younessi, 1997).

Task: Write manuals and prepare other documentation
Star rating ***

Focus: Documentation for users
Typical activities for which this is needed: Use of system, evaluation
Typical supportive techniques: Event charts, task cards

Explanation

One of the most despised tasks of the software developer is writing accompanying manuals. Developers often seem to assume that the user should either be smart enough to use it without instruction (and indeed software is becoming more intuitive to use) or, if not, should not be allowed to use it.

One of the most despised tasks of the user is having to wade through incomprehensible documentation, poorly indexed, inaccurately proofed and often downright wrong. For example, we bought our godsons a new CD drive for Christmas for their Pentium home computer. Having struggled with following the instruction manuals and returning one CD drive as broken, we finally called up a friend who said immediately 'You don't follow what it says in the manual; replace step 3 by ... and add the following two steps: ...!'

If software development is ever intended to become professional, it is of paramount importance that not only is the software usable (see Task: Undertake usability design) but also that it is documented in a high-quality fashion. One of the greatest benefits of using OT is the support for quality; but that requires high-quality documents. In one financial analysts team using OPEN at Dow Jones Telerate in Sydney, one important and permanent member of the team is the technical writer. The software from this company has won many accolades and prizes!

References

Adams S. (1992). Constant quality management (part 4 of a series). *Hotline on Object-Oriented Technology*, **4**(1), 5–8

Austin J. L. (1962). *How to Do Things with Words*. Cambridge MA: Harvard University Press

Basili V. R. and Rombach H. D. (1988). The TAME project: towards improvement-orientated software environments. *IEEE Transactions on Software Engineering*, **14**(6), 758–73

Bezant (1995). *SOMATiK User Guide*, Bezant Object Technologies, 6 St Mary's Street, Wallingford, Oxon OX10 0LE, England, 1995. (SOMATiK is an MS Windows tool that was created to support the SOMA method. A free version is supplied with (Graham, 1995a). Many of the diagrams in this Appendix were produced using SOMATiK.)

Blanchard K. and Johnson S. (1983) *The One Minute Manager*. New York: Willow Books.

Booch G. (1991). *Object Oriented Design with Applications*. 580 pp. Menlo Park, CA: Benjamin/Cummings

Buschmann F. (1995). Pattern-oriented software architecture. In *Conf. Proc. Object Expo Europe*, London, England, 25–29 September, 1995, pp. 57–66

Case T., Henderson-Sellers B. and Low G. C. (1995). Extending the MOSES object-oriented analysis and design methodology to include database applications. *Journal of Object-Oriented Programming*, **8**(7), 28–34, 56

Checkland P. B. and Scholes J. (1990). *Soft Systems Methodology in Action*. 329 pp. Chichester: Wiley

Constantine L. L. and Henderson-Sellers B. (1995). Notation matters: Part 1 – framing the issues. *Report on Object Analysis and Design*, **2**(3), 25–9

Constantine L. L. and Lockwood L. A. D. (1994). Fitting practices to the people. *American Programmer*, **7**(12), 21–7

Crowe M. K. (1993). Object systems over relational databases. *Information and Software Technology*, **35**(8), 449–61

Demming R. and Duffy D. (1996). Emerging patterns in user interface design. *Object Expert*, **2**(1), 38–44

de Paula E. G. and Nelson M. L. (1991). Designing a class hierarchy. In *Technology of Object-Oriented Languages and Systems: TOOLS5* (Korson T., Vaishnavi V. and Meyer B., eds.). pp. 203–18. New York: Prentice-Hall

Desfray P. (1994). *Object Engineering. The Fourth Dimension*. 342 pp. Paris: Addison-Wesley/Masson

Desai B. C. (1990). *An Introduction to Database Systems*. St Paul, MN: West Publishing

Dietrich W. C., Nackman L. R. and Gracer F. (1989). Saving a legacy with objects. In *OOPSLA'90 ACM Conference on Object-oriented Programming systems, Languages and Applications* (Meyrowitz N., ed) Reading, MA: Addison-Wesley

Dorling A. (1993). SPICE: Software Process Improvement and Capability dEtermination. *Information and Software Technology*, **35**, 404–17

Fenton N. E. (1994) Software measurement: a necessary scientific basis. *IEEE Transactions on Software Engineering*, **20**, 199–206

Fenton N., Pfleeger S. L. and Glass R. L. (1994). Science and substance: a challenge to software engineers. *IEEE Software*, **11**(4), 86–95

Firesmith D. G. (1992). ADM3: a language-independent, object-oriented method for large, real-time systems development. Presented at *Methodologies and Tools for Real-Time and Object-Oriented Systems Conference 1992*, 26 pp.

Firesmith D. G. (1993). *Object-Oriented Requirements Analysis and Logical Design: A Software Engineering Approach*. 575 pp. New York: Wiley

Firesmith D., Henderson-Sellers B. and Graham I. (1997). *OPEN Modeling Language (OML) Reference Manual*. 271 pp. New York: SIGS

Freeman C. and Henderson-Sellers B. (1991). OLMS: the Object Library Management System. In *TOOLS 6* (Potter J., Tokoro M. and Meyer B., eds.). pp. 175–80. New York: Prentice-Hall

Gamma E., Helm R., Johnson R. and Vlissides J. (1995). *Design Patterns: Elements of Reusable Object-Oriented Design*. Reading, MA: Addison-Wesley

Goldberg A. and Rubin K. S. (1995). *Succeeding with Objects. Decision Frameworks for Project Management*. 542 pp. Reading, MA: Addison-Wesley

Grady R. B. (1993). Software metrics etiquette. *American Programmer*, **6**(2), 6–15

Graham I. (1991). *Object-Oriented Methods*. 410 pp. Harlow, UK: Addison-Wesley

Graham I. M. (1995a). *Migrating to Object Technology*. 552 pp. Harlow, UK: Addison-Wesley

Graham I. (1995b). Business process modeling, part I. *Object Expert*, **1**(1), 74–8

Graham I. (1996a). Requirements engineering as business process modeling, part II. *Object Expert*, **1**(2), 54–6

Graham I. (1996b). Linking a system and its requirements. *Object Expert*, **1**(3), 62–4

Grosberg J. A. (1993). Comments on Considering 'class' harmful. *Communications of the ACM*, **36**(1), 113–14

Haynes P. and Henderson-Sellers B. (1996). Cost estimation of OO projects: empirical observations, practical applications. *American Programmer*, **9**(7), 35–41

Henderson-Sellers B. (1995). The goals of an OO metrics programme. *Object Magazine*, **5**(6), 72–9, 95

Henderson-Sellers B. (1996). *Object-Oriented Metrics: Measures of Complexity*. 234 pp. Englewood Cliffs, NJ: Prentice-Hall

Henderson-Sellers B. and Dué R. T. (1997). OPEN project management. *Object Expert*, **2**(2), 30–5

Henderson-Sellers B. and Edwards J. M. (1994). *BOOKTWO of Object-Oriented Knowledge: The Working Object*. 594 pp. Sydney: Prentice-Hall

Henderson-Sellers B. and Pant Y. R. (1993). When should we generalize classes to make them reusable? *Object Magazine*, **3**(4), 73–5

Henderson-Sellers B., Kreindler R. J. and Mickel S. (1994). Methodology choices – adapt or adopt? *Report on Object Analysis and Design*, **1**(4), 26–9

Henderson-Sellers B. and Younessi M. (1997). *OPEN's Toolbox of Techniques*. Harlow, UK: Addison-Wesley

Higgins K. (1997). Cultural Issues in Human–Computer Interaction, *Honours Thesis* (unpublished), Swinburne University of Technology

Humphrey W. S. (1989). *Managing the Software Process*. 494 pp. New York: Addison-Wesley

Humphrey W. S. (1995). *A Discipline for Software Engineering*. 789 pp. Addison-Wesley

Ince D. (1990). Software metrics: an introduction. *Information and Software Technololgy*, **32**, 297–303

ISO (1991). ISO 9000–3, *Quality Management and Quality Assurance Standards*

Jacobson I., Christerson M., Jonsson P. and Övergaard G. (1992). *Object-Oriented Software Engineering: A Use Case Driven Approach*. 524 pp. Harlow, UK: Addison-Wesley

Jain H. and Purao S. (1991). Distributed application development: SDLC revisited. *Information and Management*, **20**, 247–55

Johnson R. E. and Foote B. (1988). Designing reusable classes. *Journal of Object-Oriented Programming*, **1**(2), 22–35

Jones C. (1994). *Assessment and Control of Software Risks*. Englewood Cliffs, NJ: Prentice-Hall

Kitchenham B. A. and Linkman S. J. (1990). Design metrics in practice. *Information and Software Technology*, **32**(4), 304–10

Koch G. R. (1993). Process assessment: the 'BOOTSTRAP' approach. *Information and Software Technology*, **35**, 387–403

Korson T. and McGregor J. D. (1992). Technical criteria for the specification and evaluation of object-oriented libraries. *Software Engineering Journal*, **7**(2), 85–94

Lee G. (1993). *Object-Oriented GUI Application Development*. Englewood Cliffs, NJ: Prentice-Hall

Lorenz M. (1993). *Object-Oriented Software Development: A Practical Guide*. 227 pp. Englewood Cliffs, NJ: Prentice-Hall

Lorenz M. and Kidd J. (1994). *Object-Oriented Software Metrics*. 146 pp. Englewood Cliffs, NJ: Prentice-Hall

Loucopoulos P. and Karakostas V. (1995). *System Requirements Engineering*. 161 pp. London: McGraw-Hill

Lynch T. (1995). Measuring the value and performance of your IT department. In *Software Quality and Productivity. Theory, Practice, Education and Training* (Lee M., Barta B-Z. and Juliff P., eds.). pp. 183–6

McCabe T. J. (1976). A complexity measure, *IEEE Transactions in Software Engineering*, **2**(4), 308–20

McGibbon B. (1995). *Managing Your Move to Object Technology. Guidelines and Strategies for a Smooth Transition*. 268 pp. New York: SIGS

McGibbon B. (1997). Reuse strategy for large-scale legacy systems. *Object Magazine*, **7**(2), 70–3

McGregor J. D. and Sykes D. A. (1992). *Object-Oriented Software Development. Engineering Software for Reuse*. 352 pp. New York: Van Nostrand Reinhold

Marmolin H. (1993). *User Centered System Design*, UI Design AB (in Swedish), Linköping, Sweden, June 1993

Martin B. E., Pedersen C.H. and Bedford-Roberts J. (1991). An object-based taxonomy for distributed computer systems. *IEEE Computer*, **24**(8), 17–27

Menzies T., Edwards J. M. and Ng K. (1992). The case of the mysterious missing reusable libraries. In *Technology of Object-Oriented Languages and Systems: TOOLS12&9* (Mingins C., Haebich B., Potter J. and Meyer B., eds.). Sydney: Prentice-Hall

Meyer B. (1988). *Object-Oriented Software Construction*. 534 pp Hemel Hempstead: Prentice-Hall

Meyer B. (1994). *Reusable Software. The Base object-oriented component libraries*. 514 pp. Hemel Hempstead: Prentice-Hall

Mowbray T. J. (1995a). Essentials of object-oriented architecture. *Object Magazine*, **5**(5), 28–32

Mowbray T. J. (1995b). What OO architecture benefits are you missing? *Object Magazine*, **5**(7), 24–8, 85

Mumford E. (1985). Defining system requirements to meet business needs: a case study. *The Computer Journal*, **28**(2), 70–9

Nielsen J. and Mack R. L. (1994) *Usability Inspection Methods*. New York: Wiley

Paulk M., Curtis B., Chrissis M. E. and Weber C. (1993). Capability Maturity Model, Version 1.1. *IEEE Software*, **4**, 18–27

Pfleeger S. L. (1991). *Software Engineering. The Production of Quality Software* 2nd edn. 517 pp. New York: Macmillan

Pfleeger S. L. (1993). Lessons learned in building a corporate metrics program. *IEEE Software*, **10**(3), 67–74

Prieto-Diaz R. and Freeman P. (1987). Classifying software for reusability. *IEEE Software*, 6–16

Rational (1997). *Unified Modeling Language. Notation Guide. Version 1.0. 13 January 1997*, available from http://www.rational.com

Redmond-Pyle D. (1996). GUI design techniques for O-O projects. *Object Expert*, **2**(1), 24–8

Redmond-Pyle D. and Moore A. (1995). *Graphical User Interface Design and Evaluation (GUIDE): A Practical Process*. Englewood Cliffs, NJ: Prentice-Hall

Reenskaug T., Wold P. and Lehne O. A. (1996). *Working with Objects. The OOram Software Engineering Manual*. 366 pp. Greenwich, CT: Manning

Renouf D. W. and Henderson-Sellers B. (1995). Incorporating roles into MOSES. In *TOOLS15* (Mingins C. and Meyer B., eds.). pp. 71–82. New York: Prentice-Hall

Rowe A. and Whitty R. (1993). Ami: promoting a quantitative approach to software management. *Software Quality Journal*, **2**, 291–6

Rumbaugh J., Blaha M., Premerlani W., Eddy F. and Lorensen W. (1991). *Object-Oriented Modeling and Design*. 500 pp. Englewood Cliffs, NJ: Prentice-Hall

Schackel B. (1990). Human factors and usability. In *Human–Computer Interaction* (Preece J. and Keller L., eds.). pp. 27–41. Englewood Cliffs, NJ: Prentice-Hall

Schank R. C. and Abelson R. P. (1977). *Scripts, Plans, Goals and Understanding*. Boston MA: Lawrence Erlbaum

Searle J. R. (1969). *Speech Acts*. Cambridge: Cambridge University Press

Short J. E. and Venkatramen N. (1992). Beyond business process redesign: Redefining Baxter's Business Network. *Sloan Management Review*, 7–17

Smith M. D. and Robson D. J. (1992). A framework for testing object-oriented programs. *Journal of Object-Oriented Programming*, **5**(3), 45–53

Sparks S., Benner K. and Faris C. (1996). Managing object-oriented framework reuse. *IEEE Computer*, **29**(9), 52–61

Sukaviriya P. and Moran L. (1990). User interface for Asia. In *Designing User Interfaces for International Use* (Nielsen J., ed.). pp. 189–218. Amsterdam: Elsevier

Swaminathan V. and Storey J. (1997). Domain-specific frameworks. *Object Magazine*, **7**(2), 53–7

Taivalsaari A. (1996). On the notion of inheritance. *ACM Computing Surveys*, **28**(3), 438–79

Taylor D. A. (1995). *Business Engineering with Object Technology*. 188 pp. New York: Wiley

Thomsett R. (1990). Management implications of object-oriented development. *ACS Newsletter*, 5–7, 10–12

Thorne F. (1997). *MSc thesis*, University of Technology, Sydney (unpublished)

Waldén K. and Nerson J.-M. (1995). *Seamless Object-Oriented Architecture*. 301 pp. New York: Prentice-Hall

Webster B. F. (1995). *Pitfalls of Object-Oriented Development*. 256 pp. New York: M&T Books

Williams J. D. (1995). *What Every Software Manager MUST KNOW TO SUCCEED With Object Technology*. 273 pp. New York: SIGS

Wills A. (1997). Frameworks and component-based development. In *OOIS'96* (Patel D., Sun Y. and Patel S., eds.). pp. 413–30. London: Springer-Verlag

Wirfs-Brock R. J., Wilkerson B. and Wiener L. (1990). *Designing Object-Oriented Software*. 341 pp. New York: Prentice-Hall

Yap L-M. and Henderson-Sellers B. (1997). Class hierarchies: consistency between libraries. *Australian Computer Journal* (in press)

Zultner R. (1989). The Deming way to software quality. Presented at the *Pacific Northwest Software Quality Conference*. Princeton, NJ: Zultner &Co.

Appendix B
The COMN Light notation

The concepts supported by the object model in OPEN are very much in accord with emerging industry 'standards.' At present (early 1997) there is significant activity which is likely to lead to an agreed model, metamodel and, possibly, notation. Members of the OPEN Consortium have been in discussion with other leading OO methodologists, notably those affiliated with the Rational Software Corporation, in order to ensure future compatibility of models/metamodels and notation.

A methodology needs to include a means for representing the generated artifacts; it needs to contain a notational element. While only a small part of a methodology, it is, however, the most obvious part and, since choosing a methodology also implies choosing a CASE tool, it is a component of the methodology which often surfaces first and, if you do not prevent it, can take over the whole mindset.

OPEN is a full lifecycle, third-generation OO methodology. A small component of OPEN is its modeling notation (COMN) and its underpinning metamodel (an extension of COMMA). While OPEN is in a sense notation-independent, since it will support your chosen, favorite notation set, its full expressiveness is only realizable through its preferred notation, COMN. We package these (notation and metamodel) together as OML (OPEN Modeling Language = metamodel plus notation) (Firesmith et al., 1997).

Notation is the way of communicating between software developers and software users. It should therefore be designed with usability and HCI issues in mind. A poor notation can still be learned but is likely to take more time and be a poorer communication vehicle. Some well-known OO notations, for example, are sometimes counter-intuitive or contain arbitrary elements which have to be learned by rote – not a good HCI practice.

For many of us, once we have learned a notation we find no barriers – we can use the notation easily and fluently. It is like learning a programming language or learning a natural language. Some natural languages are harder to learn than others. It is generally appreciated that Chinese and English (for non-native speakers) can present almost insurmountable problems. For a francophone, on the other hand, learning Italian is relatively easy. Even becoming fluent with the basic alphabet (choose from Roman, Japanese, Cyrillic, Arabic, Hebrew and many others) can be a challenge for adults with no previous exposure. So, an interface, here the alphabet, that is unfamiliar or does not include symbols that are easy to comprehend (arguably Chinese is easier here because of its ideographic heredity) makes the syntax and semantics hard to learn. So it is with an OOAD notation.

The OPEN preferred notation, COMN, has been designed with intuition and usability in mind. Granted we cannot find internationally recognizable symbols amenable to all types of novice in every country; however, if we assume we are trying to pictographically describe the main, commonly understood, elements of OT such as encapsulation, interfaces, blackbox and whitebox inheritance, a discrimination between objects, classes and types, then designing a broadly acceptable notation becomes possible.

Semiotics is the study of signs and symbols. Those semiotic ideas were built into the MOSES notation (Henderson-Sellers and Edwards, 1994) and into UON (Page-Jones et al., 1990) both of which have had influences on COMN as well as more recent studies in interface design and notational design. OPEN has no hereditary biases from an earlier, data-modeling history. COMN has been designed from the bottom up by a small team of methodologists who, over the last decade, have worked on these issues.

COMN provides support for both the novice and the sophisticate. Here we describe only those elements necessary for beginning and, indeed, which will be found in around 80% of all applications. In a nutshell, we need to have symbols for:

- class versus type versus instance
- basic relationships of association mapping, aggregation and inheritance
- a state transition model (dynamics of individual objects and classes)
- an interaction model (dynamics of interactions)
- a use-case model (or an extension thereof)

We only have *one* model. Different descriptions (static, dynamic, use case) are just different views of aspects of the same entity.

B.1   COMN's core notational elements

This Appendix describes the 'Light notation' for COMN (and hence for use in OPEN). We aim for minimality in semantics while acknowledging that the notation is likely to evolve, especially with niche extensions such as hard real time, rôles and distribution. This will particularly result as more 'satellite' methods are merged into the mainstream of OPEN. Figure B.1 depicts the basic icons for class and object. Both class and object are similar; however, an object is 'more real' than a class so the icon is represented by a sharper icon whereas the class icon is smooth. The class icon itself is also unmistakable and cannot be confused with rectangles as used in structured hierarchy charts, for example. In MIS systems, we usually use class icons and only use object icons for

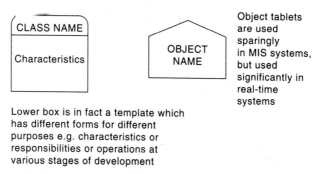

Figure B.1 COMN icons for class and object.

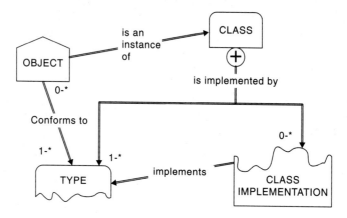

Figure B.2. COMN metamodel for the relationships between metalevel types for object, class, type and class implementation.

specific message-passing sequences (on collaboration diagrams); whereas in real-time systems it is usually object icons that dominate. Another sign used is that of a dotted line to indicate a more ethereal notion. Abstract/deferred classes are more ethereal than classes so they get a dotted outline.

The other interesting item here is how to design a notation that will 'last' throughout the lifecycle. The answer we have come up with is 'drop-down boxes.' These are attached below the icons (for all icons) and can contain information relevant to the particular phase of the lifecycle. They may contain information on characteristics, responsibilities, requirements or stereotypes, for instance. These are all types of traits.

Figure B.2 shows how these concepts are related by the core metamodel. Here we introduce for the first time into an OO notation the well-understood notion that a class is composed of an interface plus an implementation. Graphically we 'tear apart' the class icon to get the two complementary icons: the type and the class implementation. An object is then an instance of a class which also conforms to a type. Figure B.2 is an example of a semantic net (also known as

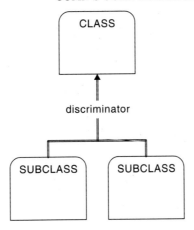

Figure B.3   Example of specialization relationship expressed using COMN.

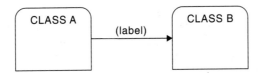

Figure B.4   Example of association/mapping relationship expressed using COMN.

class diagram) which uses COMN to describe its own metamodel. It can either be read as an example of COMN notation or as a description of a metamodel (actually it is both!).

In Figures B.3–B.6 we see the major relationships illustrated: specialization (Figure B.3), unidirectional associations (mappings) (Figure B.4), aggregations (Figure B.5) and containment (Figure B.6). Again the icons chosen are self-explanatory. Specializations are very close bindings between sub and super

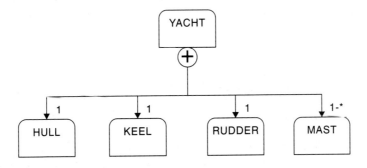

Figure B.5   Example of aggregation relationship expressed using COMN.

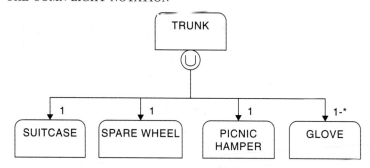

Figure B.6   Example of containment relationship expressed using COMN.

class/type. They have a very thick arrow (a double arrow is chosen as being easier to draw by hand than a thick one and easier to see when different magnifications are used in a drawing tool). A label can be used to indicate the discriminator used for the subclassing. Specialization, the default, is an is-a-kind-of relationship. Other types of 'inheritance' can be shown but the basic, encouraged is-a-kind-of gets the easiest-to-draw line. All relationships are unidirectional – as indicated by the arrowhead. Consequently, an association is always, by default, unidirectional. If no decision has yet been made, the arrowhead may be left off until a later decision adds it. This is more reasonable than permitting an unarrowed line to mean bidirectional. Leaving off arrowheads may be carelessness rather than a design decision! Mappings as used here do not break encapsulation; whereas bidirectional associations do. We believe in supporting a true OO paradigm as default.

Aggregation, although not as well defined as we would all like it to be, represents a fairly permanent binding: an 'is-composed-of' or 'part–whole' relationship. At the same time, we can see this symbol as a plus sign which represents the fact that the aggregate (here the yacht) is (often more than) the sum of its parts.

Often confused with aggregation is the looser collection concept. A good example here is what you store in the trunk of your car. The items are connected with trunk, but that connection may be highly temporary. We replace the plus symbol with a cup symbol to give the visual clue suggested by this icon of a cup and its contents.

B.2   Basic relationships in COMN

One pleasing aspect of the relationship model is its carefully structured metamodel. All relationships, as noted above, are binary, unidirectional dependencies or mappings. These can be of two major types (four when we include dynamic models). The two static relationship types are definitional (in which one thing is defined by relationship to another) and referential (in which one thing 'knows about' another).

B.2.1   Definitional relationships

We use a double arrow for the tighter definitional relationships and a single arrow for the less permanent referentials. Our default definitional node, the easiest to draw, is the is-a-kind-of which thus gets a double arrow. An is-a-kind-of relationship is good for both knowledge representation (in say user requirements/analysis) and in support of polymorphism, through dynamic substitutability. Since we discourage simple subtyping (specification inheritance) and implementation inheritance, they are represented as adornments (a blackbox and whitebox respectively at the subclass end of the arrow, to represent blackbox and whitebox inheritance).

All other definitional relationships (also with a double arrow) carry a textual label. These can be grouped into classification relationships (conforms-to, is-an-instance-of, plays-the-role-of) and implementation relationships (implements, is-implemented-by).

B.2.2   Referential relationships

All referential relationships use a single-width arrow. Associations and linkages (associations for classes, linkages for instances) have an unadorned, solid single arrow, whereas for aggregation and containment (see Figures B.5–B.7) it is adorned at the 'whole' end.

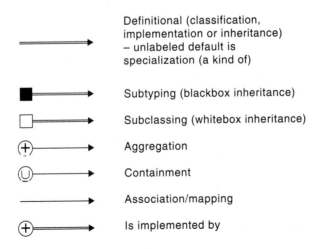

Figure B.7   The major relationship arrows in COMN.

B.2.3   Transitional and scenario relationships

There are in fact two further types of relationship: transitional and scenario. These are more advanced features, not part of COMN Light and thus not discussed here (see *OPEN Modeling Language (OML) Reference Manual* by Firesmith et al. (1997)). Transitional relationships are not used in the static model (semantic net or class models) but only in the dynamic models and scenario relationships in use-case/task-script models. Beginners can use any state transition model they choose before investigating the OML dynamic model. Similarly, although we prefer a use-case/task-script model for large systems, any version of this to help gain understanding of user requirements will be satisfactory for learning the overall OPEN approach. Interconnections between diagrams are similarly reserved for the full notation discussion.

References

Firesmith D., Henderson-Sellers B. and Graham I. (1997). *OPEN Modeling Language (OML) Reference Manual*. 271 pp. New York: SIGS

Henderson-Sellers B. and Edwards J. M. (1994). *BOOKTWO of Object-Oriented Knowledge: The Working Object*. 594 pp. Sydney: Prentice-Hall

Page-Jones M., Constantine L. L. and Weiss S. (1990). Modeling object-oriented systems: the Uniform Object Notation, *Computer Language*, **7**(10), 69–87

Appendix C
The OPEN–MeNtOR project

It is clear that a 'methodology' can have many purposes and many types of use. Thus, rather than requiring methodologies to serve all purposes at the same time, we urge development (or adaptation) of methodologies at a range of 'levels.' Three broad levels of methodology have been proposed:

(1) Complete methodologies (level 3). These are methodologies that are complete descriptions of the software development process in that they contain all the elements necessary to run a *commercial* project successfully. As such, these methodologies must support techniques and deliverables which may not necessarily be specifically OO elements, such as feasibility studies and cost–benefit analysis. These methodologies are unlikely to be captured in their totality in a single text book although the key ideas and techniques may be. These methodologies are likely to be well documented, supported by training courses, teams of external and in-house consultants and a range of software development tools. The investment necessary to develop such a methodology also implies that they are likely to be proprietary to organizations.

(2) Core/pilot methodologies (level 2). These are methodologies that are focused on a particular area of the software development process or are less complete in their description of the process. By their nature, these methodologies are often more accessible. For example, they may be published by a commercial publishing company and are likely to require less training and mentoring. These methodologies are likely to be attractive to small development shops and individual developers or even to small pilot projects trialling OT. Almost all methodologies fall into this category.

(3) Teaching methodologies (level 1). These are methodologies that are used for teaching OO development to users and students. They are likely to be less onerous and less complete in terms of documentation and definition, concentrating more on concepts than on the production of practical software.

While an organization committed to OO software development requires a fully supported and industrial-strength approach (level 3), it is also clear that there are a large number of potential users of OO techniques who require assistance in learning and applying concepts of OO development but for whom such large-scale commercial methodologies may be out of reach or too imposing. For these users, texts such as this one are more than adequate, providing as they do comprehensive guidelines and practical assistance (they are all level 2 methodologies) without the all-encompassing nature or expense of commercial, proprietary methodologies (i.e. level 3). Furthermore, it has been argued by Lilly (1994) that even these methodologies as described in the books may be too much for those coming to grips with OT for the first time and that trimmed down versions of these methodologies may be appropriate. She suggests the need for a 'Booch Lite' (actually a term already used for a trimmed down version of Booch's *notation* not the methodology) or a 'Rumbaugh Junior' (and at the language level maybe C––) for teaching and learning purposes (i.e. level 1). This is an excellent idea although one that has not yet been fully realized (see below).

The majority of published methodologies, including OPEN, are at level 2. They tend to be most available to software developers with some experience, often in both OO concepts and also some previous experience with structured methodologies. Project teams may certainly attempt realistic projects with a level 2 methodology. Indeed, a significant part of the organizational learning can occur using such a level 2 methodology; whereas small organizations may stay with a level 2 methodology and simply extend it as they go. However, many organizations will find the support (both in terms of documentation and mentoring) offered in a book plus some mentoring, either from the authors or qualified support companies, inadequate for their needs. Instead they will require the type of extensive support which is increasingly available through (often proprietary) level 3 methodologies, such as Objectory (historically, the complete version of OOSE) and MeNtOR.

The OPEN/MeNtOR project aims to consolidate the links between the level 2 OPEN method and the level 3 MeNtOR by creating a disciplined and complete third-generation software process for use with OT. This software process will then be made available to a range of users covering the three levels of sophistication identified above and summarized in the project documentation as:

- Level 1: Education – the primary purpose of this material will be to support teaching and education. The primary reference material will be a textbook, a set of course notes and exercises.

- Level 2: Public domain – the primary purpose of this material is to provide a public domain version of the software process for use by industry on smaller projects; or on pilot projects. The primary reference material will be books and papers. The process will be supported by CASE tools and some training.

- Level 3: Industrial strength – the primary purpose of this material is to provide a complete, rigorous industrial-strength software process for use in commercial software projects. The primary reference material will be industrial-strength process descriptions, supported by CASE tools, training, consulting and online tools.

The level 3 methodology is thus the repository of all knowledge. It is essentially a commercial product, a subset of which will be released into the public domain (level 2). The level 2 material is thus the entry level to the industrial-strength product.

The OPEN/MeNtOR project merges together the best practices of the level 2 method, MOSES/OPEN and the level 3 method MeNtOR. The resulting level 3 method will still be known as MeNtOR and the level 2 method known as OPEN (OPEN–MeNtOR in Australasia). (In this book it is referred to as just OPEN.)

OPEN/MeNtOR will be used as a teaching vehicle, as an entry-level method for commercial organizations and as a research vehicle to develop new approaches and techniques that will eventually feed into MeNtOR, the commercial product. Meanwhile, the MeNtOR commercial sites prove a testing ground under industry conditions for the ideas generated within OPEN, i.e. a larger user base is created than would otherwise be likely to ensue from a stand-alone level 2 method.

In due course, as OPEN/MeNtOR stabilizes, it will be possible to take a subset of this and create UniOPEN/MeNtOR (level 1) which will be an undergraduate teaching tool: including a textbook plus other teaching aids.

The collaboration between the OPEN team and Object-Oriented Pty Ltd, the purveyors of MeNtOR is being finalized (early 1997). The resulting OPEN/MeNtOR project will create, by August 1998, a new version of MeNtOR and refine and extend the description of OPEN in this and accompanying OPEN textbooks.

References

Lilly S. (1994). Planned obsolescence. *Object Magazine*, **3**(5), 79–80

Appendix D
Migration strategies

Many people and organizations are convinced of the wisdom of shifting their systems development activities towards an OO style. This may be because they have become aware of the benefits of OT, seen other companies succeeding in this way or even for that worst of reasons: because OT is new and fashionable. Even in the latter, misguided, case these companies may gain from the experience because, even should the project in hand fail, they may gain a better understanding of existing systems and development practices through the construction of an object model. People and organizations have several reasons for replacing or extending older systems. For example, a package vendor may see the move to OT as closely tied to the move to an open platform and, in turn, see this as a way of achieving greater market share since there are usually potential customers who do not (and perhaps will not) own the proprietary platform on which the old product currently runs. Vendors may wish to compete more effectively by adding value to the existing product with graphical user interfaces, management information system (MIS) features or delivery on distributed platforms. User organizations may wish to take advantage of new standards, downsizing or friendlier interfaces along with the benefits of the move to OT itself. Both types of organization will be looking to slash maintenance costs, which can account for a huge proportion of the MIS budget, and reduce time to market. However, while overnight migration is highly desirable it is seldom possible. Furthermore, gradual migration may take too long for its benefits to be worthwhile. Often the solution is to reuse existing conventional components or entire systems and packages. So, there are several available options: interoperation, reuse, extension, and gradual or sudden migration. These options are closely related but we will deal with interoperation first.

D.1 Interoperation of conventional and OO systems

There are a number of scenarios in which an OO application should interoperate with existing non-OO systems. These include:

- the evolutionary migration of an existing system to a future OO implementation where parts of the old system will remain temporarily in use

- the evolution of systems which already exist and are important and too large or complex to rewrite at a stroke and where part or all of the old system may continue to exist indefinitely

- the reuse of highly specialized or optimized routines, embedded expert systems and hardware-specific software

- exploiting the best of existing relational databases for one part of an application in concert with the use of an OO programming language and/or OODBs for another

- the construction of graphical front-ends to existing systems

- the need to build on existing 'package' solutions

- cooperative processing and blackboard architectures may involve agents which already exist working with newly defined objects

- the need to cooperate with existing systems across telecommunications and local area networks.

The first issue addressed here is how to tackle the migration of a vast system that is almost invariably very costly and tricky to maintain. The strategy recommended is to build what is known as an object *wrapper*. Object wrappers can be used to migrate to OO programming and still protect investments in conventional code. The wrapper concept has become part of the folklore of object orientation but, as far as I know, the term was first coined by Wally Dietrich of IBM (Dietrich 1989) though it is also often attributed to Brad Cox and Tom Love, the developers of Objective-C, but in a slightly different context. There are also claims that the usage was in vogue within IBM as early as 1987.

The existence of large investments in programs written in conventional languages such as Assembler, COBOL, PL/1, Fortran and even APL has to be recognized. It must also be allowed that the biggest cost associated with these 'legacy' systems, as Dietrich calls them, is maintenance. Maintenance is costly because, in a conventional system, any change to the data structure requires checking every single function to see if it is affected. This does not occur with OO systems due to the encapsulation of the data structures by the functions that use them. However much we would like to replace these old systems completely, the economics of the matter forbids it on any large scale; there are just not enough development resources. What we must do is build on the existing investment and move gradually to the brave new world of object orientation.

It is possible to create object wrappers around this bulk of existing code, which can then be replaced or allowed to wither away. Building object wrappers can help protect the investment in older systems during the move to OO programming. An object wrapper enables a new, OO part of a system to interact with a conventional chunk by message passing. The wrapper itself is likely to be written in the same language as the original system, COBOL for example. This

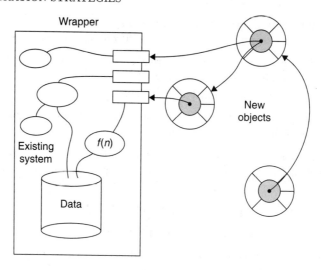

Figure D.1   Object wrappers.

may represent a very substantial investment, but once it is in place virtually all maintenance activity may cease; at least this is the theory.

Imagine that an existing COBOL system interacts with users through a traditional menu system, each screen offering about 10 options and with the leaf nodes of the menu tree being normal 'enter, tab and commit' data entry screens. This characterizes a very large number of present-day systems. The wrapper must offer all the functions of the old system as if through the interface of an object, as illustrated by the 'Gradygram' in Figure D.1 where the small rectangles on the boundary of the wrapper represent its visible operations, which in turn call the old system's functions and thereby access its data too. (The term *Gradygram* was coined to stand for the icons with operations indicated by small boxes on the boundary of a rectangle representing the object used by Grady Booch since his work on design for Ada in the mid 1980s. The Booch'93 method uses them for its module diagrams to this day and variants have appeared in several other methods.) Effectively, the wrapper is a large object whose methods are the menu options of the old system. The only difference between this new object and the old system is that it will respond to messages from other objects. So far, this gives little in the way of benefits. However, when we either discover a bug, receive a change request or wish to add a new business function the benefits begin; for we do not tinker with the old system at all but create a new set of objects to deliver the new features. As far as the existing users are concerned, they may see no difference when using the old functions; although their calls are being diverted via the wrapper. Wrappers may be small or large, but in the context of interoperation they tend to be of quite coarse granularity. For command-driven systems, the wrapper may be a set of operating system batch files or scripts. If the old system used a form or screen-based interface, the wrapper may consist of code that reads and writes data to the screen. This can be done using a virtual terminal. This is fairly easy to accomplish on machines such as the VAX though it is not always possible with systems such as OS/400 where some specialist software or an ORB may be required. All new functions or replacements should be dealt with by creating new objects with their own encapsulated data structures and methods. If the services of the old system are needed, these are requested by message passing and the output is decoded by the wrapper and passed to the requester.

So much for the propaganda! Implementing wrappers is not as easy as it sounds in several respects. Much of the literature on wrappers is aimed at deriving the necessity ORBs. When these are not available, for whatever reason, developers have to face up to the implementation details directly. One such issue concerns granularity. Most of the theoretical arguments and a good deal of the practical experience of OO programmers indicate that small objects are usually more reusable than large ones. Recall the usual set of guidelines for object design from your favorite text on the subject: interfaces should be small and simple; no more than about 17 operations per object; and so on. However, with the legacy system we are faced with a *fait accompli*; the system is as it is. There are irreducibly large grain 'objects' often present in the design of legacy systems. ORBs are specifically aimed at dealing with this kind of coarse-grain reuse. The question is whether, without such a broker, we can still gain from the use of a hand-made wrapper. Some developers find that coarse-grain objects arise naturally even with new requirements and deduce that OO models are not always appropriate. Brice (1993) for example found this in the context of geometrical image-transformation software. The data structures were straightforward but the processing required pages of equations to describe it and data-flow models were found to be the most natural thing to use (Rumbaugh (1993) has also suggested using the data-flow models in OMT to model numerical computation – a better use I think than that originally intended by Rumbaugh et al. (1991)). Here is a case where wrappers may be beneficial even with green-field developments.

The wrapper approach to migration is not the only one available. Other options include the use of ORBs, employing OODBs or proceeding in a completely *ad hoc* manner. The *ad hoc* approach is often the correct one, but there are so many ways of approaching a particular problem that few sensible generalizations can be made. The *ad hoc* approach was the only one available until the appearance of ORB and OODB products. One leading financial institution, for example, built a straight-through trading system to connect its front and back office systems using objects that effectively comprised self-describing data packets. The result was observed *post facto* to be an application-specific ORB but the work was completed before any stable commercial CORBA compliant DOMS had come to market. Furthermore, this application went beyond the CORBA specification by using self-describing data. OODBs are an ingredient of most ORB products but can be used alone to act as a repository for a hand-crafted infrastructure. OODBs are discussed and compared by Cattell (1991) and Graham (1994) also gives a guide to the literature.

D.2   Data management strategies

One of the biggest problems with the concept of object wrappers concerns data management. Using the wrapper is easy until you need to split the storage of data across the old database and some of the new objects. The object-wrapper approach seems ideal at first sight but closer examination reveals some severe data management problems. Where building a wrapper makes it necessary to duplicate or share data across the new and old system components, there are four conceivable strategies.

(1) Carry a duplicate live copy of the common data in both parts of the system and keep both copies up to date. The problem with this is that storage requirements could double. Worse still, there are real integrity issues to worry about. It is almost certainly not a viable strategy for either migration or reuse of any commercial-scale system. We will call this the *tandem* or *handshake* strategy because it requires constant synchronization of updates and retrievals. It only works when there is little or no overlap between the data of the old and new systems.

(2) Keep all data in the old system and copy them to the new objects as required. Messages to the old system cause it to handle updates. This is known as the *borrowing* strategy because data are borrowed temporarily from the wrapper. It is similar to what is done in many existing, conventional MIS applications where data are downloaded nightly from a mainframe to workstations and updates transmitted in batch too.

(3) Copy the data to the new objects and allow the data from the old system to go out of date. Again there may be integrity problems, and the wrapper may have to send messages as well as receive and respond to them; which greatly increases its complexity. Call this the *take-over* strategy by analogy with one company making a take-over bid for another.

(4) Carve out coherent chunks of the database together with related functions. This is difficult and requires a sound method of OO analysis capable of describing the old system as well as the new and/or a translation technique from original systems design documents such as DFDs. It seems the most promising approach to migration on balance. This is called the *translation* strategy because one must translate the design to an object model. It is easiest to do when the old system was originally written around critical data structures using a technique such as step-wise refinement. These structures and the programs that use them will migrate naturally to the objects of the new system. A refinement of this strategy is to reverse engineer a data model from the existing system and to identify all file access operations in relation to this model using, for example, a CRUD matrix approach. CRUD techniques are often used to organize conventional systems around their data structures. These calls can then be replaced as new objects are constructed around the entities. This improved version of translation can be called *data centered translation*. Whether it is feasible will depend on

the difficulty of obtaining a data model and the complexity of the code in which the database calls are embedded. Reverse engineering tools may prove useful within this strategy and, as Reiss (1991) points out, the most useful tools would contain an understanding of the system semantics. When doing this, one should beware of normalized entities in any data model.

The habit of normalization is rooted deep in the data analysis community and one must be aware that normalized tables do not necessarily correspond to real-world entities. Take a look at any reasonably large data model and you will almost certainly find entities with strange, hyphenated names that correspond to absolutely nothing in the vocabulary of users. Thus, one must first denormalize to get rid of first normal forms which obfuscate the description of aggregate objects and then reconstruct objects that correspond to run-time join operations. So far as reverse engineering is concerned, it can be argued that a semantically rich version of OO analysis is an indispensable tool and that its representations need not be as large or complex as Reiss maintains if they are well structured and automated support is available. (SOMA initiated such an approach.)

The above data management strategies may be variously appropriate according to whether we are migrating the system to an OO implementation, reusing its components, extending it or building a better or a distributed front-end. Assuming that our chief aim is to migrate the old system to a new OO one rather than merely to reuse its components, which strategies are feasible? The handshake strategy is flawed for all but the smallest systems, and then there must be little overlap between new and old components. The borrowing strategy may well involve tampering with the old system and is not usually viable for the purposes of system migration unless there is a clean separation between existing functions and new requirements. Borrowing does not permit data to move permanently outward across the wrapper boundary. This means that there will come a time when a huge step must be taken all at once to migrate the data out, unless a DBMS has been used for all data accesses. These strategies, as migration strategies, do grievous violence to the whole idea of building wrappers. Only the last two strategies promise to be feasible if our intention is to migrate the functions of the old system to a new one, and there are some systems where neither seems to be practical. It is also the case that the type of system, its structure and the quality and type of its documentation will affect the choice of strategy. Dietrich's original application of the wrapper concept was to a solid modeling system of considerable complexity but whose intricacy resided in its code rather than in its data management. Furthermore, his primary concern was with the reuse of the functions of a stable system rather than its reconstruction. Hence, there has been little publicly documented experience of solving the problem under consideration here.

Strategy (4), translation, will work most often, provided that the old system can be decomposed around coherent data sets and if there are, say, some existing DFDs to transform objects from by encapsulating their data stores. If not, one is faced with building a wrapper of much greater complexity using take-over: strategy (3). The latter is a far costlier option.

D.3   Practical problems with migration

Another problem arises when the old system exists and is maintained in multiple versions. For example, a commercial package for a particular industry may, over the years, have been adapted for the needs of particular clients. The cost of building a wrapper for each version is usually prohibitive. The wrapper approach will only work if there is a core system common to all the versions, and the modifications will have to be maintained separately in any case until they can be reimplemented. This was the situation on a project that I was involved with where there were around 70 versions of the product customized for particular sites scattered across the globe, with local, dedicated maintenance teams in many cases. Also, the decomposition of the existing system into coherent chunks was exceeding hard because of the long modification history. The strategy adopted was to model the system using OO analysis and first wrap the core system in such a way that new functionality (a MIS component) could be added using OO methods, leaving the core system much untouched at this stage. One feature of the problem is particularly worthy of comment. It turned out that the hardware on which the system had to run, pending a move to UNIX at some future date, did not support an OO language of any form. Thus, in the short term, the new OO components had to be implemented in a conventional language. To ensure that the new system can be fully OO in the future we had to find a way to minimize the cost of so doing. This led to the use of an OO analysis approach and the conversion of its products to conventional code. It also led to the use of an ORB, Newi, that was able to let the developers treat the system as OO while still writing code in C. We also attempted to produce an OO description of the existing system to clarify understanding and help carve out separate reimplementable chunks following a translation strategy. It emerged that treating some functions as objects instead of methods was useful. The bulk of the early effort went into designing additional features and their interface, via a wrapper, to the core of the existing system; translation tasks being deferred to the near future. Thus, it proved wise to proceed in steps:

(1) build a wrapper to communicate with new OO components using (most probably) the borrowing strategy

(2) perform an OO analysis on the old system

(3) use translation or data-centered translation to migrate

(4) utilize an ORB to implement.

Grass (1991) argues that wrappers work well for mature systems that are essentially frozen, in the context of a requirement to reduce the maintenance burden which she characterizes as 'extremely aggravating' with the panache of understatement. Her main point is that ill-structured legacy systems are costly to understand and wrap. However, even this is worthwhile if the potential maintenance savings are large enough. As with the application by Dietrich, the principal application of Grass (a parser for regular grammars) was complex functionally but not primarily a data-intensive application.

One may conclude that, until much more experience has been accumulated, the best approach to migration of legacy systems with significant data management complexity is to build wrappers that support OO front-ends and to build the required new functions within the front-ends. The tandem strategy can be used only when there is little overlap and separate databases will have to be maintained. The exceptions to this are when the existing system already has a coherent data-centered structure that facilitates translation or when the benefits of the migration are large enough to justify the cost of building a very complex wrapper along the lines of the take-over strategy. If there is an existing DBMS this can be wrapped as a whole and maintained for a long time as the wrapped functions are gradually migrated. Then, at some point, one can move all the data at once to an OODB if desired and eliminate the database wrapper. This is a special variant of the translation strategy where the database is one huge 'coherent chunk.' It is probably the ideal option for many organizations already obtaining satisfactory performance from their relational databases. A good wrapper for Oracle or Sybase, probably written in C++, is a very sound investment in terms of migration strategy.

Having decided to build a wrapper and a new front-end one needs the tools for building them. There are no specific products offering wrapper technology for migration at present but there are several ORB and GUI tools that may help with reuse.

A key problem faced by many IT departments exists where there is a mixture of essentially incompatible hardware and software that somehow has been made to work together over the years. Conceptually it is easy to see that this 'goulash' can be modeled as a system of large objects communicating by passing messages with parameters. The wrapper approach is appropriate when just one of these systems is to migrate to an OO, open platform. Rather than build a wrapper for each old system, which would be expensive to say the least, it is better to wrap the communication system in some way. One approach to this problem is the ORB idea.

Microsoft's COM/Active X technology is beginning to exhibit features that let one treat existing applications as if they were wrapped. There are now several DOMS that support wrappers, ranging from coarse-grain ORBs like the ones from Iona Technologies and Expersoft to class libraries that help with finer grain wrapping and distributed object management.

In the product migration project referred to above, it turned out – for the reasons given – that there were no suitable software tools at the outset. Therefore, our main tool was our OO analysis approach itself. It was originally intended that the products we produced would conform to OMG standards including the common object request broker architecture (CORBA). In the outcome, the Newi product was used to support both distributed object management and the use of C for OO programming. The developers of NeWI were among the first people to coin the term 'business object': a subject we will take up shortly (Simms, 1994).

Another requirement was for some sort of CASE tool or repository that would support the recording of object and structure definitions. No such tool could be found. Most existing tools allow the user to draw diagrams but are weak on the recording of textual information. The project ended up by creating its own repository tool based on existing AS/400 software. The approach was similar in some respects to that of the SOMATiK software, though lacking in the latter's code generation, graphical and animation features.

We need to deal not only with the evolution of existing systems which are important and too large or complex to rewrite but also with the evolutionary migration of an existing system to a future OO implementation. This implies the need for techniques that will let us reuse components of existing functionally decomposed systems or even entire packages within our new or evolving OO systems. To this issue we now turn.

D.4   Reusing existing software components and packages

So far we have considered the wrapper technique from the point of view of migration. Now we must consider also the problem of reusing existing components when there is no explicit need or intention to reimplement them in an OO style. Dietrich's (1989) work has shown in principle how the reuse of highly optimized algorithms or specialized functions can be accomplished using the object wrapper strategy. This can be done by defining application-level classes whose methods call subroutines in the old system. The legacy systems can be wrapped in groups or as individual packages, with the latter option offering greater potential for reuse.

There is also a need to build on existing 'package' solutions. Once again a wrapper that calls package subroutines or simulates dialog at a terminal can be built. The alternative is to modify the packages to export data for manipulation by the new system, but this fails to reuse existing functional components of the old one. Also package vendors may not be prepared to support or even countenance such changes.

Some problems which must be solved in building such a wrapper are identified by Dietrich as follows.

- The designer is not free to choose the best representations for the problem in terms of objects since this is already largely decided within the old system. Here again there is a possibility that the wrappers will represent very coarse-grain objects with limited opportunities for reuse.

- The designer must either expose the old system's functions and interface to the user or protect him from possible changes to the old system. It is very difficult to do both successfully. Generally, one should only allow read accesses to the old system, which tends to preclude the take-over data management strategy.

- Where the old system continues to maintain data, the wrapper must preserve the state of these data when it calls internal routines. This militates against the translation strategy.

- Garbage collection and memory management and compactification (where applicable) must be synchronized between the wrapper and the old system.

- Cross-system invariants, which relate the old and new data sets, must be maintained.

- Building a wrapper often requires very detailed understanding of the old system. This is even more true when migrating but still a significant problem when reusing.

Because access to the internals of package software is seldom available at the required level of detail, the wrapper approach described above will not usually work. A better approach is to regard the package as a fixed object offering definite services, possibly in a distributed environment.

Whereas data-centered translation is the best approach to migration and replacement of existing systems – while borrowing strategies fail to work – where reuse is the main concern, borrowing is a perfectly viable approach. If the existing system or package largely works, for the functions it provides, and can be maintained at an acceptable level of cost (however large that may be) then when new functions are required it may be possible to build them quite separately using an OO approach and communicate with the old system through a wrapper. This wrapper is used to call the services of the old system and give access to its database. New functions are defined as the methods of objects that encapsulate the data they need, insofar as they are new data. When data stored by the old system are required, a message must be sent to the wrapper and the appropriate retrieval routines called; borrowing the needed data. Updates to the existing database are treated similarly, by lending as it were.

It may well turn out that, in the fullness of time, the new OO system will gradually acquire features that replace and duplicate parts of the old system. Data-centered translation then becomes necessary instead of borrowing for the affected parts of the system. Therefore the step-by-step strategy recommended in the last section is indicated for many commercial systems projects.

We may summarize the conclusions of this appendix so far in Table D.1. In this table a Y indicates that a wrapper data strategy may be worth considering for a particular class of problem but not that it is guaranteed to work. An N indicates that it probably will not be suitable. A ? means: 'It all depends.' The four strategies defined above are compared with four possible reasons for building wrappers: migrating a complex legacy system to a new OO implementation; reusing its components without changing the core system; extending its functionality without changing the core and building a possibly distributed front-end to provide additional functions. Note that the last three purposes are very similar and the last two have identical Y/N patterns.

Table D.1   Suitability of data communication strategies for different purposes.

		Purpose		
Strategy	Migration	Reuse	Extension	Front-end
Handshake	N	N	N	N
Borrowing	N	Y	Y	Y
Take-over	?	N	N	N
Translation	?	N	Y	Y
Data-centered translation	Y	N	Y	Y

D.5   Combining relational and OODBs

For developers and maintainers of commercial systems, many of which have a substantial data management component, exploiting the best of existing relational databases for one part of an application in concert with the use of an OO programming language or even an OODB for another is a key issue. Generally, the interoperation of legacy relational databases and OO programming languages is best viewed as a special case of the client–server model. The reason for considering an OODB is that there are several commercial applications that relational databases are very bad at dealing with. Examples include bills of materials, document handling and, in fact, any application where there are complex, structured objects. Older generation databases were just too inflexible to use for highly evolutionary applications such as text management. For these reasons it is still the case that most of the data owned by businesses are not in a computer system at all; up to 90% according to some estimates. Further, these data do not include the business and technical knowledge on which these organizations depend. As businesses strive for a competitive edge there is an ever-increasing demand to computerize all these data along with the need to build a knowledge base, and OODBs offer a partial solution. On an application involving many complex objects, an OODB can be 100 times faster than its relational equivalent and retains the flexibility of the relational approach in terms of schema evolution too. Furthermore, OODBs offer enhanced facilities such as support for long transactions and version control. However, since most organizations have a monstrous investment in existing database systems and, besides, the relational approach works well for most record-oriented IS applications, it is imperative that moving to OODBs should not involve the abandonment of all this existing work.

There are two options available: a pure OODB or a relational system extended with OO constructs. There are several pure OO products in existence but they have not yet matured fully. Further, there is a class of applications where a relational system may be not only a more mature solution but a faster one; typically those involving few large joins such as ledger applications. One alternative is to continue with the relational model extended in various ways, as with products such as Illustra. The other is to try to make our new OODB applications interoperate with existing database systems. The first may give performance problems for certain applications, judging from early experiences, so the second is at least worth considering.

The obvious approach suggested in the foregoing is to build a generalized wrapper for the DBMS itself. For example, a C++ wrapper could be written for Sybase that converts between messages and SQL queries. Thus the object wrapper approach described above will go through in many cases and the interoperability considerations for database systems are not really any different from those discussed for general computer systems. One feature of database systems, however, does deserve separate attention, and that is the issue of data modeling. Because modern database systems are nearly always based on a data model and such a model is based on real-world entities – bearing in mind my remarks about normalization above.

One of the great advantages of a conventional database management system is the separation of processes and data, which gives a notion of data independence and benefits of flexibility and insulation from change, because the interface to shared data is stable. The data model is to be regarded as a model of the statics of the application. With object orientation, processes and data are integrated. Does this mean that you have to abandon the benefits of data independence? Already in client–server relational databases we have seen a step in the same direction, with database triggers and integrity rules stored in the server with the data. With an OO approach to data management it therefore seems reasonable to adopt the view that there are two kinds of business object: *domain* (or *shared*) objects and *application* objects. As Daniels and Cook (1993) point out, objects that must be shared are nearly always persistent. Domain objects represent those aspects of the system that are relatively stable or generic and application objects are those which can be expected to vary from installation to installation or quite rapidly from time to time and which share the services of the domain objects. This approach resurrects the notion of data independence in an enhanced, OO form. The domain objects are based on the data model and include persistent aspects of the model, constraints, rules and dynamics (state transitions, etc.). The goal is to make the interface to this part of the model as stable as possible. The application objects (including the user interface objects) use the services of the domain objects and may interact through them. This approach is reminiscent of the approach taken in the KADS expert systems development method with its knowledge level, task level and application level models of a domain (see Hickman et al., 1989). It is also compatible with Smalltalk's MVC pattern if we introduce non-business objects called *interface objects* to represent the controllers. The interface controls share access to the services of the application objects while the application objects share access to those of the domain objects. So-called 'database aware' controls appear to give direct access to domain objects but may be implemented via intermediate application objects. Typically domain objects will be found in the domain or business model and will be maintained by a team separate from application development teams; they are the central repository for reuse of business objects.

The obvious candidates for domain objects are the denormalized relations or views of a legacy database wrapped with the behavior of the corresponding business objects. Where a database that offers the capability of storing procedures in the server – such as Sybase – is in use this is even more straightforward though discipline is required to prevent direct access to data structures via SQL. All calls to the database must be via stored procedures representing the wrapper interface. In the extreme case this could be implemented by the database administrator closing off all access privileges to all users, except to the stored procedures. Developers should thus be able to refer to a clean, OO conceptual model while designing their access operations from application objects.

How then should the OO component of our database or data model interoperate with the relational part? Incidentally, I am assuming that you will eventually want to migrate all your old CODASYL and IMS applications to an OODB.

The possibilities are as follows.

(1) Object wrappers can be built for the relational system as a whole, treating it as an entire domain model. This approach offers minimal opportunities for the reuse of domain objects but may nevertheless be viable and the database wrapper can be replaced easily later.

(2) Coherent chunks of the database can be wrapped individually; perhaps allowing a phased approach. The use of stored procedures and a published object model are highly beneficial here. Opportunities for reuse are maximized by this strategy where it is feasible.

(3) SQL can be used to communicate with the relational system, which means that the new system must be able to generate SQL calls and interpret the resulting tables based on knowledge of the data dictionary and its semantics. This will usually involve the use of fairly complex AI techniques such as those used in natural language query systems such as Intellect.

(4) The relational system could be addressed through an ORB provided it either conforms to the CORBA standard or a conformant wrapper is built. Once again, use of an ORB tends to deal with the legacy system as coarse grained and the reuse potential is not as high as option 2.

A good example of interworking between relational and non-relational databases is provided by GIS. Most GIS store two kinds of data; mapping data and data concerning the attributes of the objects mapped. The performance of relational systems is poor on mapping data because of their inability to store complex, structured objects and their need to do joins to reconstruct them. For this reason the mapping data are usually stored in a proprietary file system. The attribute data are often stored in a relational database and also often shared with other applications. In many applications a change to mapping data must be reflected in changes to the attributes and vice versa. This close coupling has been a significant task for product developers. Relational systems that support BLOBS (binary large objects) can be used but they cannot interpret the data. CAD systems developers have faced similar problems. The most recent GIS, such as Smallworld, have opted for an OO approach to storing mapping data.

Loomis (1991) identifies three problems and three approaches to object-relational interoperation. The three problems are to:

(1) build OO applications that access relational databases

(2) run existing relationally written applications against an OODB

(3) use an SQL-like query language in an OO environment.

The three approaches are to:

(1) convert the applications and databases completely to OO ones

(2) use standard import–export facilities

(3) access the relational databases from the OO programming languages.

The first of these approaches is complicated and expensive, and works badly if some old system functions are to be reused or migration is gradual. The same problem referred to in Sections D.1 and D.2 arises, in that coordinating updates across heterogeneous databases is problematical. However, if you can do periodic downloads of data to the new system, the approach can be tolerated. This is exactly what we did when migrating from IMS to DB2 and building MIS extensions. The second approach relies on standards having been defined, which will depend on the application; for example standards exist in the CAD and VLSI design worlds but not in general. The best variant of this approach is to use an OODB which supports SQL gateways to your relational databases, as does GemStone for example. Here though, the application must provide a mapping between table and object views of data and, except for the simplest cases, this can be complicated. The third approach implies adopting Object SQL or SQL3.

Conventional databases let one store relations, such as 'all the children who like toys,' in a table, but not the rule that 'all children like toys.' Nor do they permit one to store the fact that when one field is updated another may have to be. Both of these kinds of relationship are easy to express in, say, Prolog or in any knowledge-based systems shell. For some time now relational database vendors have extended the relational model to allow database triggers to capture the latter kind of rule. In AI frame-based systems the support for rules is more general and less procedural in style, but there is undoubtedly a trend to enriching the semantic abilities of databases in this way. Object-relational databases, in addition, now offer facilities for defining abstract data types so that they can deal with complex data types exactly in the manner of an OODB. At present no OODB product known to the author offers explicit support for declarative rules.

One way to enhance interoperability, we are told, is to place system syntax and semantics in enterprise repositories. These days, nearly all new repositories are based on OODB technology. In some cases a mixture of I-CASE and expert systems technology is used. See, for example, Martin and Odell (1992) for the arguments for this approach. Such repositories will store an interface library and this will help systems to locate and utilize existing objects.

All these developments suggest the need for a systems analysis technique which captures not just data, process and dynamics but rules and facts of the type found in knowledge-based systems. OODBs and extended relational databases will also make it imperative that business rules are captured explicitly during the analysis process. SOMA (Graham, 1995) originally showed how this can be accomplished. Certainly, I believe that the adoption of a sound approach to OO analysis is a key part of any organization's migration strategy.

D.6   Business objects and BOMs

Arguments about whether OO development is seamless or not, whether transformational approaches are better than round-trip gestalt design or disputes about the difference between essential and system models have beset attempts to explain OO requirements engineering. I believe that lack of clarity about modeling is at the root of these disputes and has also led to a great muddle concerning the concept of a business object. In this section I want to explain my understanding of the meaning and status of modeling within OO development. Then it will be possible to explain what a business object really is.

Modeling is central to software engineering practice and especially to OO development. A model is a representation of some thing or system of things with all or some of the following properties.

- It is always *different* from the thing or system being modeled (the *original*) in scale, implementation or behavior.

- It has the shape or appearance of the original (an iconic model).

- It can be manipulated or exercised in such a way that its behavior or properties can be used to predict the behavior or properties of the original (a simulation model).

- There is always some correspondence between the model and the original.

Examples of models abound throughout daily life: mock-ups of aircraft in wind tunnels; architectural scale models; models of network traffic using compressed air in tubes or electrical circuits; software models of gas combustion in engines. Of course *all* software is a model of something, just as all mathematical equations are (analytic) models.

Jackson (1995) relates models to descriptions by saying that modeling a domain involves making designations of the primitives of the domain and then using these to build a description of the properties, relationships and behavior

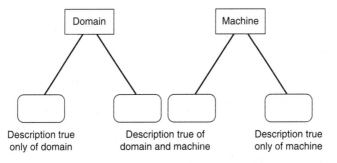

Figure D.2 M is for 'model' (after Jackson, 1995).

that are true of that domain. For example, if we take the domain of sending birthday cards to one's friends, we might make designations:

- p is a friend
- d is a date (day and month)
- $B(p, d)$ says that p was born on d.

Then we can make descriptions like: For all p, there is exactly one B. Jackson (1995) suggests that modeling is all about ensuring that the descriptions apply equally well to the model and to the original domain. In the context of computer models this might mean that the instances of a class or the records of a database are made to correspond uniquely to domain instances of our friends. Most usefully, Jackson presents this concept as the M configuration shown in Figure D.2.

The domain and the machine are different; in the domain friends do not reside in disk sectors. There are many things in the domain that are not in our model, such as our friends' legs or pimples. There are also things that go on in computers that we are not concerned with in a model, such as time sharing. The model comprises the features shared between the domain and the machine.

This understanding of what a model is can be applied to the problem of object modeling. We must understand clearly that a so-called BOM is both a model of the domain and a potentially implementable machine model. But we must begin with a model of the domain to understand and validate the requirements.

It is my thesis that object modeling is a very general method for knowledge representation. There is little that cannot be modeled with objects – provided, of course, that we do not restrict ourselves to the semantics of some particular OO programming language. We can model both the domain and the machine using objects. This is not to say that the world consists of our model objects, but it is to say that we can almost always model the domain as if it was made of objects. A good example is provided by Cook and Daniels (1994), who make a strong distinction between *essential* (i.e. domain) and *specification* models. They argue that the world is not made of objects citing by way of example the fact that the sun does not wake the birds up each morning by sending each one a message. However, if we want a correspondence between our domain and specification models it is quite permissible to model the sunrise event as recorded on a 'blackboard' object in which each instance of the class birds has registered interest. That is not what happens physically but it is a good model insofar as object semantics do not include a broadcast metaphor. There are of course many exceptions where object modeling is inappropriate, but the sheer discipline of trying to model with objects is beneficial in terms of scientific parsimony and ordered thought. For example, I doubt whether the solution of a differential equation is best modeled with objects. Here another idea promoted by Jackson (1995) may be useful. He argues that one can recognize analysis patterns (which he calls problem frames) that recur and which imply suitable modeling methods. One example is the 'simple IS frame' which indicates that a JSP approach is suitable. The arguments in this case are convincing, but generally I find that object modeling gives more chance of success than any other approach and that JSP can be accommodated as a technique within an OO approach. Kristen (1994), for one, does this within his KISS method.

Jackson's M metaphor provides us with an understanding of the correspondence between two worlds – the domain and the machine in the example above. However, if we are to apply object modeling to a realistic business problem it turns out that this is often too simplistic a view. In practice we must build a linked series of models more reminiscent of a tasty *mmmmmm* than single M. de Champeaux (1997) offers some support for this view. He distinguishes between two approaches to object modeling that he characterizes as constructivist (neat) and impressionist (scruffy). Scruffies do not emphasize the precise semantics of object modeling. They opine 'the design fleshes out the analysis' without being precise about what this means. Precision is only introduced in the implementation models when the semantics of a language has to be faced. The neats are different. They want to 'exploit the analysis computational model' and observe that analysis model are 'nearly executable.' Examples of approaches close to the spirit of the neats include those of Cook and Daniels and of de Champeaux himself. In both cases precision relies heavily on the use of state models, but this is not necessarily always the case. In SOMA, for example, there is a defined sequence of model transformations but state machines are only an optional technique. Let us examine this sequence in enough detail to illustrate the general idea.

We start by examining an entire business. If we try to build an object model of the business we soon find that it is too complex: too many people, departments, products and so on. The recommended technique is the activity grid: a matrix of the core business processes where the rows represent goals and the columns logical job descriptions. Each cell of this grid can be regarded as a (process-oriented) business area. The model is usually underpinned by a value chain analysis. We can then zoom in on a cell (or group of cells) and again try to build an object model. At this scale we have a chance of succeeding. The model transformation merely takes us from the whole business to its component processes represented in natural language. Each area has thus a mission connected with executing the process and a number of definite, measurable objectives. The next recommended technique is to regard the business area as a network of communicating intelligent agents. The agents are modeled as objects that represent people, rôles, systems or aggregates (functional units). The agents communicate with each other and with external agents: objects representing customers, etc. Communication is interpreted as consisting of abstract 'semiotic acts' or conversations. Each conversation is in support of a stated business objective. These conversations can be represented as messages with a definite structure: trigger; goal; offer/request; negotiation; task performance; handover. We now transform this agent object model to a different one by focusing on the tasks that the messages contain; we build the TOM. Task objects can be thought of as generic use cases, although a more precise theoretical foundation exists. Tasks are decomposed into smaller atomic component tasks, exploiting the aggregation semantics of object modeling. Tasks can be specialization of reusable tasks from other projects, exploiting the inheritance semantics. Tasks can also be associated with each other. For example, one task may have to *precede* another. Finally, tasks can send messages to each other asking for help when exceptions arise. This is then a veritable object model but it is *not* a model of a computer system in any sense.

We now transform the TOM into a BOM. This is a creative transformation based on the usual noun/verb technique. We make the transformation seamless using an extension of the CRC card idea. The BOM represents those business objects referred to or implied by the task scripts. But what is its status? Is it a model of the world or a model of some system yet to be implemented? The answer is that it is both. It lies exactly in the middle of a Jackson M. It abstracts what is common to the business and a future implementation model. And it is potentially executable. Tools that allow execution of such models are already available with examples including ObjecTime, SOMATiK and SES's ObjectBench.

Each business object is viewed as having its own thread of control. The BOM is inherently distributed in that no decisions about physical architecture have been made. When we begin to make such decisions we are transforming the model to an IOM. This too is a manual transformation wherein some very complex design decisions may be made. These decisions include distribution, sequentialization and optimization, and de Champeaux suggests transforming the model in three steps corresponding to these issues. We must also select a language, messaging model and persistence strategy during the design transformations. It is difficult to see how such complex transformations can be seamlessly linked back to the BOM when low-level languages are used and the need for tuning eliminates the use of code generation.

Several conclusions follow from the above argument. First among these is that object modeling cannot be seen as a single step consisting of the drawing of class diagrams and followed by refinement down to an implementation model. Such an approach – and remarkably it is the one common to most of the well-known OO analysis methods – leaves out many domain issues that should not be ignored. There must be a sequence of models. Fortunately these can be object

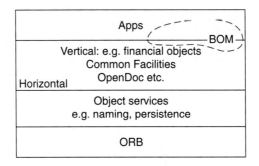

Figure D.3   One possible architectural framework.

models in nearly every case and they can be linked together seamlessly until we come to implementation. At that stage we face a trade-off between seamlessness and performance.

The argument also suggests the business object as the focal point of reuse. But our business objects are specifications not code, although they are executable specifications. This is a different view of business objects from the one emerging from the OMG currently. The latter tend to see business objects in the common facilities layer as though they were robust, reusable implementations, shielded only by IDL wrappers that cannot possibly contain a rich enough semantics to enable links back to the earlier models in the modeling sequence. Simms (1996) characterizes this as a confusion between components and business objects, pointing out that business objects can be assembled from components but that they are by no means the same thing. This is an issue that needs to be explored very carefully before companies commit themselves to third-party products masquerading as OMG business objects.

Figure D.3 offers a possible architectural framework for a company adopting OT. It is broadly based on the OMG model but indicates that there will be minimal reliance on the OMG vertical common facilities. Creating a BOM for reuse in a vertical market is actually a far harder undertaking than it would seem at first sight. This is evident from the very few commercial offerings in the finance area for example. Most commercial offerings are little more than rebadged data/process models. They are nearly always replete with false assumptions about business processes that reflect the practice of the (usually one) organization where they were first developed. Quite often they are closely tied to the semantics of a particular language; e.g. C++. Also, at the time of writing the main contender in the banking sector is strongly associated with a relational database, leading to performance problems.

The alternative is to create your own BOM. This provides a tailor-made resource, gives you more control, permits performance optimization and allows you to take advantage of new technology as it becomes available: WWW, Java, ODBMS, SOMATiK, and so on. But of course there are costs. As noted already this is no simple matter. For one thing it is often hard to decide exactly what a business object is. In the finance domain, for example, it is reasonably clear that financial instruments are good candidates for reusable business objects. However, there are well over 200 classes of this type and it is extremely difficult to form them into a robust, stable classification structure. Corporate actions are another good candidate and here there are only about 42 classes; but even this number gives moderate complexity. Pricing algorithms too can be regarded as *bona fide* objects, even though they are just processes with light data structure. The reason for this is that instruments may be priced by many algorithms, so that the algorithm is not a method of the instrument. Events – such as trades, payments, cash flows, and so on – are more problematical. Trades have complex lifecycles that could be represented by state machines, but trades in different instruments often have quite different lifecycles. So, is the lifecycle a feature of the trade, of the instrument or of the geographical location? Perhaps it is a feature of a 'relationship' object. Customers, regulators and so on are even more evidently not objects; they are relationships between organizations, departments and individuals. People are beginning to suggest that business processes are objects. If so the question that is usually ignored is whether they have the same status as object-like instruments; are they part of the same model? The task modeling approach of SOMA is a step towards answering these questions; that is processes *are* objects but in separate object model.

D.7   What needs to be done?

The main conclusion to be drawn from this appendix is that an organization migrating to OT needs to establish an OO development method. The method should help establish a clear notion of what a business object is. It should have sufficiently rich semantics to capture business rules within objects. It should have a clear process and a metrics suite.

Establishing a reuse programme within the overall process is essential. The hairies and conscripts model (Graham, 1996 and see Section 4.11.1) offers a managerial technique that encourages knowledge transfer between the reuse team and application developers. Education and training of both users and developers is also critical. OO developers can be recruited and/or retrained and tools must be acquired. The tools include languages, databases, modeling/reuse tools and especially middleware such as ORBs, gateways and transaction monitors

Teams must understand modeling. They should realize also that specification models include more than just business objects. They encompass business objectives and priorities, business processes (conversations), tasks (these are reusable objects too), business objects, links between business objects and tasks, implementation objects and components. The architecture should be the basis of the component library.

When choosing component and business object libraries, ask whether the model fits your business. Beware of data models in disguise. Make sure that performance is adequate. Take firm control over the specification of the objects, based on business needs. Use binary components only when you trust them completely. Buy or build the *right* middleware. Do not forget the business processes. Last, but by no means least, adopt a suitable method rather than just a notation of CASE tool.

D.8   Bibliographical notes

Dietrich's (1989) paper is the original source on object wrappers and is well complemented by the analyses of Reiss (1991) and Grass (1991). Some of the panels in the OOPSLA proceedings (Meyrowitz 1989, 1990) contain useful insights. Some of the data management ideas explored here are taken up and explored further by Topper (1995).

SOMA is described in Graham (1995) and much of SOMA's ideas are incorporated into OPEN. The latter book I think coined the term Business Object Model for the first time to refer to business objects in the sense used in this appendix, while Simms (1994) first used the term business object to refer to objects that could be represented as graphical icons and which meant something to the business.

Much of the material in this appendix is based on articles that have appeared through the 1990s in various conference proceedings and in the journals, *First Class*, *Object Magazine* and *Object Expert*. These articles are not included in the reference section.

References

Brice A. (1993). Using models in analysis. *Computing* (27 May), 41

Cattell R. G. G. (1991). *Object Data Management*. Reading, MA: Addison-Wesley

Cook S. and Daniels J. (1994). *Designing Object Systems*. Hemel Hempstead, UK: Prentice-Hall

Daniels J. and Cook S. (1993). Strategies for sharing objects in distributed systems. *Journal of Object-Oriented Programming*, **5**(8), 27–36

de Champeaux D. (1997). *Object-Oriented Development Process and Metrics*. Upper Saddle River, NJ: Prentice-Hall

Dietrich W. C., Nackman L. R. and Gracer F. (1989). Saving a legacy with objects, *OOPSLA'90 ACM Conference on Object-oriented Programming Systems, Languages and Applications* (Meyrowitz N., ed) Reading, MA: Addison-Wesley

Graham I. M. (1994). *Object-Oriented Methods*, 2nd edn. Harlow, UK: Addison-Wesley

Graham, I. M. (1995). *Migrating to Object Technology*. Harlow, UK: Addison-Wesley

Graham, I. M. (1996). Hairies and conscripts: making reuse work *Object Magazine*, **6**(6), 82–3

Grass J. E. (1991). Design archaeology for object-oriented redesign in C++. In *TOOLS5: Proc. 5th Int. Conf. on Technology of Object-Oriented Languages and Systems* (Korson T., Vaishnavi V. and Meyer B., eds.). New York: Prentice-Hall

Hickman F. R., Killen J., Land L. et al. (1989). *Analysis for Knowledge-Based Systems*. Chichester: Ellis Horwood

Jackson, M. (1995). *Software Requirements and Specifications*. Harlow, UK: Addison-Wesley

Korson T., Vaishnavi V. and Meyer B. (eds.) (1991). *TOOLS5: Proc. 5th Int. Conf. on the Technology of Object-Oriented Languages and Systems*. New York: Prentice-Hall

Kristen G. (1995). *Object-Orientation: The KISS Method*. Harlow, UK: Addison-Wesley

Loomis M. E. S. (1991). Objects and SQL. *Object Magazine*, **1**(3), 68–78

Martin J. and Odell J. J. (1992). *Object-Oriented Analysis And Design*. Englewood Cliffs, NJ: Prentice-Hall

Reiss S. P. (1991). Tools for object-oriented redesign. In *TOOLS5: Proc. 5th Int. Conf. on Technology of Object-Oriented Languages and Systems* (Korson T., Vaishnavi V. and Meyer B., eds.). New York: Prentice-Hall

Simms O. (1994). *Business Objects*. London: McGraw-Hill

Topper A. (1995). *Object-Oriented Development in COBOL*. New York: McGraw-Hill

Bibliography

Recommended texts: Only books are included in this section although we acknowledge that many of the ideas expressed here were first published as journal papers. Authors, while not necessarily cited, are hereby acknowledged for their invaluable contributions.

Alexander C. (1979). *The Timeless Way of Building*. Oxford: Oxford University Press

Booch G. (1994). *Object-Oriented Analysis and Design with Applications* 2nd edn. 589 pp. Redwood City, CA: Benjamin/Cummings

Firesmith D., Henderson-Sellers B. and Graham I. (1997). *OPEN Modeling Language (OML) Reference Manual*. 271 pp. New York: SIGS

Gamma E., Helm R., Johnson R. and Vlissides J. (1995). *Design Patterns: Elements of Reusable Object-Oriented Design*. 395 pp. Reading, MA: Addison-Wesley

Gilb T. and Graham D. (1993) *Software Inspection: Effective Method for Software Project Management*. Reading, MA: Addison-Wesley

Goldberg A. and Rubin K. S. (1995). *Succeeding with Objects. Decision Frameworks for Project Management*. 542 pp. Reading, MA: Addison-Wesley

Graham I. M. (1995). *Migrating to Object Technology*. 552 pp. Harlow, UK: Addison-Wesley

Henderson-Sellers B. (1996). *Object-Oriented Metrics. Measures of Complexity*. 234 pp. New York: Prentice-Hall

Henderson-Sellers B. and Bulthuis A. (1997). *Object-Oriented Metamethods*. New York: Springer

Henderson-Sellers B. and Edwards J. M. (1994). *BOOKTWO of Object-Oriented Knowledge: The Working Object*. 594 pp. Sydney: Prentice-Hall

McGibbon B. (1995). *Managing Your Move to Object Technology. Guidelines and Strategies for a Smooth Transition*. 268 pp. New York: SIGS

McGregor J. D. and Sykes D. A. (1992). *Object-Oriented Software Development: Engineering Software for Reuse*. 352 pp. New York: Van Nostrand Reinhold

Martin J. and Odell J. J. (1995). *Object-Oriented Methods. A Foundation*. 412 pp. Englewood Cliffs, NJ: PTR Prentice-Hall

Meyer B. (1988). *Object-Oriented Software Construction*. 534 pp. Hemel Hempstead: Prentice-Hall

Meyer B. (1995). *Object Success: A Manager's Guide to Object Orientation, Its Impact on the Corporation and Its Use for Reengineering the Software Process*. 192 pp. Hemel Hempstead: Prentice-Hall

Page-Jones M. (1995). *What Every Programmer Should Know About Object-Oriented Design*. 370 pp. New York: Dorset House

Reenskaug T., Wold P. and Lehne O. A. (1996). *Working with Objects. The OOram Software Engineering Manual*. 366 pp. Greenwich, CT: Manning

Riehl A. J. (1996). *Object-Oriented Design Heuristics*. 379 pp. Reading, MA: Addison-Wesley

Taylor D. (1995). *Business Engineering with Object Technology*. 188 pp. New York: Wiley

Tkach D. and Puttick R. (1994). *Object Technology in Application Development*. 212 pp. Benjamin/Cummings

Waldén K. and Nerson J.-M. (1995). *Seamless Object-Oriented Architecture*. 301 pp. Prentice-Hall

Wirfs-Brock R., Wilkerson B. and Wiener L. (1990). *Designing Object-Oriented Software*. 368 pp. Englewood Cliffs, NJ: Prentice-Hall

Name Index

Subject Index